JEWELRY:
QUEEN OF CRAFTS

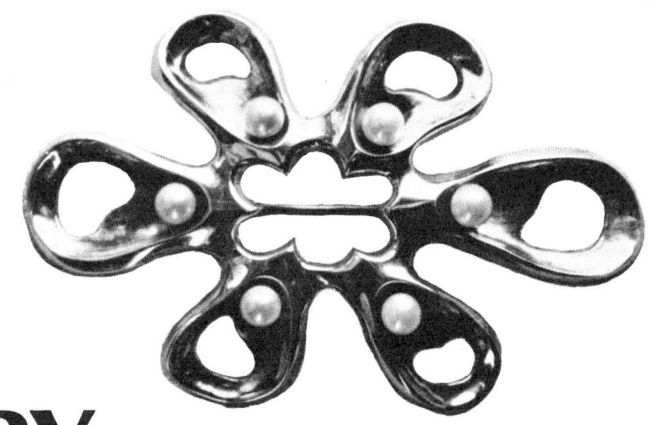

JEWELRY: QUEEN OF CRAFTS

William R. Sanford

55758

The Bruce Publishing Company, New York
Collier-Macmillan Limited, London

© Copyright, William R. Sanford, 1970

All rights reserved. No part of this book may be reproduced or transmitted in any form or by any means, electronic or mechanical, including photocopying, recording or by any information storage and retrieval system, without permission in writing from the Publisher.

Library of Congress Catalog Card Number: 77–116783

THE BRUCE PUBLISHING COMPANY, NEW YORK
COLLIER-MACMILLAN CANADA, LTD., TORONTO, ONTARIO

Made in the United States of America

ACKNOWLEDGMENTS

This book is largely the result of association with many people over a considerable period of time. Friends and associates over the years have freely given encouragement and help from their many fields of work or recreation. Many artists, craftsmen, jewelers, lapidaries, rockhounds, dentists, and laboratory technicians, students, teachers, and other writers also have contributed knowledge passed on to the reader. My debt to them is large and I regret that I must leave them unnamed because of their number. But to all I wish to express my appreciation by a heartfelt "Thank You."

Special thanks are extended to Senior Simon Ybarra, teacher at Instituto Allende, Mexico, for getting me started on the fascinating jewelry craft and to Mr. Lyle Whittier for his technical help.

WILLIAM R. SANFORD

Cast earrings. Texture was made in the wax model by chipping with a sharp pointed knife.

CONTENTS

	PREFACE
1	CHAPTER 1 Introduction
4	CHAPTER 2 Design
19	CHAPTER 3 Materials
26	CHAPTER 4 Tools
39	CHAPTER 5 Jewelry Working Techniques
135	CHAPTER 6 Jewelry Without Solder
143	CHAPTER 7 Jewelry Using Solder
147	CHAPTER 8 Cast Jewelry
152	CHAPTER 9 Gems
163	CHAPTER 10 Simple Lapidary
174	APPENDIX
181	GLOSSARY
188	BIBLIOGRAPHY
191	INDEX

PREFACE

This man's ring has a conservative but very popular mounting. The stone is jade.

Each day, some new product or tool is invented, and some new concept is discovered. Ideas and innovations of merit should be accepted and put to full use. I have tried to incorporate the newest techniques and methods in this book. Some recently published books still cling to describing and suggesting the use of antiquated tools and methods. Using some of these obsolete methods now, when faster and more efficient techniques have been developed, would hamper a professional jeweler. One of the reasons for writing this book is to bring to the student, craftsman, and reader the latest and most efficient techniques.

I believe that most textbooks, scientific books, and books on specific or technical subjects should have a rather complete glossary, one that explains the writer's language and forms a basis for communication. Because I believe that this communication is so necessary, I have devoted a large section of this book to describing completely the materials, tools, and techniques of jewelry making.

When reading, pausing midsentence to find a word in a dictionary can be distracting and frustrating, especially when many technical words are not listed in a standard dictionary. Definitions of words and terms are often given in context when a book has little or no glossary. This often means locating the word in the index, making a choice among several entries, and then going back to the text of the book. It is hoped that the Glossary entries in this book will save the reader this time and trouble.

Besides providing new information, I have tried to avoid giving the reader unnecessary information. Today, a wide variety of commercially manufactured products and tools for jewelry making can be bought. They are of excellent quality, fairly priced, and are available in a wide variety. Lengthy descriptions and discussions of how to make products and tools that are commercially available has therefore been avoided. This does not preclude experimenting with new materials, ideas, and techniques.

The tempering of steel is a necessary part of the jeweler's craft, but the jewelry maker's shop is not a blacksmith's shop, and this subject is included only to a limited degree.

The making of a jig that is not really necessary; the mixing, grinding, washing, and processing of enamel; the gluing of abrasive cloth to sticks; and the many other similar activities are time consuming. This time, that is spent on these activities, is not the essence of a craft or art. This time would be of more value if it were devoted to the task of making jewelry. And, a better piece of jewelry would be the result—better in both design and craftsmanship.

I have been directly connected with teaching for a number of years: first as a U.S. Navy instructor, later as a U.S. Army arts and crafts director, and then as a teacher in civilian adult education programs. From these experiences has come the firm belief that a systematic progression of activities in a craft program is the best approach to advise for the best results. This book is organized, therefore, to guide the reader from the simple to the more complex. The teacher may use this sequential pattern as a guide in planning lessons. And finally, material is included that, it is hoped, will inspire the interest of the advanced student, craftsman, or professional in new and challenging areas.

Lapidary is included in this book, which is primarily devoted to jewelry, for two reasons: First, the two crafts are nearly inseparable and complement each other. Second, many high school classes, college classes, and adult education classes now include both arts, either together or separately. The lapidary section is not comprehensive, nor was it meant to be. Many excellent books exist for those who wish to continue in this area.

No one writer, no one small book can hope to satisfy the needs of everyone on a subject as diverse as jewelry making. This book will accomplish the purpose for which it was written if it stimulates the interest of some readers, helps others in craftsmanship, and inspires the creation of well-designed, beautiful jewelry.

Cutouts reveal the finger beneath and give an airy light look to a ring.

CHAPTER 1
INTRODUCTION

Several elements of the design of this gold pendant can be chosen and used for the design of matching earrings.

Jewelry making is a happy craft. It is doubtful whether any other craft or art gives as much satisfaction and happiness to as many people: to the designer and maker, a sense of satisfaction and accomplishment; to the receiver, a sense of joy and appreciation. The work may be sold to a dealer, who is well aware of worth and beauty and enjoys handling and discussing each piece as well as selling it.

An especially well-designed and well-executed piece of jewelry is unique for several reasons. Jewelry is extremely individual. It has been made with the personality, tastes, likes, and dislikes of a specific person in mind. Less tangible, but nevertheless considered and incorporated in the designed piece, are the physical features of the wearer: a person's figure, size, coloring, posture, age, and social status. Jewelry not only reflects light, but mirrors the person who wears it.

2 Jewelry: Queen of Crafts

There are advantages in making jewelry which are absent from many other crafts. Jewelry requires relatively little space for a good work area, and it does not require a great number of tools nor a large outlay of money to get started. The serious craftsman may later want to add to his basic tools, but this can be done when the need arises. The hand tools which I carried in my fishing tackle box to Mexico were sufficient for the work necessary to earn a master's degree in handwrought jewelry.

The expense of materials can be what you want it to be. Good synthetic stones and cultured pearls may be bought for about two dollars, and the silver to set a pearl in a ring will cost even less. From this humble start, the cost can go up to almost any amount, especially when gold and precious stones are used.

Interest lags and dims in a craft when the hobbyist has made all the ceramic ashtrays, block prints, leather hand-tooled belts, end tables, mosaics, copper tooled pictures, enameled gadgets, and so forth, that the average home can use. But a woman never has too much jewelry, and a drawer will hold the results of virtually endless hours of work.

If a person is interested in jewelry, he will have almost limitless possibilities for continued stimulation. Many enthusiasts are never able to pass a jewelry store without looking over its display. Someone fortunate enough to travel around the world will be drawn to store displays and museum exhibits; to the pearls of Japan; to the jades of Hong Kong; to the rubies, sapphires, and elaborate settings of Bangkok, India, and Rangoon; to the treasures of King Tutankhamen's tomb; to the dozens upon dozens of jewelry shops in Jerusalem's bazaars; to the ancient works of Greece and Rome; to the filigree in Yugoslavia; to the fabulous shops on the Ponte Vecchio in Florence; to the smart modern stores in Lucerne, Paris, and London, with the Crown Jewels thrown in for good measure; to the gold and filigree of Spain and Portugal; to the treasures of Tomb 7 in Mexico; and of course to the displays in major cities of the United States.

Another source of inspiration can be used-book stores, where books on jewelry may be found. These are scarce, but when a jewelry book is found, it is likely to be a little gem in itself—out of print perhaps, but containing information and illustrations that cannot be found in recently published books. The nucleus of many an idea may be lurking between the old covers.

If you know values and do not get carried away, another source of fun and profit is attending auctions. The objects to be auctioned usually can be viewed a day or two before the actual auction, which is advertised in the newspapers well in advance of the auction date. Auctions are also held by local police departments, and, in California for example, the state auctions the contents of unclaimed bank safe-deposit boxes once every four years.

Huge exhibits by lapidary societies are given in many parts of the country, in which all types of cut and polished stones are shown and sold. Finished jewelry is also shown, the design and workmanship of which have been improving year after year.

Reading, looking at others' work, working at the craft—all will eventually lead to better and more interesting results. When more is known of the art than just the mechanics, something more than mediocrity will emerge from the bench of the craftsman. It is hoped that this introduction to jewelry making will encourage interest and show how exciting the craft can be. Jewelry is more than a few hunks of metal and chunks of stones assembled so that they may be worn.

CHAPTER 2
DESIGN

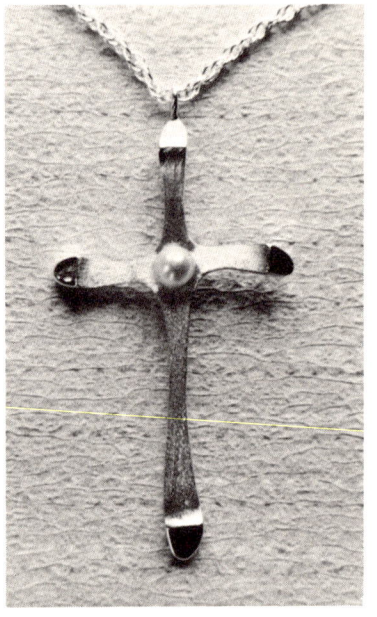

A small but noticeable deviation from symmetrical design adds interest to this simple pendant cross.

Design is construction in thought—craftsmanship is construction in materials—appreciation is the reconstruction of both processes in the mind of the beholder.

Design is the root from which all jewelry grows. Without this basic ingredient, jewelry is a collection of materials; with it, a meaningful piece of work results. Design construction is really the juxtaposing of various components into an understandable order. An example can be made of a small pile of pebbles lying on the ground. Lying there in a heap, they are just a pile of pebbles. But these same pebbles can be arranged in figures, such as squares, triangles, and circles (*Figure 1*). They can also be arranged in the shape of an arrow to give direction or of entwined hearts to symbolize love. Flower and animal figures might be depicted, and a human being coming

A

B

A Handwrought silver pendant. Abstract, insectlike design with mounted green agate.
B A scalloped bezel and bead wire surrounding the turquoise stone add a little sparkle to this silver pin.

C

D

C Silver drop earrings for pierced ears.
D Free-form gold pin with 4 mm. white pearls—Florentine textured.
E Carved Oriental Jadite mounted in a silver and brass ring mount.
F Silver and topaz used for pin and earring set.
G Silver and Alexandrites make a good color combination.

G

E

F

H   Silver Bola ties. Left — Persian and New Mexico turquoise and red coral. Middle — Mexican jelly opals. Right — jasper with gray-and-white quartz inclusion.
I   Silver pendant fused into one piece from many scrap pieces.
J   The single-celled Ameba furnished the basic design idea for this gold and ruby pin.
K   Aventurine and silver always make a good combination.

L   Titania mounted in a man's gold ring. Stone is mounted lower than the surrounding metal for protection.

M Cast silver pin with pearls; textured and oxidized for surface contrast.

Design   5

upon them would know that only another human being could have been responsible for the pebbles being placed in such a planned arrangement or design. Ability in design may be developed at any age by observation and application.

Many people are needlessly afraid to attempt their own designing. But when their perseverance and hard work have

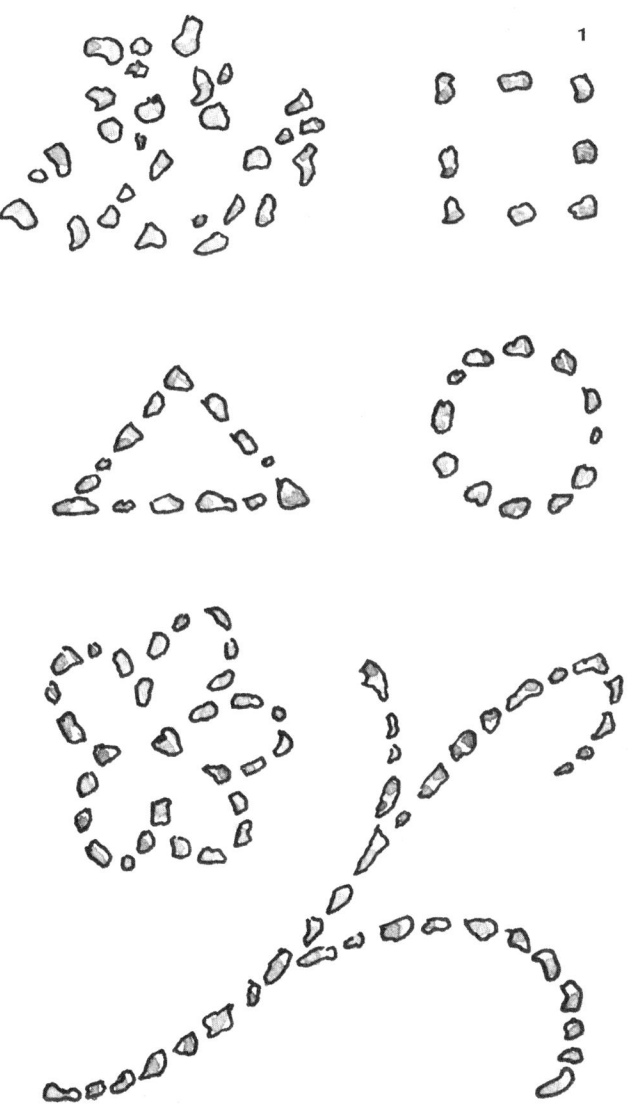

1

produced a good design, they are delighted and have more confidence in their ability. Although all abilities are not equal, everyone does have more design "sense" than he suspects.

Design is an intangible. No two people solve a design problem in the same way, nor should they. A certain designed piece may be an object of great beauty to one person, and an object of little attraction to another. There really is no valid argument against the fact that something you think is good design—is good. Or that something you think is poor design—is poor. There are, however, basic rules that tend to hold design within a structure which provides understanding and necessary order.

A design problem may be approached and solved in as many ways as there are people. We all follow basic elements of design in our everyday life. We all know what a line is, and we understand its function; a square piece of paper is recognized as having special dimensions and shape; a tiny bouquet in a huge vase is disquieting; a flowing spiral of feathers is melodic —all of these are examples of design. And so you can see that everyone, whether he realizes it or not, has a good start in understanding and recognizing good design. Creating a design is, however, a conscious enterprise, and unconscious familiarity with some design elements, while of great help, is not sufficient for the craftsman. Clear definitions and their application are necessary for good design. The explanations which follow are to be taken as guides to thinking rather than as unbreakable rules. Once learned and understood, the designer will not have to use a list of the design elements as a checkoff. What he sees as he works, either in a sketch or in working the materials themselves, will tell him whether his design is what he expects and wants.

LINE

In geometry, a line is a one-dimensional figure that can go on and on forever. Most people think of a line as being a mark made by a pen, pencil, or brush—and as a continuous mark, whether it is straight, curved, or angular. There is still another way of thinking about a line, and that way is the most valuable to the designer: it is the line that the eye naturally follows, or the imaginary line. To illustrate, draw a straight line, a triangle, and a curved line. Now, use dots, dashes, or any other symbol that you want and place these marks at spaced intervals, arranging them in a straight line, a triangle, and a curved line. This illustrates the idea of a line as eye movement: the eye following from one mark to the next creates its own line.

2

The pencil mark, or the draftsman's line, is used to show outer edges and to indicate shapes which will be cutout or negative areas, appliqué or built-up areas, or textured areas. Lines can also represent chasing and engraving (tiny lines made by tools), both in the drawing of the jewelry design and in the jewelry itself. When using wire for jewelry, line is indicated by the wire itself. Filigree is usually a design of pure line, using gold or silver wire.

The aesthetic line is the one to be most considered: it is the line that the eye takes. When a design is transferred to a piece of metal and the metal is cut along the outer line, only the aesthetic image remains. The line now indicates the edge of the metal. The same thing happens when a texture on a piece of metal borders an untextured surface, or when a decorated surface borders a plain surface, or where metal meets stone in a setting (*Figure 2*). Lines can convey tranquillity, stability, direction, vitality, continuity, balance, rhythm, activity, excitement, and many other feelings (*Figure 3*). These can be used separately or in combination to achieve various effects. The type of line that predominates will influence the "feeling" of the jewelry, and the viewer will respond to that "feeling."

SHAPE

For the purpose of jewelry designing, shape should be treated as a two-dimensional concept: it is the surface enclosed by the outermost lines of a design. If cutout areas are part of a design, these areas (sometimes called negative shapes) affect the entire design. For example, a circular shape without a cutout is similar to a coin; with a concentric cutout the shape is that of a washer (see *Figure 4*).

Shape, like line, can indicate feeling—stability, direction, excitement. A shape in the form of a triangle can be stable if

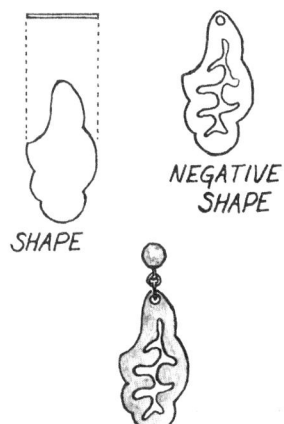

3

4

8   Jewelry: Queen of Crafts

it rests on one of the three sides. Or it can be an example of extreme instability if it is balanced on the vertex of one of the three angles. Almost any pointed shape will inspire a feeling of movement and direction toward the point. A bursting star, with its many points, gives the feeling of excitement.

The shadow of any object cast upon a screen will reveal the object's shape. In designing, shape is the starting point for drawing or arranging materials. The goal of the designer should be to create a pleasing shape that has originality and interest and is appropriate for a piece of jewelry.

Shape follows the skeleton of line: it is the picture plane of a design. The addition of another element of design, form, can put life into the shape of a design (see *Figure 5*).

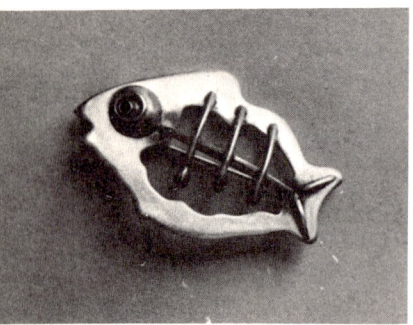
5

FORM

No photograph of a statue, however skillful, can compare with seeing the actual statue. The photographic chemicals in a camera and the artist in his painting both work on a two-dimensional surface and can give only the illusion of a third dimension. Shadow, perspective, and color help to create this illusion. But jewelry need not be limited to two dimensions. Forming the metal so that various depths, mountains, and plateaus appear and adding auxiliary shapes can make jewelry three-dimensional and exciting from any direction. The element of shape in design plus the element of form becomes a whole (*Figure 6*).

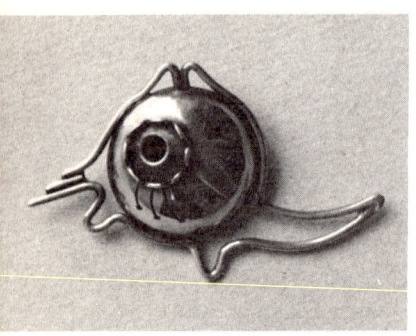
6

Form means that many planes of light reflection are possible, and there can be pleasant convex and concave areas. Lines and shapes that only hinted at the design show full depth and scope through the addition of form. Exciting shapes, like the bursting star, seem not only to spread out, as before, but to advance toward the viewer or to retreat from him. Freedom and dynamic force are combined with shape to produce form.

Form is sculptural in character, and cast jewelry easily and effectively lends itself to three-dimensional design. Form creates volume, so let us discuss this as our next design element.

VOLUME

Volume is a design element in jewelry making. It concerns the use of materials as well as the overall form. When I started working with lost wax casting, my first attempt was a man's ring. The design called for a feeling of massiveness, and in the final carved wax model this was achieved. A friend who was

Design 9

more familiar with the technique than I pointed out that although the outside of the model was very attractive, the ring had too much volume: it was heavy and clumsy and too thick. I took his suggestion and hollowed out the inside, which could not be seen when the ring was worn. This reduced the volume of the material; and it also saved some material; and at the same time it improved the feel and balance of the ring without changing the finished appearance. I had made an error common for beginners, and I was indeed grateful for my friend's advice.

The amount of forming to give volume varies greatly. Forming sometimes will improve a piece of jewelry by giving it more depth and interest, but exaggerated forming will destroy an otherwise good design. A round brooch that is 2 inches in diameter would look ridiculous if it were formed to extend forward 4 inches. For both practical and aesthetic reasons volume should be considered when designing jewelry. *Figure* 7 shows the relationship between shape, form, and volume.

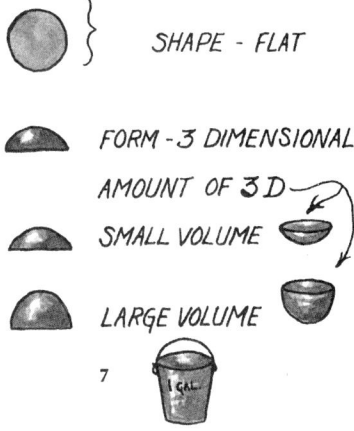

STRUCTURE

Some jewelry designers give little thought to anything but appearance. Think ahead when you are designing. The ring, the pin, the pair of earrings, the necklace—all are meant to be worn. A design that looks perfect on paper may not be appropriate for wearing. This practical and necessary factor in jewelry design is not as restricting as it may at first appear. Usually a small modification in design, combined with thoughtful and careful forming, can allow a craftsman to work around problems and still keep his original concept of design (see *Figure* 8). Most jewelry relies upon findings, such as hooks and clips, for wearability, and there must be a place to attach these findings to the jewelry. For example, a pin that has a hole where the hinge must be placed can be redesigned to leave a small area where a hinge may be soldered (see *Figure* 9). When a portion of the design cannot be changed without altering the overall design, it may help to reinforce the area in another dimension, and in this way preserve the character of the piece.

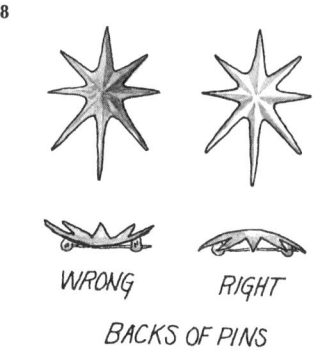

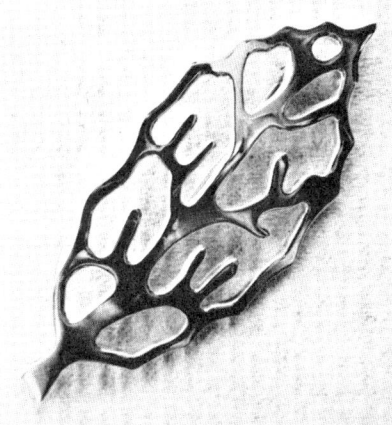

10 Jewelry: Queen of Crafts

PROPORTION

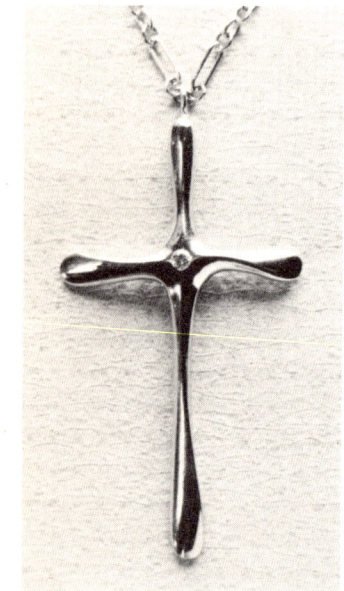

11

BALANCE

Thought must be directed toward the material used. Jewelry should not bend out of shape, bend in the middle, or have projections which will snap off easily. Gold is much stronger than silver, and designs suitable in gold may not be appropriate in silver.

PROPORTION, BALANCE, UNITY

These three elements of design are grouped together because of their close relationship. They all have separate and distinct meanings, yet to convey their meaning for jewelry design it is preferable to consider them as a unit.

Proportion

Proportion has two places in design: external and internal. The external is the relationship of the jewelry to the wearer (more will be said of this later in the chapter). The internal is the relationship of the sections, areas, spaces, or parts of the jewelry to each other and to the piece itself. A small, delicate pendant is lost if suspended on a chain having large heavy links like those shown in *Figure 10*. Large stones usually demand large settings; and small stones, more delicate settings. A design might be made, however, with the stone as the main interest and with the setting as small and as subdued as possible, or a small stone might be set in a large area where its purpose is mainly for accent (see *Figure 11*). This would appear to be out of proportion, but the design and placement can make the settings and the stones appear in proportion. Designs vary so greatly that this element is felt by the observer rather than described.

Balance

Balance is another element that is felt rather than defined. There is little trouble in achieving balance when symmetry is used: when opposite sides are identical, balance is achieved. The feeling of balance is not so easy in a design that is asymmetric, such as that of the pendants shown in *Figure 12*. Similar shapes, textures, colors, and elements of decoration will create the feeling of balance when repeated throughout a design. Curves will balance curves and angles will balance angles regardless of the curvature or angularity. The feeling of weight in balance can be thought of as a teeter-totter. Two children of equal size balance each other at an equal distance from the center. This would be like symmetry in design balance. The father, playing with his child, has to move much closer to the center of the board in order to balance the child's

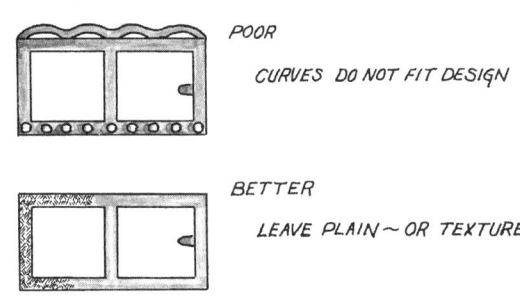

UNITY

weight. This would be asymmetric but would give balance. In the latter case, the feeling of balance demands that the placement of weight should be off-center to look correct. Designs with large masses or eye-catching centers concentrated in one area tend to be out of balance. Rearrangement of the elements can put the design into equilibrium.

Unity

Unity, as applied to fine arts in a dictionary definition, is "the arrangement of all the parts of a work of art that produces a completely harmonious effect." The parts of a work of art are the results of the use of design elements, which have to be harmonious before the work has unity. Unity may, however, be lost in other ways, such as changing style or theme in a design (see *Figure 13*).

A design that is meant to be quite ornate should not slip into modern sleekness. And the converse is true: designs which have a feeling of simplicity should not be cluttered.

Many times a design with an exotic theme is desired, and this is fine if only one theme is used. To illustrate, aboriginal art suggested the mask and the use of bone for the earrings in *Figure 14*. A handwrought chain, instead of a manufactured one, was used to further carry out the primitive feeling. Buddhist temples in Burma and Thailand, with their upturned roofs, suggested the design for the gold pendant in *Figure 15*. Carved

12   Jewelry: Queen of Crafts

light green Oriental jade was used with the complicated pendant outline to further capture the feeling of intricacy so typical in this art form. Chinese landscape painting was the basis for the design in *Figure 16*. Green jadeite was again chosen for mounting because of its close association with Oriental peoples and its contrast to yellow gold. Consistency in theme is the factor in these cases that achieves unity.

DECORATION

In discussing design elements, concern has centered on the building of jewelry, on line, shape, form, volume, structure, proportion, and balance, all of which contribute to unity in good design. But just as a room is not completed until it is painted and furnished, so jewelry is usually not complete without adding another element. This element, composed of several techniques, is decoration, or, more precisely, the surface treatment and the use of color.

Many pieces are left without embellishment of any kind; they depend on form and surface treatment for beauty and interest. A mirror finish may sparkle and glitter to fully enliven one form; a matte finish may give a feeling of richness to another. A combination of both in different areas can lend interest and draw attention to different components of the design. Oxidizing, or coloring, can attract the eye over and around the design and emphasize form in height and depth. Texture differences on two identical pieces can make them feel and look entirely different. Peening, scratching, brushing, Florentine engraving, acid etching, using abrasive wheels of varying degrees of coarseness, and matting tools—all are used to change surface texture for decorative purposes without making additions. These methods are only a few of the possibilities of texture. Experimentation and personal taste will dictate the suitable texture. *Figure 17* gives a few decorative techniques.

Besides texture, many other methods of decoration are used to create interest and beauty. Appliqué of additional shapes, various enameling techniques, engraving (other than Florentine), granulation, niello, addition of bead wire (*Figure 18*), dapped pieces, shot, stones, pearls, or contrasting metals —these are only a few of the other materials and methods used in decoration. These additions can give a feeling of rhythm when they are repeated in sequence. Additions having different shapes or having the same shape but different sizes will lend contrast and variety to a design.

Color may be present in one metal or in combination with other metals. Coloring, or oxidizing, has been mentioned

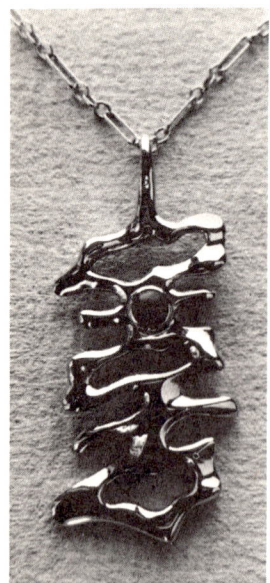

16

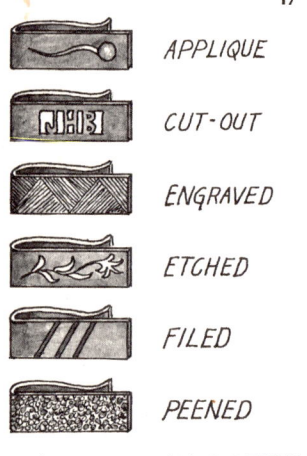

17

APPLIQUE
CUT-OUT
ENGRAVED
ETCHED
FILED
PEENED

SAME PIECE — ALL DIFFERENT DECORATION

18

Design   13

under surface treatment. Transparent, translucent, and opaque stones and enamels furnish a rainbow of colors to accent a design or to act as a center of interest. Textures of stones vary greatly, from hard brilliance to soft matte. This difference in stone texture may be used to advantage in matching or contrasting with a metal. Color should be given the same careful consideration as other design elements. Placement, color, quantity, variety—all should be considered when planning design, but color is exceptionally eye-catching and can improve or destroy design.

FUNCTION

Jewelry has little function other than to be ornamental. Watchbands, shirt studs, cuff links (*Figure 19*), some brooches, belt buckles (*Figure 20*), tie tacks (*Figure 21*), tie clips, and a few hair ornaments are about the only wearable jewelry that has any useful function. This is quite fortunate for the designer, in that he is almost completely free to design with one goal in mind: creating beauty.

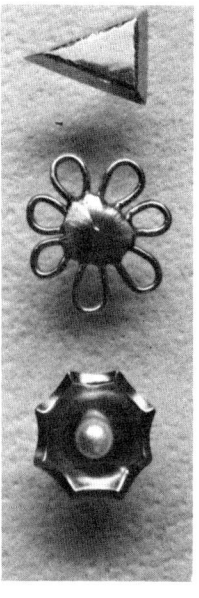

22

23

24

25

Jewelry does have some minor purposes, but the designer need not concern himself with them. One of them is the "storytelling" function: the engagement ring and the wedding ring are perhaps the best examples in our culture (*Figure* 22). Religious jewelry has similar significance, and the crosses shown in *Figures* 23 and 24 have a symbolic connection with the Christian churches. The abstract design of a six-pointed star, symbolic of the tribe of King David in the Old Testament, are pictured in *Figure* 25. In the nineteenth century the wearing of jet jewelry meant that the wearer was in mourning for a loved one or a monarch. Other examples abound, but for our purposes they cannot be listed here.

Some people find that trying to design on paper is next to impossible. Actual manipulation of scrap material, of pieces of

Design   15

wire and paper, or of a combination of lines and materials may help to develop a design. This is fine—there is no set rule. It sometimes helps to mark a simple outline enclosing the limits in size of the piece being designed. This gives a start, a reference space for doodling, and if the design is held within these limits, there is no need for redrawing. Don't worry if the design has been made too large or too small. There are only two cases where careful, painstaking drawing is necessary: if you are a student and have to do it for a grade or if you are preparing a special order for a customer. Generally do only what is needed to carry out the work. If one line or one scrap of wire carries the entire message to you, it is time to get to the bench and start working.

The most common design error for the beginner is to accept his first idea. First solutions are not always the best. If one is made that has possibilities, keep it, but it should be modified, rearranged, turned over, added to, or subtracted from. Flexibility while designing as well as while working will many times uncover unplanned but excellent solutions to a problem. Be ready to recognize these "happy accidents" and to make use of them. Frequently, a design is started with something specific in mind, and ends up being entirely different. Like a kaleidoscope, one little twist might be all that is needed. A design is seldom born in full detail. Play with each idea. Sometimes it is best to set the design aside for a time in order to get the best results.

I had the oddly shaped baroque pearl pictured in *Figure 26* for a long time before I had the idea for its use. After several

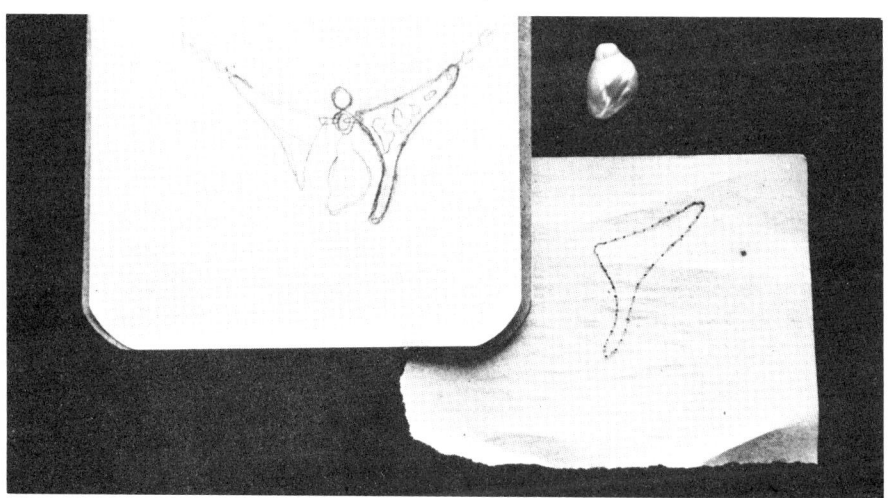

26

16   Jewelry: Queen of Crafts

sketches, the rough one in my notebook was selected and a copy was made on tracing paper for design transfer to wax. *Figure 27* shows the two wax carvings completed and ready for casting. The finished piece is shown in *Figure 28*. For appearance and practical reasons, the design was changed as the work progressed. Connecting links were added at the bottom to make it hold its shape better when worn, and two pearls to balance the changed appearance were added to the bottom. The silvery blue-green pearls resemble the iridescent colors of insects and harmonize with the yellow gold.

27
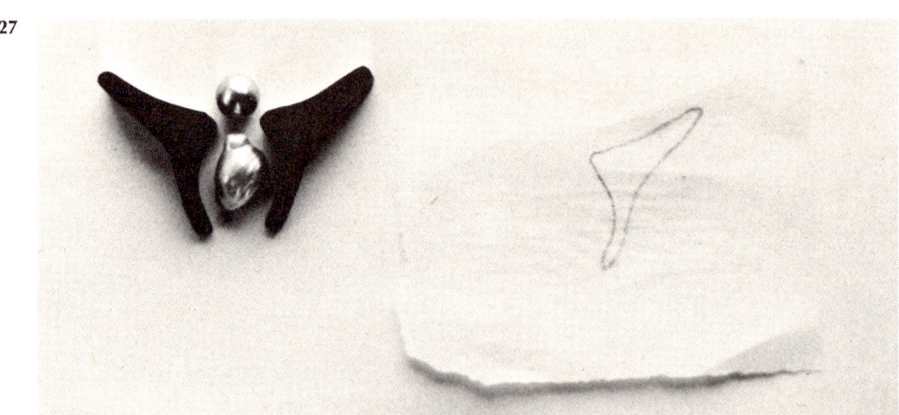

28

 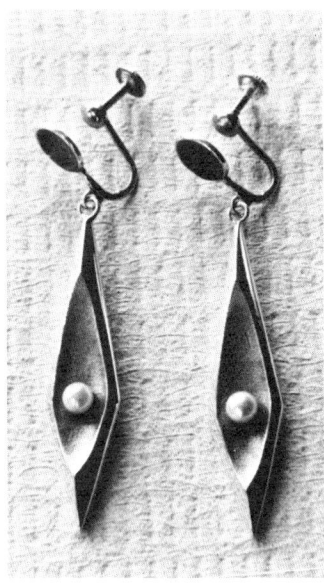 

29   30   31

Good design may also be used for physical enhancement. Here are a few examples: large bracelets make the hands look smaller (*Figure 127*); long or large rings tend to lengthen fingers (*Figure 29*); and dangle earrings lengthen a round face (*Figure 30*). Flamboyant and conservative designs should have their counterparts in personality. Color also is a factor because of its effect in complementing or pleasantly contrasting with the wearer's complexion.

The elements of design can be thought of as building blocks placed together to make a structure, and that structure is an article of jewelry. Upon completion, jewelry usually can be placed in three design categories: realistic, abstract, and nonobjective. Other names are sometimes used, but the distinctions remain the same.

Realistic Design

Realistic design, as the name suggests, attempts to produce something which looks like a natural object. A jewelry piece designed as a flower, which has the lifelike, general outline of the petals, pistils, stamens, stem, thorns, leaves, and leaf veins, is realistic in design. The leaf in *Figure 31* is realistic; there would be no doubt in anyone's mind that representing a leaf was the intent of the designer.

32

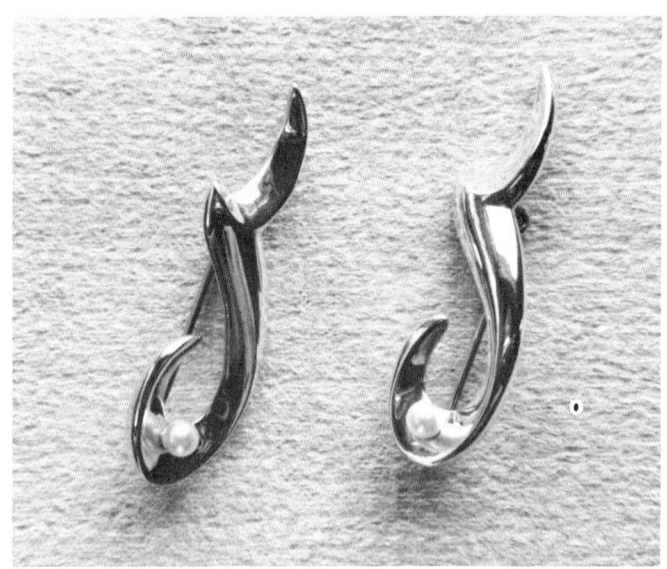

33

Abstract Design

Abstract design, as the earrings in *Figure 32* show, is rather far removed from nature. The design shown here could have popped into mind after looking at a sprouting seed, a blade of grass, an iris petal, a piece of seaweed, or a pennant fluttering from the masthead of a passing yacht. The earrings could represent all or any of these items, but only the suggestion, or essence, is present. The actual idea for this design came from the shape sawed away as waste from the leaf in the previous figure. It showed possibilities as an abstract design, and so another was made in a mirror image to create a pair.

Nonobjective Design

Nonobjective design is on its own: it is not intended to portray anything, real or abstracted. The matched pair of pins in *Figure 33* were designed with nothing specific in mind. They do not try to copy anything in nature and they carry no suggestion of anything, as an abstract design would. They have a pleasing shape, form, volume, metal color, and texture, which together make up a design in itself.

This completes the discussion of jewelry design except for this advice: Do not be timid, intimidated, or fooled. If a design idea has any merit, try it at least once. If you have followed your inspiration and feel a design possesses beauty and you are satisfied with the outcome, let it stand as is. Design should not be stilted by conformity or concern about acceptance.

CHAPTER 3
MATERIALS

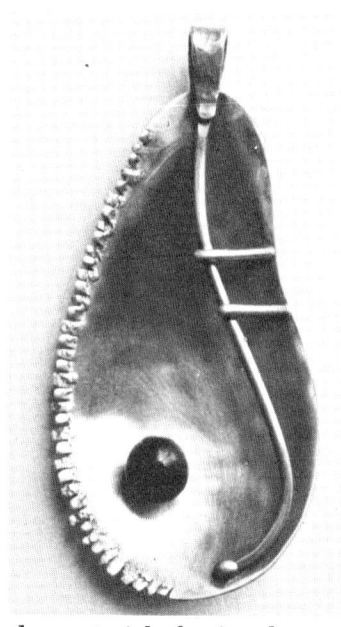

Adapted shell design marks this silver shell pendant. Partial fusion was used on the left to represent the shell mantle. Brass wire suggests depth. A black seed was mounted to balance design and create interest.

Compared with the materials required by other crafts, the materials for jewelry work are few and inexpensive. Many are household items and can be bought in grocery stores, dime stores, hardware stores, or drugstores. They can be bought in small lots and do not deteriorate if properly stored. The list below may seem formidable at first glance, but not all items are necessary for all work, and they do not have to be purchased at the same time, but only as a need for them arises. Others can be used for several purposes, and substitutions can be sometimes made for the more common items.

METAL AND STONES

Gold sheets, wire, casting pieces, solder
Silver sheets, wire, casting pieces, solder
Copper and brass sheets, wire, solder
Findings to match metal used
Cabochons, faceted stones, pearls

If you have not worked with gold before, order small sheets of 22 or 24 gauge for the basic metal, and 26 or 28 gauge for bezel work. Gold is stronger than silver, and so gold articles can be made of thinner gauge sheets. Expenses may be reduced by ordering one large size of wire, 14 or 16 gauge, and drawing it to smaller sizes as required. Further savings can be made by ordering casting pieces instead of sheets. Small sheets of gold solder are preferable to wire solder. All forms of gold and gold solder should be ordered by color and karat.

Silver is less expensive than gold, and a wider selection of metal may be stocked. Sterling sheets 3 by 6 inches are large enough to cut out nearly any jewelry piece. Gauges 20 and 22 are most commonly used, but heavier, 14 or 16, gauges are needed for ring shanks, and 26 or 28 gauge for bezels. Fine silver is better than sterling for bezel work. Sterling wire in assorted sizes and shapes can be purchased by the foot—again larger gauges can be made smaller with a drawplate. Sheet hard solder of three different melting temperatures—easy, medium, and hard—can be bought in small quantities because they are used sparingly. See *Figure 34* for the exact size of gauges in sheet and wire.

Copper and brass sheets and wire are inexpensive in com-

SHEET	WIRE			
B & S Gauge	ROUND B & S Gauge	HALF ROUND B & S Gauge	SQUARE B & S Gauge	RECTANGULAR, B & S Gauges
12	9	5/16" base	8	4 x 16
14	12	6	12	6 x 18
16	16	10	14	8 x 22
18	18	15	18	8 x 26
20	20	FLAT		
22	24	18 B & S x 3/8" wide (10 gauges hard) for tie and money clips.		
24				
26				

Courtesy of Allcraft Tool and Supply Company, Inc., Hicksville, N.Y.

parison to silver and gold. The usable gauges for work are comparable to silver, but the appropriate solder is the lead-tin soft-solder wire that is sold in hardware stores.

Findings should match the metal to which they are to be attached. It is false economy to buy cheap findings of any kind; they not only detract from a well-made piece but do not work as well and soon wear thin or fall apart.

Cabochons may be bought in a wide selection of sizes, shapes, and materials. They are the easiest form of stones to set, and their cost ranges from a few cents to several dollars each. Faceted stones, especially the synthetic ones, are stocked by lapidary and jewelry suppliers in different styles, sizes, and materials. Cultured pearls are also part of their stock. Quality, size, color, roundness, baroque form, salt- or freshwater type, three-quarter grinding—all determine pearl prices, and prices vary considerably between dealers. The differences in price are greater with pearls than with stones, and it is best to shop around before purchasing pearls, keeping quality, as well as price, in mind.

Metals and stones are the most expensive materials for the craftsman, but of course they form the finished product of his jewelry. Most of the following materials are expendable and are used to execute the work.

CASTING MATERIALS

Cristobalite investment (plaster containing silica for better refractory properties)
Borax
Wax (block, sheet, wire, utility wax)
Debubblizer
Chalk or soapstone
Sheet asbestos

Jewelry and dental supply companies sell all of these items. Household borax is found on grocery and drugstore shelves. Carving wax comes in block form in three grades of hardness: blue is flexible, purple is semiflexible, and green is hard and brittle. Either blue or purple is good for jewelry work.

Utility wax is sticky and very useful for combining parts made from Karvex and wires. Sheets and wire have many uses, and larger gauges are used for attachment and placement of pieces for casting. It may be best to buy a small box of assorted thicknesses of sheet and a box of wire of different gauges until you are familiar with their use.

A debubblizer is a liquid which is painted over the waxes before placing them in the plaster to reduce bubble formation;

a small bottle is all that is needed. Chalk or soapstone is used to mark the flasks when more than one item is being cast at a time. Kind of metal and quantity is measured in the amount necessary to cast each flask, and unless the flask is marked it is very easy to put in the wrong metal or amount. Sheet asbestos is used to line the flasks to form a cushion during expansion and contraction and also to key the plaster into the flask. It is cheaper to purchase this from sheet metal shops than to buy it precut into strips from suppliers. Asbestos is also used to line the crucible before heating and melting metal. Scraps can be shredded for use in hard-soldering operations to protect previously soldered joints.

CEMENTING MATERIALS

Pearl cement
Pearl cement solvent
Epoxy cement

Cementing is seldom done on good jewelry—pearls are perhaps the only exception. The cementing materials are supplied by jewelry firms. Pearl cement and cement solvent may be used, but the epoxy cements, which are mixed from two tubes or bottles, are colorless when they harden and work as well, if not better. They are found in almost any hardware store. Removal is made easy by slightly heating the metal and removing the pearl before it gets hot; no solvent is necessary.

CHASING AND REPOUSSE MATERIALS

Pitch
Paint thinner

Prepared pitch from jewelry suppliers is well worth the price; mixing your own is a messy job. Paint thinner bought at paint and hardware stores is used to remove the pitch which clings to the chased article. Thinner does the job as well as turpentine and costs less.

DESIGN TRANSFER MATERIALS

Chinese white
Carbon paper
Transfer paper or tracing paper
Pencils
Beeswax
Water-soluble glue

These common items need little explaining. An exception might be the Chinese white, which comes in small blocks from jewelry suppliers and costs but a few cents. Poster paint can be substituted, but the Chinese white is superior because it does not chip away as easily.

ENAMELING MATERIALS

Gum tragacanth or a commercial liquid substitute
Scale-Off or a similar protective product
Enamels in various colors, threads, chunks, and powder

Gum tragacanth is the old standby material for holding enamels in place for firing. Commercial liquid products are good on level surfaces and are easily applied, but the gum solution is better for sloping areas, and additional enamel can be applied over the first coating after it has dried before firing.

Scale-Off, Fire Coat, or similar commercial preparations of scale and oxide preventative liquids should be used with silver or copper on the exposed metal during firings to prevent the formation of oxides.

Enamels are made as powdered frit, chunks, and threads. They are supplied in a wide range of colors. Craft stores supply enamels and enameling equipment.

ETCHING MATERIALS

Asphalt varnish
Sulphuric acid
Pyrex tray
String
Paint thinner

Hardware stores furnish all these ordinary things except the sulphuric acid, which can be bought in small bottles at drugstores. Jewelry firms also carry these supplies, but sulphuric acid cannot be sent if an order is made for shipment by mail.

LAPIDARY MATERIALS

Dowels, wood
Sealing wax
Tin oxide

Lumber companies have assorted sizes of wooden doweling. Short lengths, 4 to 5 inches long, cut from ⅛-, 3/16-, and ¼-inch dowels make excellent dop sticks for working cabochons. Seal-

24   Jewelry: Queen of Crafts

ing wax holds the stone to the dop stick. A dollar will buy enough of both sticks and wax for several months' work.

Tin oxide is a polishing agent which is sold by the pound. It performs nearly all necessary stone polishing jobs and is usually stocked by lapidary and jewelry supply firms. Other oxides exist but should not be bought until the need arises.

The various silicon carbide wheels could be mentioned here but will be considered under Tools, Chapter 4, because they are an integral part of the lapidary machinery even though they wear and are expendable.

OXIDIZING MATERIALS

Liver of sulphur (potassium sulphide)
Commercial oxidizing solutions
Old brushes
Toothpick cotton swabs
Iodine crystals
Alcohol

Liver of sulphur is carried in chunk form by druggists. Because it deteriorates quickly, it is inferior to commercial oxidizing liquids, which are not expensive and if properly stored, retain their strength for long periods of time. Small inexpensive brushes or old brushes should be used for application of oxidation solutions. Cotton swabs on toothpicks are practical because they can be used once and then thrown away. Gold is not oxidized by these solutions, but by iodine crystals bought at drugstores. One-fourth teaspoon of crystals made into a saturated solution with alcohol will be enough to oxidize hundreds of dollars' worth of gold jewelry.

SANDING, SMOOTHING MATERIALS

Emery cloth, dry-type backing
Emery cloth, wet-type backing
Crocus cloth
Bobbing compound for buffing
Tripoli
Rouge
Steel wool
Scotch stone or Carborundum stone

Only the ordinary dry-type emery cloth is needed for work on metal pieces. A few sheets of medium and fine grit, along with a sheet of crocus cloth, will be enough to smooth many articles by buffing. Emery cloth for working while wet is more expensive and is needed only for use on enameled work. Bobbing compound is needed only if work has to be done quickly, otherwise tripoli and rouge will fulfill all buffing requirements. Only fine steel wool is used on jewelry, and a little goes a long way. Scotch stone or Carborundum stone is useful for smoothing hard-to-reach places but is seldom needed if a worker has a flex-shaft tool. All these items are inexpensive and can be bought from jewelry supply companies, craft shops, and local hardware stores.

SOLDERING MATERIALS

Soft-solder flux, paste
Hard-solder flux, prepared
Toothpicks
Small brushes
Sparex No. 2 or sulphuric acid
Pyrex container for pickling
Alcohol
Borax
Iron binding wire
Shredded asbestos
Yellow ochre or Scale-Off
Charcoal block or asbestos pad

Most of these items and their use are described in Chapter 5. Toothpicks are ideal for applying the paste soft-solder flux, and small dime store watercolor brushes are used for the liquid hard-solder fluxes. Sparex No. 2 is by far the best pickling solution. Alcohol and borax can be used separately for cleaning, as a flux when mixed together, or combined to form a thin solution for a protective coating over pieces to reduce oxidation. Alcohol is required for the alcohol lamp if it is used for soft-solder sweating jobs. The lamp is also used in wax work for casting.

MISCELLANEOUS MATERIALS

Strong detergent soap
Scrub brushes (or old toothbrushes)
Clean cloths
Small can of light oil

All materials should be bought with discretion. Only what is necessary should be bought, and then only in small quantities until you know how much work you will do and how long the materials will last.

CHAPTER 4
TOOLS

An extension of one of the twelve points of this pendant is attached to the chain. Balance is maintained by the reverse curve of the extension.

Generally the materials for jewelry making can be listed according to their use. Buffing compounds are used only for buffing, enamels only for enameled work, and flux only for soldering. Tools, even though designed for a specific purpose, can be used in many different ways. A pair of pliers, for example, can be used to hold metal while filing, sawing, bending, texturing, buffing, and polishing. Some tools are not as versatile as pliers but most can be used in various jewelry working techniques. A small ball peen hammer can be used for riveting, bending, straightening, forming, and texturing.

The tools listed below are essential for the beginning craftsman, or they are used for the most common techniques. This is followed by lists of tools that can be added to the necessary basic tools to make working easier and quicker or to per-

Tools 27

form operations which cannot be done without them. Common tools are listed but not illustrated or numbered.

BASIC HAND TOOLS

   1.*Jeweler's saw frame, 5½- or 6-inch adjustable
*See corresponding numbers in Figure 35.
      Jeweler's saw blades, #2 (medium)
   2. Combination bench pin and anvil
      Small bench vise, 2- or 3-inch jaws

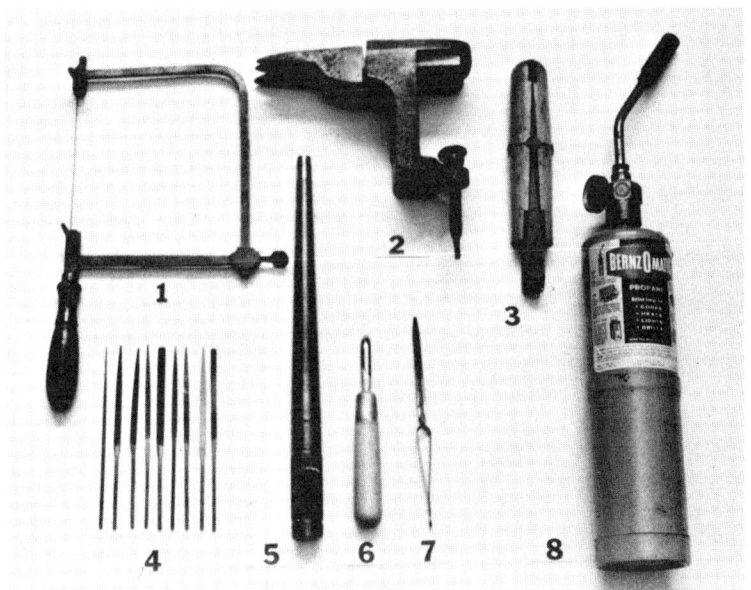

35

   3. Ring clamp
      Flat-nose pliers, 5- or 6-inch
      Round-nose pliers, 5- or 6-inch
      End nippers or side-cutters
      Center punch
      Scriber
      Steel rule, 12-inch
      Dividers, small, steel, 4- or 5-inch
      Metal shears, 7- or 8-inch
      Ball peen hammer, small, 7- or 8-ounce
      Rawhide mallet, 1½-inch face
   4. Jeweler's files, set, 5½- or 6-inch
      Flat file, 6- or 8-inch double-cut
      Half-round file, 6- or 8-inch double-cut

5. *Ring mandrel,* graduated, steel
   Plastic emery-cloth holder
   Hand drill
   Twist drills, assorted sizes between #1 and #60
6. *Burnisher,* straight
   Small tweezers, 3- or 4-inch
7. *Tweezers,* cross-locking, 6-inch
   Copper tongs, 8- or 9-inch
   Charcoal or asbestos soldering block
8. *Propane torch* (Bernz-O-Matic)

ADDITIONAL HAND TOOLS

1.*Jeweler's saw frame, 2¼-inch adjustable. If only one saw frame is included in a worker's tools, the 5½- or 6-inch frame will do all cutting, but it is awkward for small work. The smaller 2¼-inch frame is much easier to use after a design has been cut from a sheet.

Hack saw frame and blades. These are necessary for cutting heavier pieces, such as steel rod used to make stamps and chasing tools.

Chain-nose pliers, 5-inch.

Half-round pliers, 5-inch. One face is flat, the other round for forming heavier metal used for ring shanks. The curved jaw allows bending without scarring the metal.

Parallel-jaw pliers, 5-inch. These are used for heavy work and can substitute for drawtongs.

2. *Rivet-setting pliers, 5-inch.* Although these are not used extensively, they are very helpful when riveting the pins in all hinge joints. They never scar the metal as can happen when riveting with a hammer. The rivet is set with one squeeze of the handles.

Center punch, automatic or spring-loaded. This is a versatile little tool that can be used not only for center punching, but also for riveting or setting prongs and bezels. Buy the type on which the tension of the spring can be adjusted for light or heavy blows.

3. *Spring gauge.* This is a small spring-type outside caliper. It is calibrated in douzièmes (a French measurement) and millimeters and is used to measure the diameter of stores and stone-setting burrs. It also measures the thickness of inside areas of metal and wax patterns which cannot be measured in any other way.

4. *Sliding calipers.* This measures inside diameters or widths of holes and outside diameters or thicknesses. Measurements are given in thirty-seconds of an inch and in millimeters.

**See corresponding numbers in Figure 36.*

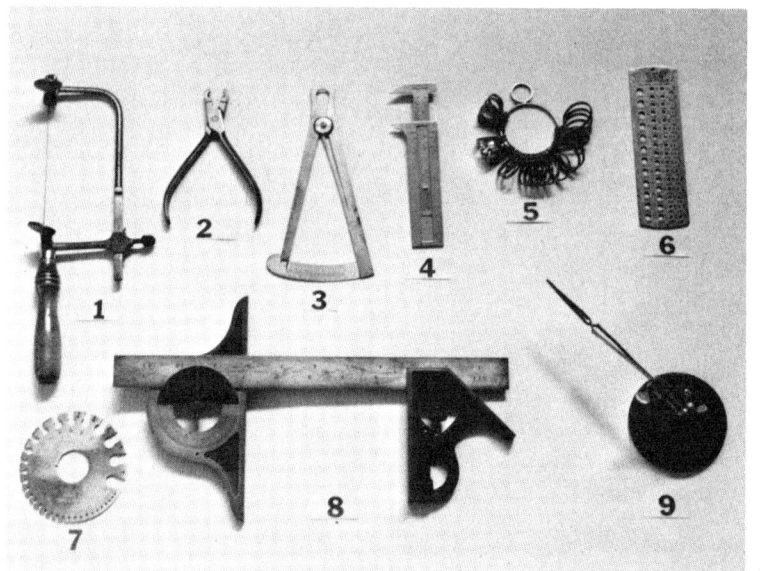

Rods, tubes, stones, drills, and so on, can be measured with this pair of calipers.

5. *Ring gauges, set.* For finding a correct finger size, the sizes on these gauges match the markings on the steel ring mandrel.

6. *Drill gauge.* There are different drill gauges for lettered drills, drills measured by fractions of an inch or by decimals, and numbered drills. Jewelry work usually employs only numbered drills from #1 to #60, so only the numbered-type drill gauge is necessary. The decimal equivalents in thousandths of an inch are shown on the gauge for each number.

7. *Wire and sheet gauge.* Measurements given are those in the Brown and Sharpe Gauge—the accepted American gauge. The other side shows decimal equivalents in thousandths of an inch.

8. *Square or combination square.* The demountable steel rule in the combination square can serve for the 12-inch steel rule listed under BASIC HAND TOOLS.

9. *Mounted tweezers (third hand).* This is an invaluable little cast-iron mount for holding cross-locking tweezers for soldering. With the tweezers and work held steady and in a fixed position, both hands are left free for torch and soldering poker manipulation in small or complicated soldering operations.

Electric soldering iron. The heavy-duty type with broad flat-tip surfaces is useful for tinning large surfaces for sweat-soldering.

Riffle files. A set of 4 to 6 is recommended if no flex-shaft machine is included in tool equipment.

File card or brush. This removes metal chips from files.

Straight peen hammer, 7- or 8-ounce. A tool for riveting in hard-to-reach places and for texturing.

30   Jewelry: Queen of Crafts

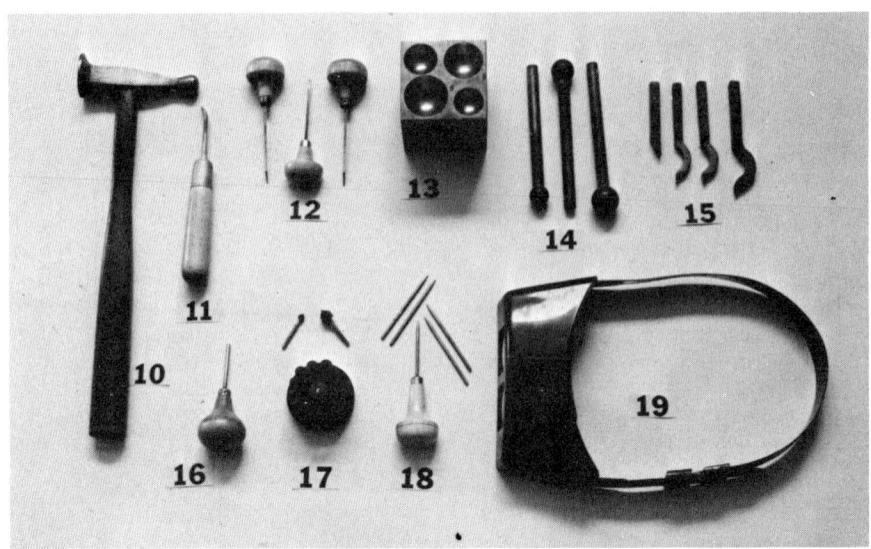

10. Planishing hammer. The broad polished head of this type of hammer performs work without marring the metal.

Chasing tools (matting tools). These come in sets of 25 or more but can be purchased individually. These tools are needed for chasing and repoussé. The tools or punches can also be made inexpensively (see TEMPERING, Chapter 5).

Chasing hammer. This hammer has a broad face and a spring to the small handle, which makes it better than ordinary hammers for chasing.

Nail sets. These are useful for texturing, especially when several sizes are included.

Pitch bowl, cast iron with leather holding ring. This is ideal equipment for chasing and repoussé work, but it is expensive to buy for occasional work. A pitch-filled shallow can or pan with a canvas bag filled with sand makes a good substitute for the craftsman who seldom forms metal by these methods.

11. Burnisher. A burnisher with a curved tip is almost necessary for setting stones. It can be used for prong setting or burnishing bezels.

12. Gravers. These tools are made in many straight and curved shapes (see ENGRAVING, Chapter 5). Only a few should be purchased as a start because in jewelry working they serve supplemental rather than professional purposes. One each of the round, flat, knife, diamond, and lined gravers, all with handles, will serve well unless a worker wants to pursue more complicated work.

Shellac stick. Small work is held securely and is easily manipulated for engraving on this small tool, although the pitch bowl can be substituted.

Engraver's ball or block. This is a very expensive item, recommended only if engraving comprises most of a craftsman's work with jewelry. The shellac stick or pitch bowl will fulfill the needs of others.

Carborundum or India oilstone. Used for sharpening gravers and other tools, these should be of fine grade.

13. Dapping die. This is made from wood, brass, or steel in three different overall cube sizes. The large steel dies are recommended because they have a wider selection of holes and hold up better under use. They are worth the expense if a die is necessary in shop equipment.

14. Dapping punches. Sets range from 1 to 3 dozen or are sold individually from ⅛ to 1½ inches in diameter. A half-dozen assorted sizes will do most work with the assistance of ball bearings and wooden punches (see DAPPING, Chapter 5).

Lead block. This is used for backing while punching and forming. A 5-pound block purchased at hardware stores or plumbing shops is large enough.

Hardwood block. This serves the same uses as the lead block.

Drawplate. Plates of different-shaped holes—square, round, and half-round—make it possible to vary shape and size of wire without stocking many types and sizes. This saves a great deal of expense, especially when working in gold.

Drawtongs. These should accompany the drawplate if much drawing of wire is done; otherwise, parallel-jawed pliers make a good substitute.

15. Hand stamps or hallmarks. These are needed only when selling jewelry pieces claimed to be sterling, a specified karat gold, or handmade. Stamps are made straight and curved styles to make it possible to stamp inside ring shanks or in two pieces because of the number of letters involved, such as Hand Made. Individual stamps or hallmarks to identify the craftsman can be designed by him and made by jewelry suppliers. They are reasonably priced and add interest and prestige to the article.

16. Stone pusher. This may be used for both prong and cabochon bezel settings.

17. Stone-setting burrs, set. These are needed when any amount of round faceted stones are to be set.

18. Beading tools, set. These are also necessary when any amount of stones are to be set in prong settings.

19. Binocular magnifier. Ordinary jewelry work can be

32   Jewelry: Queen of Crafts

done without glasses if you do not need them for reading. For close work and inspection everyone needs magnification, and the binocular magnifier which can be used with or without reading glasses is best. They come in various focal lengths and should be tested before buying. If this cannot be done, the medium sizes are usually best.

CASTING EQUIPMENT

Steel spatula. One end is flat, the other pointed. When heated, it is used for wax transfer, manipulation, and smoothing.

Small carving knives, set. Assorted sizes and shapes in the small set are used for carving wax.

1.*Alcohol lamp or Bunsen burner. One of these two heat sources is necessary for heating the spatula or for flame-smoothing wax.

2. Scale. One is needed for wax and metal weighing. The amount of metal to replace wax in casting is determined by equal water displacement of metal and wax. The metal to be used is usually ten to twelve times heavier than the wax model. An inexpensive scale which registers in pennyweights (troy weight) will be accurate enough for this work.

3. Graduate, glass. Investment plaster and water should be accurately measured for good results. The regular photographic measure of 16- or 32-ounce capacity can be bought inexpensively at a photo supply store.

Casting machine. These machines come complete and include flasks, flask tongs, sprue formers, crucibles, and counterweights. Specifications of the machine with accessories are listed in the catalogues of supply companies. Kerr is one of the largest names in casting supplies and equipment. Their equipment is carried by nearly every jewelry and dental supplier, which makes replacement and replenishing of parts and material easy.

Burnout oven. Good casting depends upon melting and proper burnout of wax before casting. The heat required is 1200 to 1400° F, with a means of raising the heat gradually over a period of 5 to 6 hours. An electric oven with rheostat control and thermocouple temperature indicator that has this temperature in its range and will hold two or three flasks at a time is almost necessary. Burnout ovens made for the purpose are expensive. In the larger sizes electric kilns with front-loading doors for enamel work are less expensive. Vented gas ovens are very good and are usually less costly to operate. Individual needs, the amount of money which can be invested,

*See corresponding numbers in Figure 37.

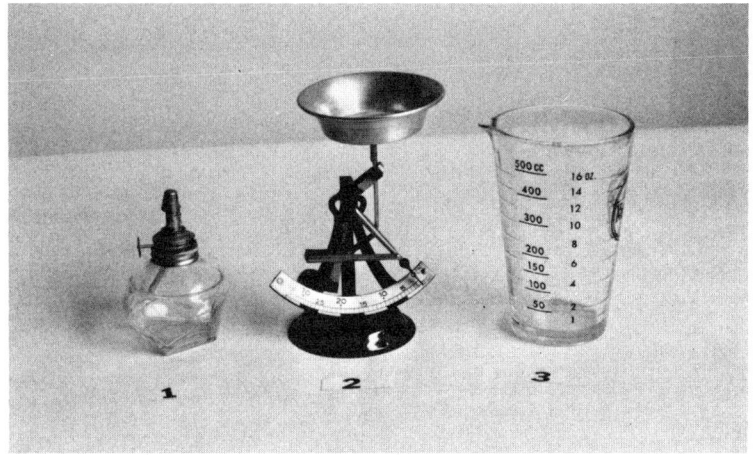

the relative cost and availability of gas and electricity—all must be considered when buying a kiln.

ELECTROPLATING, ELECTROSTRIPPING EQUIPMENT

The process and equipment used are explained in Chapter 5 under ELECTROPLATING. No special equipment other than the electrical current control unit and the chemicals are needed.

ENAMELING EQUIPMENT

Sieve, small, 1- to 2½-inch diameter. This is used for enamel application (see *Figure 38*).

Spatula, small, 2- or 3-inch. This is used for enamel placement, but toothpicks or wire flattened on the ends will do.

Steel wire, 8- to 10-inch lengths. Sharpened on the end, these are used for swirling melted enamel for design.

34   Jewelry: Queen of Crafts

Wire screen, monel metal. The firing pieces rest upon this in the kiln.

Stilts, stainless steel. Their use is the same as above when both sides are enameled.

Spatula, small, painter's. This is needed for transferring pieces on and off the stilts or screen.

Carborundum stone. This grinds and smoothes enameled surfaces.

Enameling kiln. An inexpensive electrical hot-plate type is on the market which is sufficient for small work. The burnout oven (see CASTING EQUIPMENT) can be used for all other enameling work if one is available.

SOLDERING EQUIPMENT

Prest-O-Lite (acetylene unit) (see *Figure 39*). This is an excellent source of heat for soldering, better regulated than the propane-burning Bernz-O-Matic torch. The B tank of 40 cubic

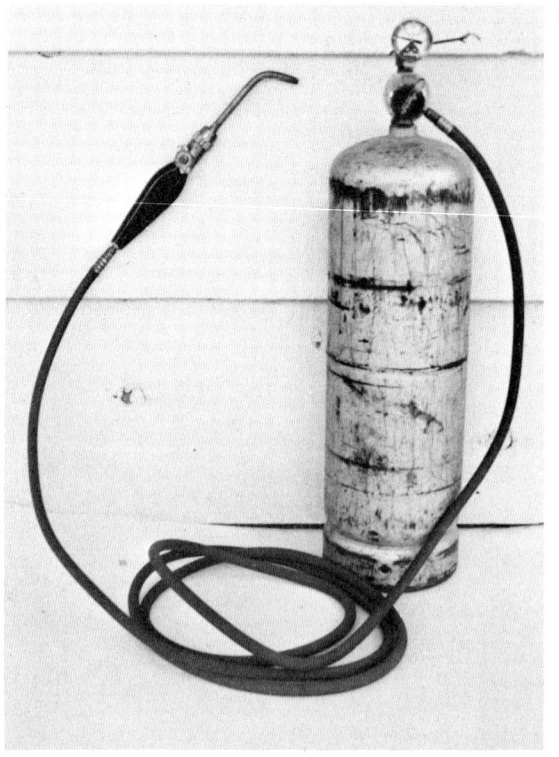

39

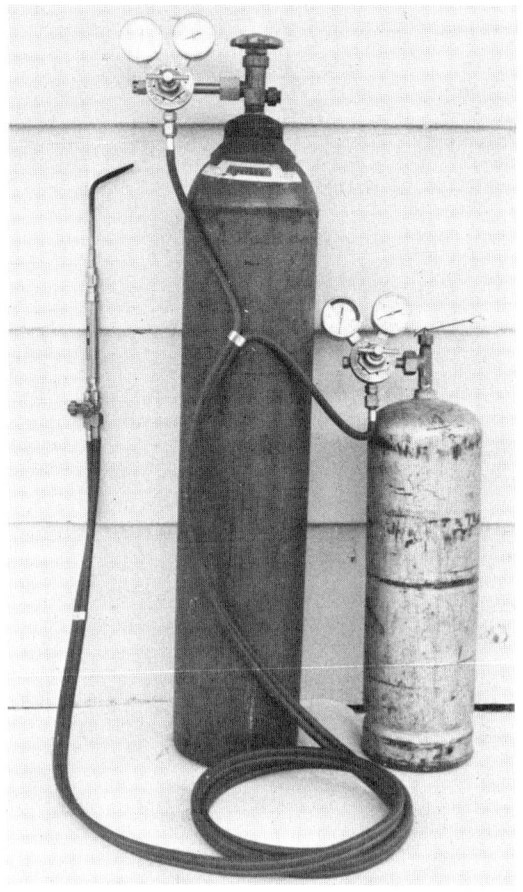
40

feet capacity is the best size for small shops. A regulator valve, hose, torch, and assorted tips make up the full unit. Flame size is regulated by a valve on the torch handle and by the size of tip used. A #3 tip for heavy work and a #1 tip for smaller work are sufficient for good soldering. Air is automatically drawn into the torch chamber for proper combustion.

Acetylene and oxygen unit (see *Figure 40*). This is more expensive equipment but it has refinements found in none of the others. The B tank can be used for an acetylene source, but another regulator, hose, and torch are required. An oxygen tank of 80 cubic feet is easily handled and matches the B tank in size. These can be rented, bought, or leased for twenty years. Leasing is the best arrangement for most workers because it is less expensive than renting and any maintenance work on the container or valve is taken care of without charge by the company that owns it. Separate gauges are needed for both tanks to show both pressure in the tank and pressure delivered to the torch (this can be regulated on the gauge). Separate hoses connect to the torch, which has valves for still further regula-

36 Jewelry: Queen of Crafts

tion of pressure. Tips are made in a number of sizes, but #0, #2, and #4 tips are needed to control heat ranging from the temperature used for soldering to that of melting metal for casting. The Victor Company is a supplier of these items, and the firm's agencies are found in almost any city of any size in the United States.

Gas and oxygen unit. These units use household gas instead of acetylene combined with oxygen for fuel and are a very good source of heat. The torches for this type are different from those used with the acetylene-oxygen unit, and so one type or the other must be chosen before buying the equipment. If possible, try both to determine which one you prefer.

Gas and compressed air. No special advantage can be credited to this form of heat. It uses the cheaper household gas but requires either a bellows or air pump and tank equipment to furnish air pressure. Other units require a large initial expense because of tank purchase or lease, but refills for them are very reasonable.

POWER EQUIPMENT

Drill press. Usually, jewelry work does not warrant buying a drill press; however, in a shop or classroom that is used by many people a drill press can be an easily justified purchase.

Buffing motor. If you do a large quantity of work, it will soon become apparent that power buffing is the best way to buff and polish. If you go to the expense of buying a motor, buy a good one. The price difference between a ¼-HP motor and a ½- or 1-HP motor is not great, and the larger motors will not be slowed or overloaded during heavy buffing work. A 1-HP motor, double-shaft, with sealed bearings and braking device is ideal. Good heavy motors may be bought at second-hand stores and are superior to a new, underpowered one. The double shaft with tapered right and left spindles allows both buffing and polishing buffs to be mounted at the same time, so that constant changing is not necessary.

Dust collector. Some form of dust collector should be provided for the buffing machine. It can be a metal hood with a tray of water, a motor-driven collector with a filter, or a complete unit which includes both the buffing motor and filtered collector. The price varies widely; only the craftsman can know which type is best for his needs.

Flex-shaft tool (see *Figure 41*). This small tool makes little noise, is easily handled, can be used for drilling, grinding, sanding, buffing, polishing, texturing, cutting, and, with an additional attachment, can be used for hammering, stone setting, and riveting. It is highly recommended for anyone making jewelry to any great extent. Sold as a unit, it includes foot rheostat to control the speed up to 14,000 RPM, small motor, flex shaft, and handpiece with tool chuck. Usually the chuck furnished with the machine is a hand-grip tightening type, which tends to allow the small tools to work loose after a period of time. A Jacobs chuck holding device in the handpiece, the same as used in drill presses, is far better and can be substituted for the supplied handpiece at a reasonable exchange cost when first purchased. The motors are rated at $\frac{1}{15}$-HP and $\frac{1}{10}$-HP; the more powerful motor is recommended and felt to be well worth the extra expense. Suppliers that stock the machine also stock the necessary mandrels, grinding wheels, cutting wheels, silicon-carbide grit-impregnated rubber wheels, wire buffs, cloth buffs, and brushes for use in the machine.

LAPIDARY EQUIPMENT

Equipment for lapidary work is almost prohibitive for the jewelry maker. It is unsound to buy machinery worth hundreds of dollars to cut stones which can be purchased reasonably. Jewelry and lapidary firms sell cutting and grinding units which vary in number of wheels, size, and cost. They often sell separate parts which a handy worker can use to construct his own grinding and polishing equipment. Stone slices or slabs can also be bought at fairly low cost. Lapidary work has become popular during the last few years and many clubs have their own equipment for their members' use. Schools often include lapidary in their evening adult programs. Whenever possible it is better to take advantage of these two sources than to purchase machinery immediately. It will also give an idea of the type and size of equipment that is best for the worker if he desires to buy his own later.

A note on tools. Some people feel that the more tools they own the better their work will be. This is not true unless the craftsman knows how to use each tool to the best advantage. It is far better to have a few good tools than to have a large number of inferior ones. Good tools deserve good care and a craftsman should take pride in their upkeep. Frequent cleaning, oiling for lubrication and to prevent rust, and sharpening where needed will lengthen the life of tools and make them easier and safer to work with. A matched set of tool items may look handsome when displayed but many times includes pieces which will never be used. I have homemade tools, tools made by different United States companies, tools which were made in England, Italy, Germany, Sweden, Mexico, and Japan. None are matched or expensive, but all were bought because they were judged the best to do the work. Each tool proved itself over the years.

CHAPTER 5
JEWELRY WORKING TECHNIQUES

The pearl mounted in the central cutout area in this pendant appears to be floating in space. The manner in which the pearl was pegged accounts for this illusion. The same design appears in Figure 70, page 61, used as a pin but turned upside down. Designs should be turned around and viewed for different applications.

Before starting actual work on jewelry, consider the various processes and techniques used in making, decorating, and finishing jewelry. The comprehensive list below includes some techniques used in the making of all types of jewelry, others are used only occasionally, and some are used only in special situations. Following the list, a short description of each of the techniques will follow in order to give the reader an overall knowledge of what they are and how and why they are used. The list is arranged alphabetically for easy reference; later, these techniques will be presented as the need arises in the actual process of making jewelry.

	Page		Page		Page
Annealing	40	Electroplating	68	Pickling	96
Appliqué	41	Electro-		Piercing	97
Bending	42	stripping	69	Polishing	98
Buffing	43	Enameling	69	Repoussé	100
Burnishing	45	Engraving	74	Riveting	101
Carving	45	Etching	76	Sanding	102
Casting	47	Filing	79	Sawing	103
Chasing	57	Finding		Soldering	107
Coloring	58	application	81	Stamping	113
Dapping	61	Forming	87	Stone and	
Drawing		Fusing	88	pearl setting	115
transfer	62	Granulation	90	Stoning	127
Drawing wire		Laminating	92	Tempering	128
and tubing	64	Oxidizing	94	Texturing	130
Drilling	66	Peening	94	Trumming	133

ANNEALING

This is a process used to soften metal by subjecting the metal. The jewelry worker uses annealing on the metals he is working and occasionally on steel tools that need tempering. The latter use is part of the tempering process and will be discussed later.

All metals, after repeated working, such as hammering, drawing, stretching, bending, and twisting get hard and brittle and lose their qualities of malleability and ductility. If work is continued after this stage is reached, the metal tends to crack or break. After annealing, the metal regains its original state and work may be continued. The annealing process may have to be repeated several times depending on the working of a piece of metal. When drawing wire through a drawplate to reduce its size, the wire should be annealed after two or three size reductions. Other formed metal will have to be judged for stiffening by feel. The process is simple and takes little time, so it is best to anneal when in doubt, rather than to risk cracking. If a piece is completed about the time annealing becomes necessary and removal of all stress and strain is desired, the heat from hard-soldering the findings will do the annealing at the same time.

Place the metal to be annealed on a charcoal or asbestos soldering pad and apply heat evenly over all areas; use a soft blue flame. When all parts of the metal have reached a dull red color (1000 to 1200° F), the flame is removed and the metal allowed to cool. Cooling can be hastened by quenching in a pickle solution after the red color has left. Annealing also cleans the piece. Overheating is to be avoided, so annealing should be done where the light permits the accurate judging of color. Flux may be applied if the worker finds it difficult to

judge the temperature color—when the flux melts the annealing temperature has been reached. A long piece of wire is wrapped into a small coil (*Figure* 42) and held together compactly by binding wire and then annealed. This heats the wire evenly and minimizes the danger of burning the thin wire. If steel binding wire is used, do not quench the roll until the wire has been removed, as a stain will be left on the metal.

A precaution should be taken whenever heat is applied to metal. At temperatures required for any hard-soldering or annealing, fire scale results if the heat is at all prolonged. This scale results from oxidation of the alloy metal being driven to the surface. Sterling silver is particularly susceptible to fire scale and much work is required for its removal. Scale appears as a dull gray covering of the normally white color of sterling or fine silver. If pieces are dipped into a saturated solution of borax and alcohol before soldering or annealing, fire scale can be prevented or greatly reduced. The alcohol burns, leaving a thin white coating of borax which keeps the surface from collecting oxides.

APPLIQUE

Appliqué is the attaching of a piece of metal upon another for design purposes (*Figure* 43). Hard solder is usually used to hold the two pieces together. Riveting is seldom used on jewelry, and soft solder should be avoided as much as possible

42   Jewelry: Queen of Crafts

44

because of its color difference and low strength. Appliqué is not limited to the addition of only one piece; many pieces of the same or different metals which have different colors may be joined. When a number of pieces are soldered together, the soldering should be done in stages rather than in one operation. The pieces may overlap into or over voids in a design, or one appliqué may be on top of another. Appliqué is used in hand-wrought jewelry to give depth. In cast jewelry it is seldom used, unless another metal of different color is required. The top two pieces in *Figure 44* are appliquéd over the next lower pieces to complete the pin and pendant at the bottom. The soldering technique is discussed fully later in this chapter.

BENDING

There are few pieces of handwrought jewelry that have not gone through a bending process when it was made. Bending as discussed here is forming to a degree, but forming will be taken as a separate process. Wire and metal strips are bent to be used as appliqués or to serve alone as a completed piece (*Figure 45*). The bending may be done by hand, using different types of pliers, or the metal can be placed in clamps or a vise and beaten to the proper bend. Metal strips, such as ring shanks, may be bent by placing them over half-round cutouts of wood, and a ring mandrel may be used to bend them into the round. If bends of identical curvature and size are required,

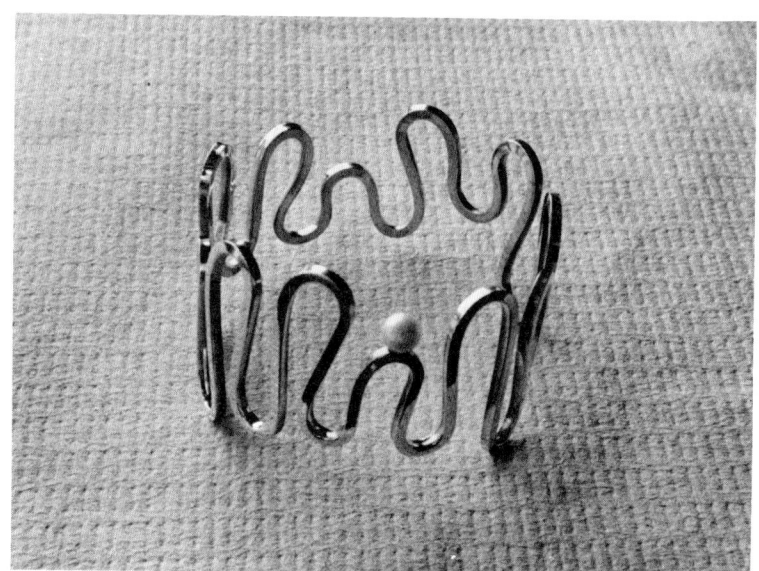

45

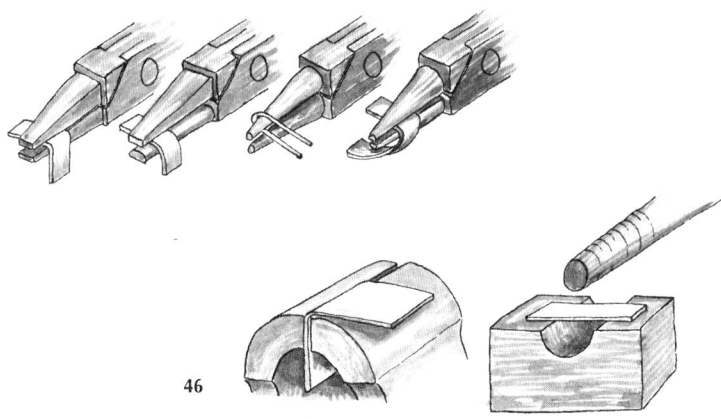

46

as for links in a chain, nails may be driven into a wood block and wire wrapped around in the pattern desired. In a bend the metal on the inside of the curve has to contract while that on the outside expands. When strength is needed after a bend has been made, it is best to use a bend having the largest possible radius. *Figure 46* shows some of the means used to bend wire and sheet metal.

BUFFING

This is a finishing process that can be done either by hand or by using power-driven buffing wheels. Before buffing, all undesirable tool marks, scratches, pits, or foreign matter, such as flux, should be removed by pickling, scraping, or using fine emery cloth. This preliminary work is important, for buffing should be limited to putting a smooth finish on a piece. Buffing is done in two steps. Tripoli, a limestone mixed with a waxy material, which comes in blocks or bars, is used first. It is fast cutting when used on buffing wheels and removes fine scratches left by the emery cloth. Final polishing is done with rouge. The base of rouge is iron oxide, which puts a final high gloss on the metal. Cleanliness while working is important. Separate wheels are used for tripoli and rouge, and the work should be scrubbed to remove all tripoli before buffing with rouge. Buffing compounds exist that work faster than tripoli, and there are different types of rouge for metals such as platinum, but ordinary tripoli and rouge are all that are needed for the buffing of gold, silver, copper, and brass. Stitched flannel buffing wheels work best with tripoli; muslin wheels should be used for rouge. The block or stick of tripoli or rouge is touched to

47

the wheel for only a second while it is turning and this is sufficient to charge the cloth. Bristle brushes are useful for articles such as those shown in *Figure 47*.

Buffing looks easy to do, and it is if these suggestions are followed. Work should always be held so that the wheel will slide off and not dig in and pull the work from the hands. *Figure 48A* shows the correct position to hold work; *B* shows the improper way. Contact should be made relative to the axle at an angle of about 4 to 6 o'clock, and the top of the piece should not come in contact with it. The article is turned around so that the top (now the bottom) is buffed next. Very small pieces may be held in pliers or a ring clamp. Chains are buffed with a board for a background and are turned to get all sides. *A note of caution here.* Chains are easily caught while buffing, so make certain that the chain is held in a perpendicular position, held tightly on the backing board, with only slight pressure against the wheel (*Figure 48C*).

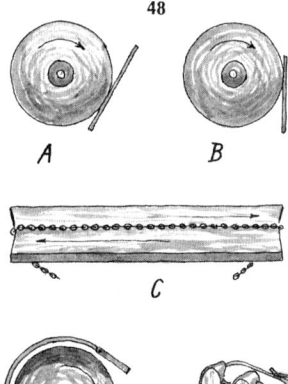

48

Detail may be lost very quickly while buffing and sharp outline may be obliterated. Square wire or parts having a square cross section can become rounded almost immediately if the slipoff action is not observed. If heavy fire scale or deep scratches show at the start of buffing, stop buffing and with a fine emery cloth remove the defects. Small scratches are best buffed out. Hold the piece so that the scratches are placed crosswise to the face of the wheel, otherwise they may be gouged deeper. It is best to use moderate pressure. Too little pressure tends to cut away details, while pressing too hard may result in the piece being torn from the hands.

Jewelry Working Techniques   45

When a wire buffing wheel is used either for cleaning or for texturing, safety goggles or glasses of some kind are necessary because the small wires might become detached. *Figure 48D* shows a wire wheel guard with an extension window for viewing the work in safety, and goggles.

BURNISHING

Burnishing is a rubbing or smoothing process done with a burnishing tool. The tool is curved in two directions at the tip similar to the outside of a long thin spoon. It is highly polished, and when used to smooth and turn metal, it leaves a bright polished surface. The main use of a burnishing tool is to set stones by bending the bezel over the stone. Stone setting and the use of the burnishing tool are described later in the chapter.

Burnishing leaves small marks which are polished surfaces. These may be used to advantage because they texture the metal. If their direction and placement is right the article will have the feeling of antique craftsmanship. *Figure 49A* shows a curved burnisher from a side view and a straight burnisher from a top view. In *Figure 49B* the metal is burnished in one direction in order to rub out scratches or to give a texture. *Figure 49C* shows a bezel which is being bent and burnished over a cabochon-cut stone.

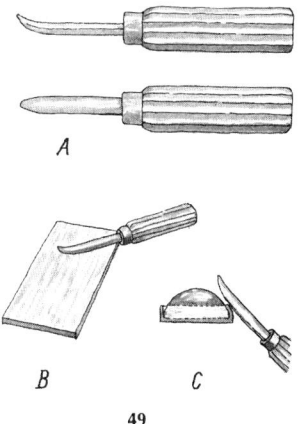

CARVING

Carving in metal is not an important technique because it is seldom used. Gravers which have round, pointed, and flat cutting edges are used for this purpose. Small amounts of metal are removed in the form of small chips. Removal of metal or solder in hard-to-reach places using gravers cannot be called carving. Carving is more a forming and decorating process than a cleanup process. Metal carving is slow and tedious work. When extensive depressions are used on a cast article, the carving is done on the wax model before casting.

Carving in wax is really "making" the article. Casting in metal faithfully reproduces the wax model. It leaves only finishing—smoothing, stone setting, and finding application—to be done. The most popular wax is an opaque, solid, model maker's wax, which comes in block form. The wax can be sawed, scraped, whittled, drilled, filed, or burred, and it can be sanded and smoothed by rubbing with a cloth. It can be fused with a heated tool to add additional wax or to replace a broken part. Three grades of flexibility are available; the medium grade gives the qualities most generally needed for carving.

50

51

52

In carving a ring, the size needed and the overall dimensions of the ring are determined by the thickness of the shank and the design used on the front of the ring. This means the view if the ring was placed on a table and looked at from above. Dividers may be used to scratch the circle of the ring size on the wax. Leave ample wax for carving around the edges of this circle. This piece is sawed from the block. A hole is drilled all the way through in the middle of the circle to facilitate the carving. Small knives are used to enlarge the drilled hole to finger size. From time to time the model is slipped on the ring mandrel to check the size. Care should be taken to keep the hole as round as possible—emery cloth wrapped around the mandrel at a smaller size will show high and low spots when the ring blank is rubbed over it. When one ring size too small is reached, the emery cloth is used to sand out the rest of the ring by twisting the blank around the mandrel over the emery cloth. It is best to leave the model slightly undersize, allowing for removal of metal when dressing and polishing. One-fourth to one-eighth of a size is the correct allowance for this. The inside of the ring is then completed.

If the ring design is symmetrical, the shank location can be scratched in the wax for guidance in cutting. Excess wax is carved away until the final design is almost reached; then it can be scraped, filed, and sanded to the final shape.

This technique is also used for carving other pieces, such as pins and pendants. The shape outlines are scratched onto a block of wax having enough thickness to allow for the three-dimensional form, and using the jeweler's saw are sawed out. If the article has cutouts, a small hole is drilled for insertion of the saw blade and the piercing is done. Carving and smoothing to the designed form completes the models for the casting process.

Jewelry Working Techniques

Carving is cutting away, while modeling is the adding of material. Both means are used separately or together to form wax patterns.

The wax chipped from a carving can be saved, but care should be taken to keep it free of dirt. The chips can be slowly melted so that no volatile material is lost.

Adding a small amount of candle wax improves the working quality. Disposable aluminum pans are ideal for melting and cooling.

Figure 53 shows how a wax block is shaped into a rough blank for carving. (A) A circle is inscribed which will be the size of the hole to be drilled (B). (C) Surplus material is then sawed away and (D) lines are marked around the piece to show the location of the shank. The ring blank at E is ready for carving.

CASTING

The process used here is known as cire-perdue, the lost wax method of casting. This is not a new process; ancient civilizations used it and recorded the process on stone and papyrus. The basic principle is simple enough. The piece to be cast is first made of wax. The wax is surrounded by plaster material which will withstand heat. A hole, or wax passage, is left in the plaster leading to and connecting with the wax pattern. The wax is melted away, leaving a cavity in the plaster in the same form as the pattern. This cavity receives the molten metal, and when cooled the plaster is removed, revealing the metal replica of the original wax form. Refinements have been made, but the process is substantially the same. Dental investment is now used in place of the plaster material. The investment does not expand and contract while setting up and undergoing the heating necessary to melt the wax and to receive the molten metal.

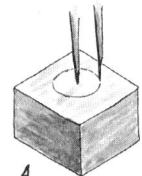
A
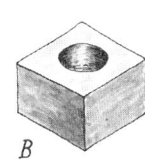
B

C
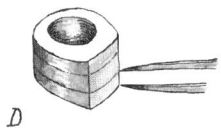
D
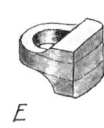
E

53

Two methods better than pouring metal into the mold have been devised: one, a vacuum to suck the metal into the mold; and the other, a casting machine which thrusts the metal into the mold by centrifugal force. The centrifugal method will be described because the materials and equipment come within the scope of a majority of craftsmen. Also, everything needed for centrifugal wax casting is commercially available, and the process itself has proved to be highly successful.

Wax is available in shapes other than blocks. Sheets of various thicknesses and wire of different gauges and shapes are available. Some waxes are hard and brittle, others are tacky and sticky and may be used for holding pieces together. Round wax wire in gauges 8 and 10 is the most widely used because it connects the wax model to the sprue, and some is used for each piece to be cast.

Several items are necessary to prepare a flask for casting. The flask itself, a bottom to the flask, which contains the sprue former, sheet asbestos to line the flask, a liquid debubblizer to free the model of bubbles, a vibrator of some kind, a bowl and spatula for mixing, and the investment. Also needed is a source of heat for melting wax, such as an alcohol lamp, and a small tool to apply the wax.

Flasks of various sizes and sprue formers are included with the purchase of a casting machine. A vibrator is expensive, however, substitutes may be made. For some years, I used a Vibro Tool to shake a small board mounted on rubber matting as a vibrating platform.

Another expensive item is a vacuum, which consists of a bell jar under which a flask is placed after being filled with investment and subjected to the vacuum created by a motor and pump. If much professional casting is done, this kind of vacuum is worth the expense because this process removes all bubbles.

Proper placement of models in the flask and vibrating will remove all but the smallest bubbles, which will look like very small beads on the metal of the finished casting. These are not much of a problem to remove unless they are in the most intricate part of a pattern. Again, placement in the flask allows some control over bubbling. Bubbles always rise, and if these sections are uppermost, vibrating tends to pull them away from the mold. Most bubbles will attach themselves to the underside. Models with large flat areas can be placed on a slant to facilitate slipoff of bubbles so they may rise and become free of the metal.

Using a ring, for example, the finished wax model is attached to the sprue former by means of wax wire (*Figure*

Jewelry Working Techniques 49

54). A 1-inch length of 8- or 10-gauge wire is held against the shank of the ring; melted droplets of wax are used to make the connection. A small, pointed, spatula-shaped tool or a wire, such as a straightened-out paper clip, is heated over an alcohol lamp and used to pick up small chips of wax. Bits left from carving will serve well. The small drops are placed at the juncture of wire and model to weld the two pieces together. Enough wax is placed in this way to make a fillet, or funnel-shaped form, coming up to the wire. Sprue formers are made of either metal or rubber, but both have a hole at the top of the cone which is filled with sticky wax. As a rule the shortest workable amount of wax wire between model and sprue is best. Cut off the wire attached to the ring, leaving about ¼ to ½ inch, and stand this up on the sticky wax in the sprue. Test the location of the model in the flask by slipping the flask over it and setting it down. There should be no less than ⅜ inch between the sides and top level of the flask when filled with investment. If the model is correctly placed it can then be wax welded to the sprue former in the same manner as the other weld was made on the ring. The model and flask are now ready for the investment.

54

If liquid debubblizer is available, dip or carefully paint the model and wire sprue. Cut a piece of asbestos paper long enough to cover the inside of the flask and wide enough to expose about ¼ inch on both ends of the flask. This exposure of a small amount of the flask at each end keys the investment, while the asbestos allows better distribution of heat and acts as a cushion between the model and flask. Wetting the paper will make it adhere to the flask and stay in place. The flask is then put on the sprue former. If a metal one is used, it can be held by placing several small pieces of sticky wax between the outside of the flask where it meets the sprue former. If a rubber former is used, a rubber lip holds the two together so that there is no loss of investment from the bottom. *Figure 55* shows a cutaway flask set over the mounted wax ring and resting upon the sprue former base. Dotted lines indicate where the sticky wax is placed around the base to seal it for the investment. The inside of the flask has been lined with asbestos.

Next, investment is mixed with water according to the manufacturer's instructions. Flask sizes and investment vary, so it is a good practice to record accurately the amount of investment and water used for a particular size flask to avoid waste on later casts. Roughly, the investment necessary to fill a flask when mixed will be about one and a half times the flask volume when dry. Mix plenty for the first time and cut down on the amount the next time if too much has been

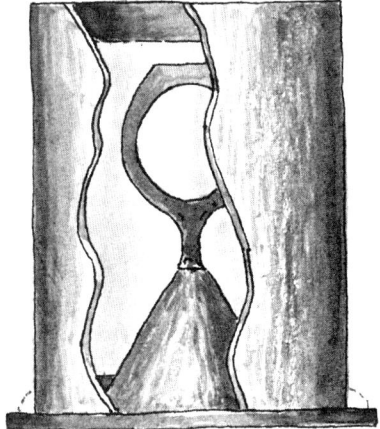
55

mixed. The investment should have a thick, creamy consistency for best results. When the investment has been sufficiently mixed, the bowl is vibrated to remove bubbles, and the mixture is poured down the sides of the flask rather than on and over the model. If a vacuum is available the flask is subjected to this treatment; otherwise more vibrating is necessary to free the mold of bubbles. The flask is then set aside to allow the investment to set for 10 to 15 minutes. The sprue former may then be pried off to reveal the cone-shaped indentation left in the bottom and the exposed end of the wax sprue wires. This completes the preparation of the flask for casting.

One point has been omitted from the preparation: the amount of metal which must be ready to cast. The amount of metal needed to form a ring and sprue can be easily judged.

Metal weighs about twelve times as much as wax. Find the weight of the wax, multiply it by 12, and the answer will be the amount, by weight, of metal to be used. To this weight must be added the amount necessary to form the conical sprue. A metal sprue button may be added to the weight needed for the models, or a fair guess may be made to fill the cone between half-full and full. Graduated flasks may also be used to measure the amount of metal necessary by water displacement; the amount of water displaced by the wax and sprue must be matched by an equal displacement of metal.

The amount of metal for more complicated pieces and combinations of pieces in the same flask is harder to judge. Care must be taken that the cone-shaped sprue does not become overloaded and spill metal; about half-full to full is sufficient to provide reserve metal for shrinking into the model while contracting during cooling.

Now let us go back to the ring. After the sprue former has been pried off and while still damp, the casting arm on the casting machine should be balanced with the flask in place. The metal used will offset the weight of the water lost during burnout, so only the invested flask need be placed on the arm. Counterweights on the machine are used to balance the flask as closely as possible. The next step is the burnout.

Burnout ovens may be gas-burning or electric. Flames should not come in contact with the flask, and some means of venting should be provided. A pyrometer is essential because the control of the heat is very important. To allow gases and wax to flow freely out, the flasks should be placed in the oven on stilts rather than directly on the oven floor. The flask is placed in the oven resting on stilts, sprue end down. At least 1 hour is allowed for the investment to set up before the burnout is started. Nothing varies so greatly among craftsmen as

Jewelry Working Techniques 51

the amount of time allowed for burnout. This varies from bringing the flask up to casting temperature as quickly as possible, to 13 hours or more. Burnout equipment varies, and large flasks take longer than small ones, but normally a 5- to 6-hour burnout is safest and will accomplish the task. Do not invest a flask and wait a week before casting, as the flask must go into the oven while damp. If the flask is invested one day and cast the next, wrap it in plastic to avoid evaporation.

When the oven temperature reaches about 300° F, moisture coming from the vent will be noted for an hour or more while the water in the investment is being driven off. When this water vapor has evaporated, gradually raise the temperature until 4 or 5 hours later a temperature of 1250° F has been reached—this is casting temperature. If a black or gray stain still appears on the sprue end of the flask, burnout is not complete; continue the burnout until the investment shows a clear, clean white before casting.

The casting machine is wound up at this point—three turns for small flasks, five for large flasks—and the holding bar is set to keep it in position. Metal which has been placed aside for this flask casting is now put into the crucible of the casting machine, sprinkled with flux, and melted. A slate or carbon rod is used for stirring the metal to bring impurities and oxides to the top. A crucible lined with asbestos is best for gold; a flux-coated crucible is best for silver. The flask is placed in the casting arm cradle, the crucible pushed against it to be sure of alignment with the sprue, and the metal is checked to make certain that it is still in a molten state. It should stir easily and the flux should float on the surface, moving as the torch is moved. A soft flame is used throughout melting. When the metal temperature is correct, the arm is released, forcing the metal into the mold as it spins. The flask should be cooler than the furnace temperature before receiving the metal, but the work of placing the flask in the cradle and rechecking the metal should be done quickly lest the flask cool off too much and result in incomplete casting. The machine is allowed to come to a complete stop by itself before removal of the flask and setting it aside for cooling. In 10 to 15 minutes the flask is placed in a bucket of water, which will steam and boil, helping to disintegrate the investment. The casting is removed, scrubbed, and placed in acid pickle for further cleaning. Cutting the model from the wire sprue completes the casting.

Figure 56 shows two rings attached to the sprue former ready for the flask to be placed over it and the investment to be poured into it to the top, as shown in *Figure 57*. *Figure 58* shows the bottom of the flask after the sprue former has been

56

57

58

59

Jewelry Working Techniques   53

pried off—the ends of the wax model appear at the bottom of the cone-shaped depression. *Figure 59* shows the flask placed in the burnout oven on ceramic stilts, so that the wax can freely flow out of the investment as the temperature increases. The casting machine with counterweights, flask, and crucible positions are shown in *Figure 60*. The rings in *Figure 61* have been cast and cleaned up and are ready for sawing off the sprue button and wire.

There are bound to be some failures in your first attempts at casting. Fortunately most of the failures leave clues, so mistakes need not be repeated. For example, when the sprue button cools with an indented top, it indicates the metal was too hot; the sprue button might be convex if the metal was too cold; and if it is level, the metal was about right. If excess oxidation is present on the piece, one reason may be that the metal was overheated or too little flux was used. If the casting is not complete, it could be because of underheating. Incomplete burnout may also cause too much oxidation, and a pitted surface can reveal overheating of the metal. Breakdown of the investment, because of shock or overheating for an extended period of time, will show as small fins extending from the pattern. This may also be caused by trying to burn out too rapidly or by vibrating the investment too long, causing a fracture after the investment has started to set. Fins may

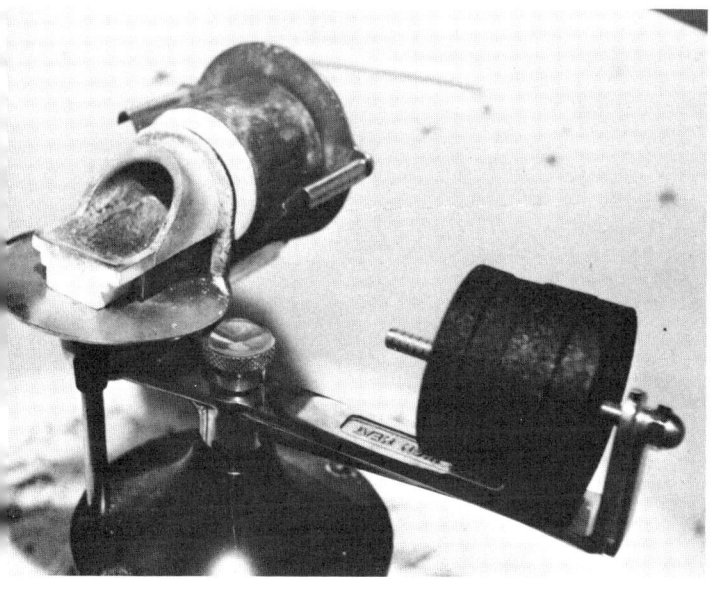

60

61

appear where the investment is weak from excess water or insufficient mixing. Cracks causing fins may be due to pressure failure, as when the metal strikes a flat surface or the pattern is too close to the top or sides of the flask. Incomplete castings may be due to the metal not being hot enough, broken investment blocking the passage, or sprues too small to carry the metal to all parts before cooling. Too much or too violent vibration may even dislodge the pattern from the sprue and no casting will result. The air filling the cavity must be forced out through the pores of the investment by the inrushing metal, so enough centrifugal pressure is needed to accomplish this. Perhaps a complete casting would have resulted if an additional turn or two had been given to the machine. Dirt and excess flux may pit surfaces. Too little metal may be used, and then parts of the pattern which extend above the level of metal entry will be cut short of metal. And air bubbles in the investment, of course, are the cause of the small metal beads clinging to the casting. An otherwise good casting may be cracked by too early quenching. Remember that the hot flask full of investment is like a baked potato, much hotter inside than is sometimes suspected.

If some of these faults appear in the castings, vary the amount of heat for metal and heat and time for the flask burnout. Cleanliness, and this includes the metal used, is very important. It should be clean of grit and grease and should contain no solder. Crucibles can become loaded with impurities and flux; boiling in water will dissolve these, and after drying, the crucible will be as good as new. After a little experimenting a near-perfect casting can be achieved.

A mistaken idea is held by some craftsmen and writers that the lost wax method of casting is best suited for mass production and does not provide the individuality that handwrought jewelry does. Nothing could be further from the truth.

It is true that mass production makes use of this method, but only as a preliminary step. Handwrought jewelry could be duplicated in mass as easily as pieces that have originally been cast in wax. As stated before, either method of making jewelry is chosen to facilitate the work. In some cases, to cast would be doing things the hard way. Some pieces that lend themselves to the casting process might require an undue amount of work to produce by handwrought methods, and the results would be inferior. An example of this could be the casting of a pair of earrings made entirely of wire. Why manipulate wax wire and go through the casting process and the following cleaning and buffing when the metal wire is available and can be bent to shape, soldered, and finished in much

less time with economy of cost and effort? And conversely, why do difficult carving or build up metal by additional sheets in some area of a design to give a sculptured effect, when attaining this sculptured effect is the main advantage of lost wax casting? The argument concerning individuality does not make sense. A carved wax model has within itself as much of the elements of design and individuality as a finished hand-wrought article.

The step following casting, which has been developed and used for mass production, is the use of rubber molds to reproduce wax models from an original. Small commercial shops make good use of this method. A pair of earrings is designed, carved, cast, and finished (*Figure* 62). A brass or iron sprue is soldered to the earrings so that they look like the original wax earrings with the wax sprue wire attached (*Figure* 63). These metal models are placed between sheets of uncured rubber and vulcanized (*Figure* 64). After this curing of the rubber, the mold is split apart, and the earrings and attached sprues are taken out, leaving a cavity in the mold, the exact impression

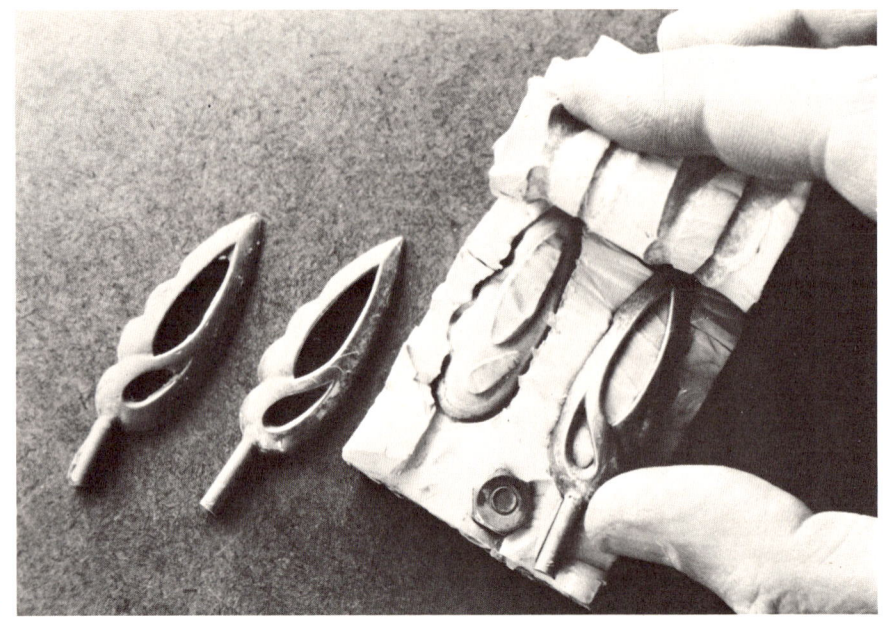

65

of the embedded earrings (*Figure 65*). (Before vulcanizing the two halves of the mold are keyed so that they will always go back together in the same relative position when and after cutting has been done.) The mold is held together, and melted wax is forced under pressure into the hole left by the sprue. The wax fills the earring and sprue cavity in the rubber. A few seconds later the mold may be opened and the wax earrings, complete with attaching sprues, can be lifted out (*Figure 66*). They are now ready for attaching to the sprue former and can go through the casting process. A dozen or two dozen may be made and cast at the same time, depending upon the capacity of the casting equipment. Large flasks may hold many pieces at a time, and the models can be sprued to a central wax

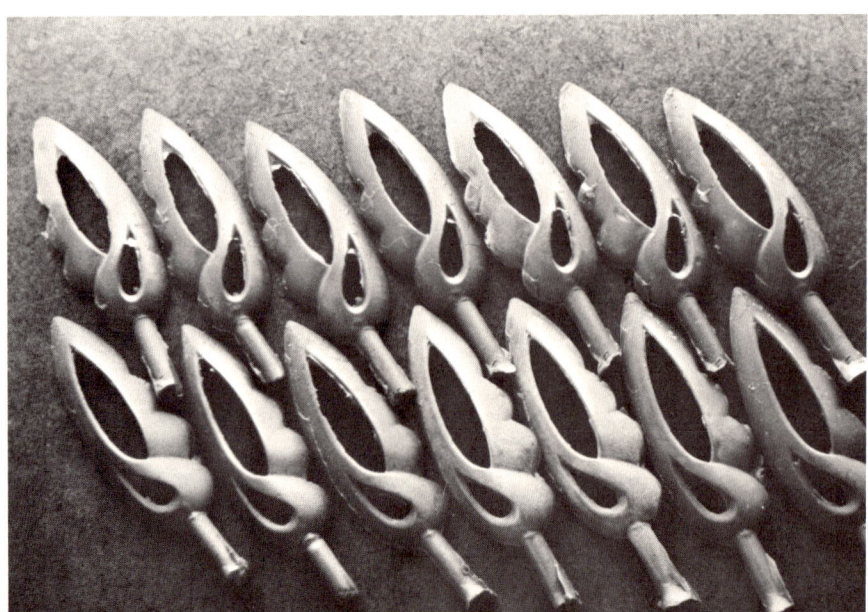

66

Jewelry Working Techniques   57

trunk, the result looking much like a Christmas tree. The advantages of this form of reproduction are quite evident.

CHASING

Chasing is a decorating and forming process. The steel tools which are used have a wide assortment of shaped ends. A chasing hammer and some sort of backing material are needed to lend support for the metal being worked upon. Except in very few instances, chasing and repoussé work are used together, one method depending upon the other for final results. In fact, in one modern language, both terms are synonymous. The terms as used here will have some distinction: chasing is the work performed on the front of an article (*Figure 67A*), while repoussé is the work done from the back (*Figure 67B*). Used together, the result is shallow sculpture, or bas-relief.

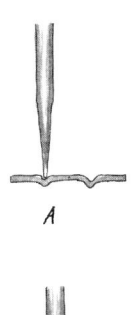

A

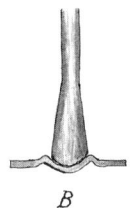

B

An example of the use of chasing alone would be the veining of a leaf or the indentation of the metal to form a simple outline. A lining tool similar to a small blunt chisel is used to form the lines by blows from the chasing hammer. In order to get a smooth line, the leading edge of the liner is tilted slightly, so that it may be slid along the line, while the top of the tool is tilted slightly away from the worker. The tool is moved forward a small space with each blow, and the overlapping indentations form a uniform groove (see *Figure 67C*). Backing for this type of work may be a lead or wood block. Larger, rounded chasing tools for repoussé work can be moved back and forth and held in various positions to form smooth raised surfaces, as shown in *Figure 67D*. If, after the chasing has been finished, the piece has become uneven, it may be straightened out by placing it between paper or cloth and gently tapping with a mallet.

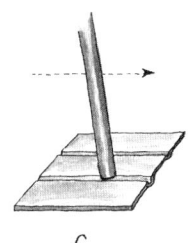

C

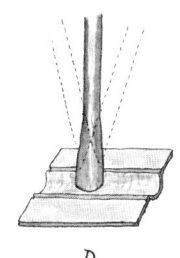

D

67

When both chasing and repoussé are used, a better backing is needed so that work done on one side will not be lost when the other side is being formed. A heavy, half-spherical, cast-iron pitch bowl filled with pitch and having a leather ring base which allows position changes is ideal. However, any container which will hold the pitch and article securely while the work is being done will suffice. It is best to mark the design by light scratches in a piece of metal, leaving an excess border all around. The metal is to be stretched, and if the design itself is cut out first before working, it will be stretched and warped out of the original shape. Upon completion of the forming, the outline of the design is sawed out, including any cutouts in the article. The surface of the pitch is warmed and melted slowly by a torch so as not to burn it, and the article to be chased is set into the pitch after being lightly oiled on the back. For better holding, the pitch along the sides can be folded over the top slightly so as not to interfere with the design. The chasing of the lines is then done. If the lines are to be deep, go over them lightly the first time and follow up by going over them again. The article is removed from the pitch by warming and then being lifted from the pitch with tweezers or by prying off after chilling. Kerosene will remove all adhering pitch, and if more cleaning is desired, a short time in the pickle solution will bring the piece down to clean metal. Now the piece is turned over and placed in the pitch the same as before, and the repoussé work begins, using rounded dapping tools to bump the metal down in the direction opposite from that made by lining tools. Here again the work should be done gradually if the design has any appreciable depth. It was pointed out under ANNEALING that metal becomes brittle after continued working and will crack if not annealed frequently. Chasing and repoussé stretch the metal in order to form the design, and so annealing should be done during both processes. There is no limit to the number of times a piece may be worked, turned over, and worked from the other side. Very high relief can be obtained if the metal is always kept malleable. There are no set rules; the design may have to be chased from the back and dapped from the front. If very sharp lines are required for distinctness, they should be done last to avoid tearing the metal.

The "pitch" used for this work is composed of pitch, plaster of paris, and tallow. Pitch is inexpensive. Unless a great deal of repoussé is to be done, it is better to buy the amount needed from a jewelry supply house than to get involved in a sticky, unpleasant job of mixing. Some books listed in the Bibliography contain proportions and mixing instructions for anyone who wishes to make his own pitch mixture. A chasing hammer is not a must, but again, if much of this type of work is done, it will be found superior to an ordinary hammer because of the wide face and the spring in the handle. Simple tools may be made from nails to do the work on thin metal if a tool necessary to fit the job is not among the set of chasing tools. Leather-working tools may also be called into service. A whole set of tools may be made from ¼-inch tool steel rods which are cut, formed, polished, and tempered as described later in this chapter under TEMPERING.

COLORING

Time changes the colors of such metals as gold, silver, copper, and brass. Depending on the design, color can be good or bad.

Jewelry Working Techniques 59

Some jewelry pieces look their best with the finish fresh and shiny; others pick up a richness and depth from the color change which time brings on. *Figure 68* shows the use of oxidation on an etched piece to give contrast. The lower right section below the dotted line shows how the design elements are nearly lost without the contrasting effect of coloring. There are chemical changes which can be used in the shop to hasten the time process. The term "oxidation" is generally used to describe this process, and the resultant work is described as having been antiqued or oxidized. Most chemical changes are effected by sulphur compounds which form sulphides rather than oxides, and so the term "oxidation" is incorrect. This can be noted if rubber is placed in contact with silver; very shortly the silver will pick up a dark finish because of the sulphur in the rubber.

Various sulphides, such as barium sulphide, ammonium sulphide, and potassium sulphide, may be used. Potassium sulphide, also known as liver of sulphur, is most commonly used. It may be purchased inexpensively in most drugstores in lump form. Its disadvantage is decomposing and losing strength after a period of time even though sealed tightly in a dark bottle. Ammonium sulphide is a liquid and is the base of commercial oxidizing solutions, which may be purchased from supply houses; breakdown and loss of strength is not as noticeable.

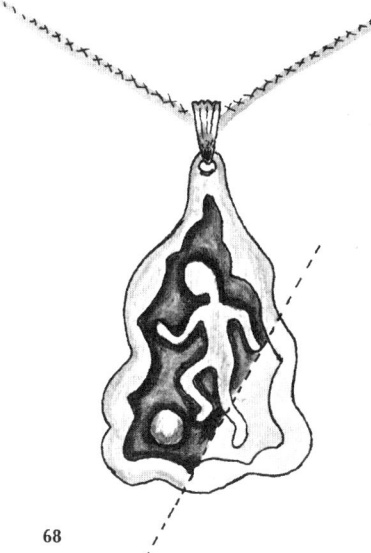

68

All metal work must be completed on an article before coloring. This includes soldering the findings where necessary, buffing, and polishing. Wax coatings may be placed on stones already set, but it is advisable to set them after the coloring has been done. Any metal piece to be colored must first be clean and free of dirt and grease for an even distribution of color. Gold and silver will take color evenly if scrubbed in soap and water and left in a warm pickling solution for a few minutes. (This will help pieces having areas hard to scrub.) Copper and brass may be dipped into a bright dip, which is composed of equal parts of nitric and sulphuric acids into which a pinch of salt has been added. When making this dip, add the sulphuric to the nitric acid. Because of chemical reaction, heat will result from this mixture. Upon cooling the dip is ready for use.

If liver of sulphur is to be used for coloring, a small piece, about a half-inch cube, is dissolved in a pint of warm water. The piece may be placed in the solution while the chemical is hot (below boiling) or while cold; much quicker action takes place under heat. The article may be heated and dipped into a cool solution, or the solution may be applied by swab to the article and gently heated with a torch. The latter gives

60   Jewelry: Queen of Crafts

better control where oxidation is limited to an area or to specific places on an article. Silver and copper turn in color from dark straw, to blue, to black; the piece may be removed at any time. Soap and water scrubbing and rinsing should follow removal to stop all coloring action by the chemical. Care should be taken that the piece is removed when black has been reached, because the sulphide will build up and chip off. If this happens, recleaning and recoloring are necessary.

Nickel silver and brass do not react to sulphur compounds for coloring. A solution of butter of antimony (antimony trichloride) and water will give a blue to black finish depending upon time, heat, and strength of the solution. Karat gold, such as in *Figure 69*, may be given colors ranging from dark straw through brown to black. A saturated solution of iodine crystals and alcohol is used. The iodine may be purchased at any drugstore. In heating the article and swabbing it with the iodine solution, be very careful because the fumes are very poisonous.

69

Polishing follows the coloring and may be done by machine or by hand. The buffing wheel should be used only if the construction of the piece is such that the wheel can safely ride over the colored areas and highlight only the desired ones. For pieces which do not lend themselves to power buffing, a cloth rubbed on the tripoli bar and wrapped around the finger will allow full control of color removal. Rubbing in a similar way with rouge will restore the original high luster. If the coloring for antiquing was done, the color should be removed so that the highlights are where the object would naturally receive wear and polish. This is the usual way of finishing. Color may be graduated from bright metal to black, or a distinct line may be left at the juncture. Appliqué is especially enhanced by coloring, which gives it depth.

The texture of the metal will greatly influence the color. A matte finish, shown in *Figure 70,* will appear like velvet with no sheen, while a shiny surface will look like satin even though the amount of color applied is the same. Peened surfaces, if polished by using a hard flat stick, will look like net. Steel wool rubbed over an oxidized area will give still another effect, while scratches made with a sharp tool can change the appearance entirely. *Figure 71* shows a triangular pin with scratched lines made tangent to the cabochon-cut opal stone.

If anyone is interested in chemistry as well as in jewelry, formulas and coloring procedures other than those given here may be found in two books listed in the Bibliography: *The Design and Creation of Jewelry,* by Robert von Neumann, and *Hand Made Jewelry,* by Louis Wiener. Coloring is meant to accent and enhance a piece of jewelry. Because of the ease of

70

71

applying, coloring should not be used indiscriminately on and over everything, and most certainly not to cover poor workmanship. If poorly used, colorful hues, such as the blues, greens, browns, and golds, can add a garish touch that may ruin an otherwise good work, especially if they compete with colored enamels and stones or detract from other forms of decoration, such as texture. Dark gray and black oxidizing on a jewelry piece—the antique effect—may also be used to harmonize with certain types of clothing.

DAPPING

Dapping is a forming process used for making partial spheres, or dome, in metal. The coin used as a tie tack in *Figure* 72 was slightly dapped to remove the flat starkness of the coin. Dapping punches with spherical heads of assorted sizes are used with a dapping die to make the desired size and depth of dome. The die is a steel, brass, or hardwood cube with half-sphere depressions cut into each of the six sides. A circle is cut from light- to medium-gauge metal, that is, 20 to 26 gauge, placed in a hole in the dapping die, and struck down with a dapping punch to form the dome. The lighter gauges of metal usually work well, as a dome has considerable strength because of its form.

72

Dapping punches of graduated sizes come in sets of a dozen up to two dozen, with diameters of $5/32$ to $3/4$ inch. Dapping dies have as many as 22 half-sphere depressions, ranging in size from $3/16$ to 2 inches in diameter. This provides a very wide range of sizes and forms.

A disc can be given a domed form ranging from a half-sphere to one having only a slight curvature. Dapping will

62 Jewelry: Queen of Crafts

decrease the diameter of a disc; the disc diameter becomes smaller as the dapping becomes deeper. This must be taken into account if a dome of a definite diameter is needed. The diameter to use in cutting the disc can be easily determined. A piece of soft wire pressed into the depression on the die having the desired curvature will measure the rise of the dome. Measure and mark the wire with the required diameter across the curve. This piece of wire when straightened will be the diameter to use in cutting the disc.

To allow for the thickness of the metal always select punches that are slightly smaller than the depression to be used in the die, as in *Figure 73*. After a disc has been cut it is placed in a depression larger than the one which will give the disc the final dapping. A punch of proper size is then used to set the metal down, and the process is repeated in the smaller, final depression with a still smaller punch. Rotating the disc and punch while working will ensure a smooth, even surface. Filing followed by sanding on a flat surface will level the edges of the disc for soldering.

Dapping may be done in the middle of a sheet of metal, using both the punches and dies. This has the disadvantage of scarring the metal where it passes over the edge of the depression in the die. This type of dapping is done best on a hardwood block, lead block, or pitch bowl, as described under CHASING. The metal should be annealed if dapping is done in a sheet where the metal stretching is much more pronounced than when forming a dome.

Dapped work is used in other ways besides making decorative domes. The concave surface serves well as a cup for stone and pearl settings for rings and earrings. It is also the method used for making hollow beads: two half-spheres are soldered together to form round beads. Discs that are less deeply dapped and soldered make the flattened sphere beads and squash blossoms seen in Indian jewelry.

A note on punches. Steel ball bearings of assorted sizes substitute well when dapping discs. Wood punches can also be made from 1 to 2 inches in diameter by rounding the ends of pieces of wood roughly the size needed for proper dapping. Rotation of both the work and the wood punch will give a perfect dome.

DRAWING TRANSFER

Designs drawn on paper are transferred in several ways to the metal to be cut or worked. In all cases, the metal should first be thoroughly cleaned with fine steel wool or, if the work is to

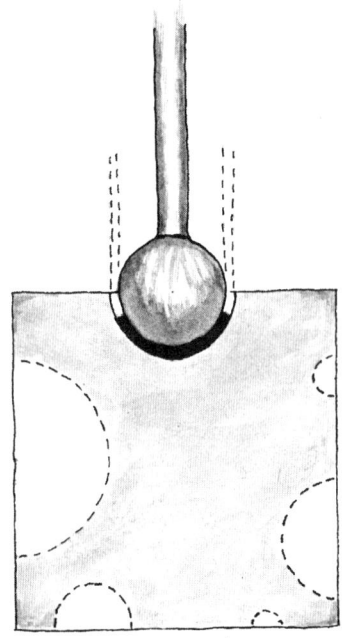

73

be free of fine scratches, by using soap and water or dipping the metal in a hot pickling solution for a few moments. A simple and direct method of transfer is to glue the design onto the metal. Any water-soluble glue will do and is preferable to rubber cement or paste. After drying, the metal with the attached design is ready for working. If there are negative areas or holes in the design, a hole is first drilled for inserting the saw blade, and then the cutout spaces are sawed away. The outline of the piece may then be sawed. Lines which are not to be sawed but are to indicate placement of a stone or appliqué may be transferred by gently pricking through the paper with a sharp scriber or awl. Soaking in water will remove the paper design.

Tracing is another transfer method. Ordinary carbon paper can be inserted between the design and the metal and all details traced. A white transfer paper is made for use over metal that is superior to the regular carbon paper and can be purchased at craft supply houses. A better, clearer transfer is made if the metal is given a thin coat of tempera or poster paint. Chinese white tempera comes in small inexpensive blocks and may be applied with a moist fingertip or small soft brush. After drying, the tracing is made with carbon paper and a clear line results. All carbon lines should be lightly scratched over before starting work, as handling smudges or rubs off the tracing lines. The tempera is then washed off and the scratches are used as guides.

When a delicate and intricate design is to be transferred another method may be used. The design is retraced with graphite or carbon paper underneath but facing upward so that the design shows on the back of the paper. The metal is warmed and beeswax is rubbed over it to form a thin, even coating. When dry and cool the paper is placed on the waxed metal and the design is well burnished. After carefully removing the paper, it will be found that the beeswax has picked up the design from the back of the paper. Scratching the design for permanency, followed by warming the metal and wiping it clean, completes the transfer.

Machinist's layout stain or fingernail polish may be used to cover the metal for another means of design transfer. No carbon paper is used; the design is scratched directly through the stain onto the metal. This method is desirable when using a precut design pattern or making duplicates. Lacquer thinner will remove the stain or nail polish.

For most purposes the tempera and carbon-paper transfer method fulfills all needs. However, the transfer of a design for lost wax casting calls for another method of working. The

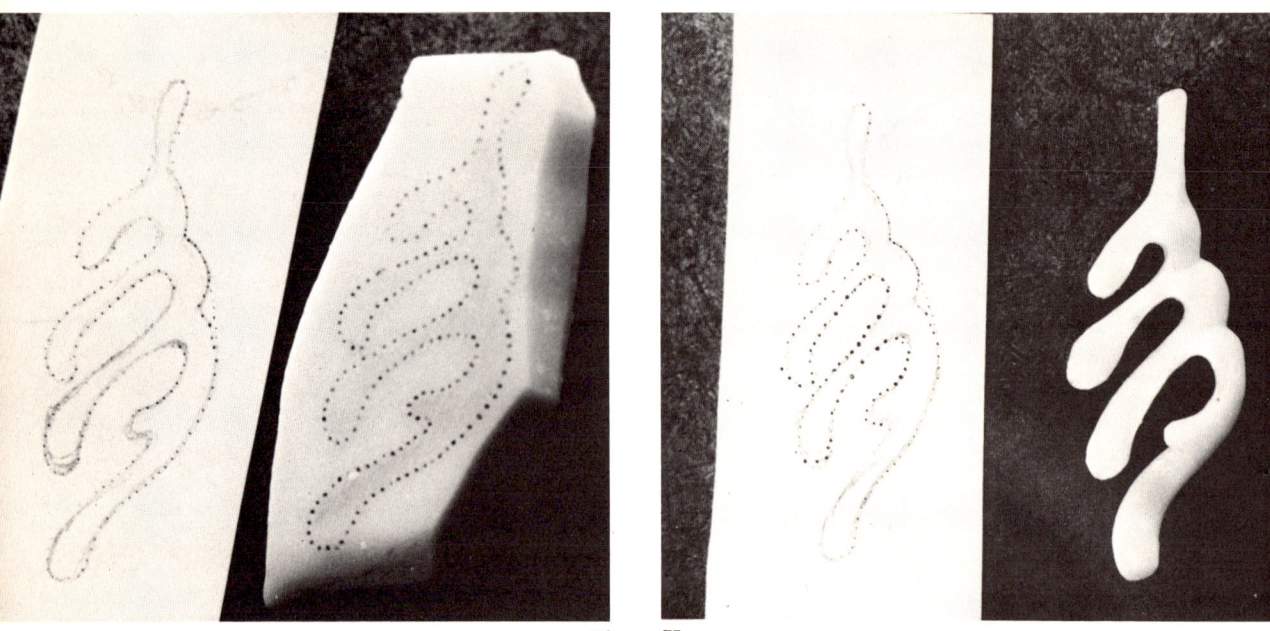

74   75

design is placed on the wax instead of the metal. Carbon or transfer paper will not work on wax, so the design is pricked at closely spaced intervals through the paper and into the wax. Most carving waxes are dark in color, making the small marks difficult to see. This can easily be remedied by rubbing powdered chalk or Chinese white into the holes, or if the wax is white, India ink can be used.

Figure 74 (left) shows a sketch for a design which was used for a pendant. The block of wax on the right has the design pricked into it and is ready for sawing along the dotted line and carving. The wax block is about half an inch thick to allow deep curvature. The finished carved pattern is shown in *Figure* 75. The white wax does not show the form in the photograph, but it is nearly half as deep through the middle as it is wide. This design can also be used for pins when turned in the opposite direction.

DRAWING WIRE AND TUBING

Jewelry supply companies have large assortments of wire in different sizes, cross sections, or shapes, and in different metals. Common wire shapes are round, half-round, oval, square, rectangular, and triangular. The metals are copper, brass, fine silver, sterling silver, and karat gold of different colors. For the craftsman or the small shop to attempt to stock all the various sizes and shapes in different metals is nearly impossible. The expense in silver would be considerable, and prohibitive in karat gold. The drawing of wire is a means of keeping this inventory down and offers ready access to any shape and size of wire needed for any particular job. Drawplates and draw-

Jewelry Working Techniques 65

tongs are not inexpensive but will pay for themselves; savings made by ordering larger amounts of larger gauges will soon offset their cost.

Drawing is done to reduce the size of or to reshape a wire. No metal is lost in the process; the wire lengthens as it is being reduced. The plate itself is made from heavy tempered steel through which graduated holes of a particular shape have been made. These holes are tapered from back to front. Plates are made that have only one shape of holes of various sizes; others have two or more different series of shapes in the same plate. The wire to be drawn should be in the annealed state, and one end should be filed to a tapering point about an inch long (*Figure 76A*). Beeswax is rubbed over the wire for lubrication, and the tapered end is placed through a hole slightly smaller than the wire. The tapered hole acts as a funnel, so the wire goes in the back with the pointed end in front. Considerable pull is necessary to draw wire, and the drawplate should be made secure in a vise which will not scar the plate (*Figure 76B*). The pointed end of the wire is pulled through the hole with the drawtongs. This is repeated through the same hole after the wire is rubbed again with beeswax. Further reduction is made by repeating the process in the next-smaller hole, always pulling straight through the hole and applying beeswax each time. The wire should be annealed to reduce brittleness after it has been reduced three or four times. Annealing not only will make further reduction easier, but it will keep the wire from breaking. Less drawing is necessary if the wire to be reduced is the same shape as the finished wire. Round wire drawn into square wire must compress into corners; square wire must have the corners squeezed into a round hole. In all drawing of wire do not skip any holes between the one used first and the finishing-size hole.

The drawplate has a use other than that of wire reduction or of changing cross section. Small tubing for hinges, for example, can be made by drawing from thin, 24- to 28-gauge, metal strips. A strip of metal slightly over three times wider than the diameter of the tube needed is cut carefully so that the

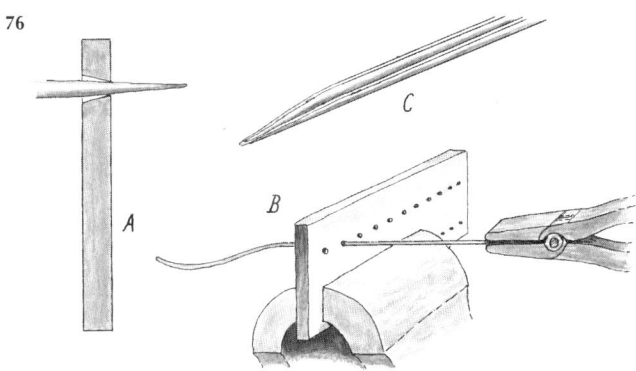

76

sides are exactly parallel. This ensures an even joint in the tubing when the edges are drawn together. *Figure 76C* shows a taper given to one end for insertion into the drawplate hole. The initial bending must be made by creasing the strip lengthwise into a U, or gutter, form. The strip can be laid over a groove made in a hardwood or lead block and set down by using a dull chisel, a chasing tool, or a length of rod or wire; the latter causes the least scarring on the metal. The outside of the strip is rubbed with beeswax and the drawing is done the same as for wire.

Twisting can be held to a minimum if another person tightly holds the back end of the strip with pliers as it is being drawn through the plate. A knife held in the strip joint just behind the drawplate hole will also help in keeping the tubing free of twist. Turpentine or paint thinner, followed by washing in soap and water, will remove the beeswax. The tube may be soldered after drawing, and this will also anneal it. Then it can be carefully straightened with a rawhide mallet in the groove of the hardwood or lead block used to give it the initial creasing. Another time through the drawplate in a smaller hole after cleaning and pickling gives a final smooth finish to the tube.

If a tube has to fit exactly around a wire, as for a hinge, the wire may be used as a core while drawing. The wire should be oiled and care should be taken so that the strip does not bind the wire so tightly that it cannot be removed. Short lengths work best. Removal is done by placing the wire through a hole in the plate which is too small for the tube to pass through and pulling the wire out.

DRILLING

Drilling is by far the most common method of making holes in metal for jewelry work. Twist drills are made in various sizes, and different methods of numbering are used: fractions of an inch, letters, meters, and numbers. Numbered drills are most frequently used by jewelry makers; the numbers run from 1, which is .228 inch, to 80, which is only .013 inch.

The metal to be drilled should be laid on a metal plate or hardwood block and center-punched where the hole is to be made. This keeps the drill from creeping (*Figure* 77A) and gives a positive start to the drilling. A drill press, hand drill, or flexible shaft may be used with the twist drill. The drill should be placed as far into the chuck as possible to avoid breakage. Using a drill press, because it does not have the wobble of a hand-held drill, is sometimes best. The flexible shaft is ideal

Jewelry Working Techniques 67

for smaller drills and for drilling where the piece cannot be easily placed on a flat base. The work should be backed with a wood block whenever possible. This makes a cleaner hole and leaves less burr on the back (*Figure 77B*). Only pliers that will not scar the metal should be used to hold the work. The most critical time in drilling is when the drill first emerges from the back—when the drill usually breaks or hangs up and spins the metal instead of cutting through.

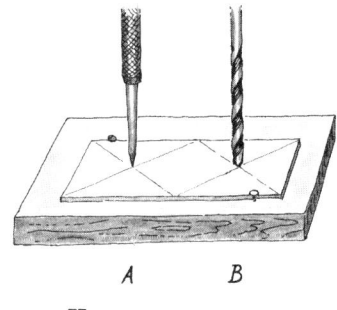

77

A hand vise or ring clamp is used when drilling small pieces with the flexible shaft. Always hold the drill perpendicular to the work or the drill will creep or break. If a slanted hole must go through a piece for a diagonal effect, clamp another piece of metal or hardwood next to the center-punch mark for support in starting the hole. Another way is first to drill a small perpendicular hole and then carefully to ream the hole at an angle with a larger drill.

As a rule, higher speeds are used with smaller drills rather than with larger ones. Speed can be reduced as the drill starts to break through. If the drill sticks it often helps to rotate the chuck by hand the last few turns to prevent breakage. Backing up and starting again with more speed and less pressure works well too. The "feel" for which is best will come with experience. A lubricant, such as light oil, turpentine, or beeswax, should be used for better and faster work; it also prolongs the life of the drill. Beeswax works best for small drills and is the least messy. The tip of the drill is turned into a block of wax before drilling, and this should be repeated several times if the hole is deep. Use no lubricant when drilling pearls.

Drills are made from carbon steel or high-speed steel. Both work well with the metals used in jewelry. The high-speed drills last longer; they cost slightly more but are worth it. Either type can be resharpened with a little practice by stoning or with an emery wheel. *Figure 78* shows the angle to be ground on the cutting edges (59°) and the smaller angle (12°) made at the same time for clearance. The edges should be ground to the same angle and length so that both cut evenly at the same time to make a straight, true hole. Care should be taken not to overheat the drill while grinding, because this will remove the temper. This can be prevented by dipping the drill in water. No color change in the drill should appear while grinding.

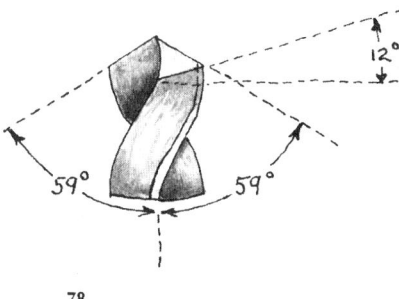

78

The real function of a drill is to make a hole, but large drills can be used by hand to remove burrs from small holes. Drills are used in stone setting but only to drill a hole smaller than the stone to be set. The seat for the stone should be cut with a stone-setting burr, not a drill. See Simple Lapidary, Chapter 10, for drilling stone.

ELECTROPLATING

Small boys are delighted when someone breaks a mercury thermometer. A small ball of mercury can be picked up on a penny and rubbed all over it to produce a silvery, shiny, slippery coin. Mercury was employed by the ancients from Italy to Mexico to plate objects. The mercury was mixed with powdered gold to form an amalgam. The article was covered with this amalgam and then heated to vaporize the mercury and leave a covering of gold. Today there are chemicals which plate metal by being wiped on with a cloth or spread on with a brush which is connected to the article by a length of wire and flashlight batteries.

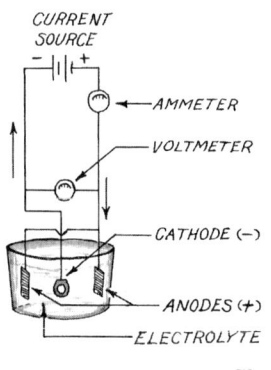

79

Electroplating uses direct current electricity and a liquid called an electrolyte, which contains compounds of the metal to be used for plating in solution. Direct current travels in one direction only, from the anode (+) to the cathode (−) terminal, when a circuit is completed. A bar of metal which furnishes the plating metal is attached to the anode (+) terminal, and the object to be plated is connected to the cathode (−) terminal. Both are then submerged in the electrolyte so that they do not touch each other, and the current is turned on (*Figure 79*). The flow of electricity strips metal off the bar connected to the anode, carries it across the separating solution, and deposits a thin layer of it on the connected jewelry piece. The process is simple, and the equipment not too expensive. Metal can be plated as lightly as one millionth of an inch thick. The cost of thinly plating a jewelry piece even with gold is insignificant, and it can be given a heavy plating for only a few cents.

Plating can be used to contrast metal colors by covering areas not to be plated with lacquer. After the plating, the lacquer is removed with lacquer thinner. This method is effectively used to plate recessed areas that have been etched or other depressed parts that receive little wear.

Plating is done for two main reasons: (1) to cover a metal which tarnishes easily and irritates, or (2) to cover a less valuable metal in an attempt to enhance its appearance. Some people cannot wear silver because their body acids and perspiration quickly tarnish it, and the tarnish in turn blackens clothing. Others find that silver irritates their skin. Rhodium, which is unaffected by body acids, is often used to plate silver pieces, especially chains which might have close contact with the body. Gold is plated over silver, and silver is plated over brass, copper, or nickel silver in order to cover the less valuable

Jewelry Working Techniques 69

underlying metal and lower the cost of production. Costume jewelry is nearly always plated to cover the cheap metal used.

Plating has many valuable uses and is certainly a most important working method in many fields, but the writer feels that a good piece of handwrought jewelry should stand upon its own merits by choice of metal, good design, and workmanship, and not require plating to prop it up.

ELECTROSTRIPPING

This is a cleaning process for metal which follows buffing and polishing and is employed just before plating by commercial firms or the more elaborately equipped small shops. It can be described as a process opposite to electroplating. Plating deposits metal on a jewelry piece; stripping removes impurities and metal by the same electrical process used in reverse. Electroplating has been described above, so there is no need to go into this stripping process extensively. The same unit for electroplating can be used for electrostripping. All manufacturers supply full information on voltage, amperage, solutions, and attachment of parts for both processes for their particular units. Because the units vary in cost, complexity, and capacity, follow the instructions of the manufacturer for the best results. Adequate cleaning can be done without stripping; there is no point in acquiring plating equipment just for cleaning, but, stripping does make for better plating results.

ENAMELING

Among the decorative techniques used for jewelry, enameling has one of the longest histories. The technique was known to the Egyptians, Phoenicians, Assyrians, Greeks, Romans, Etruscans and later spread as far as Ireland and Byzantium. Drop earrings were made by the Greeks about 300 B.C. In the Middle Ages enameling spread first to China and later to India and Japan. Unexcelled perfection in enameling technique was achieved at the end of the nineteenth century in Carl Fabergé's work for the aristocracy and the Czar of Russia. Enameling through this long history had progressed from simple application of enamel in dapped depressions to Fabergé's method of *en plein*, the covering of large plains of surfaces with flawless enamel. *Figure 80* shows enamel placement on a flat surface.

Besides Fabergé's coverage of large unbroken areas and the practice of dipping wire into molten enamel for the making of drop earrings, five different methods are now employed for enamel application. They are basse-taille, champlevé, cloisonné,

80

70   Jewelry: Queen of Crafts

Limoges, and plique-à-jour. These methods use the same enamels, which vary from transparent to translucent to opaque, all having a wide range of colors.

Figure 81 shows these five types of enamel application in exaggerated cross-sectional views; the enclosed white areas represent enamel and the shaded areas are metal: (A) basse-taille, (B) champlevé, (C) cloisonné, (D) Limoges, (E) plique-à-jour.

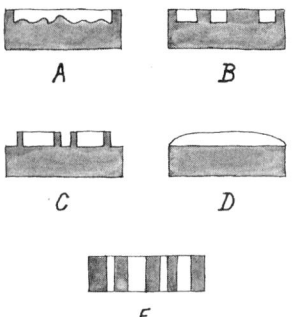

81

Basse-taille

This method is used to fill a carved or engraved sunken area with transparent enamel. The bottom of the depression may be textured or have a tooled or engraved design. Differences in the transparent-enamel thicknesses covering the design produce variations in color and light reflections. When finished, the enamel may be sunken or flush with the surrounding metal.

Champlevé

This method resembles basse-taille as a means of applying enamel in sunken areas, such as those formed by leaving uncarved metal as separators between sunken areas, pierced pieces soldered to backing pieces, acid etchings, or depressions in castings. Translucent and opaque enamels may be used here. Enamel color and shape plus the metal separators give this method its charm.

Cloisonné

Metalwork in this method is additive rather than subtractive, as in basse-taille and champlevé. Thin strips of metal or flat wires are soldered or laid edgewise upon the metal to be enameled. These cells are then filled with enamel and fired. A mosaic or inlaid effect can be achieved with cloisonné.

Limoges

This method may be thought of as a painting enameling. An enamel background of opaque color is applied and usually fired first. This is followed by carefully placing enamel grains to form a picture or design upon the background; the piece is then fired. A third firing of transparent, colorless enamel (flux) over the entire area brightens the colors and completes the work.

Plique-à-jour

This is a method best described as giving the stained-glass window effect. Transparent enamels are used to allow light to pass through the work, and narrow metal strips are formed to the desired pattern and soldered together without backing to create a grill or filigree. The strips, requiring little curvature, can be drawn through a drawplate, giving a slight cupping to the strip which will help to key the enamel after firing. The assembled cells should be leveled off after soldering by stoning or rubbing over emery cloth on a smooth surface. Metal of heavy gauge can be pierced to form cells instead of using strips. All cells, whether made from soldered strips or cutouts, should be of small size. Plique-à-jour is a delicate process because no metal backing to the enamel is provided. Metal and enamel shrinking and expansion during firing tend to crack the enamel if cells are too large.

The assembled or cutout design is placed on a flat mica sheet, and the enamel is placed in the cells. Mica is not affected by the heat and will leave a smooth undersurface that does not adhere to the enamel.

Metals most commonly used in jewelry enameling are copper, fine silver, and special enameling gold. Sterling silver may also be used, but it has the drawback of slightly changing the color of some enamels; it also picks up scale during firing. Fire scale can be held to a minimum by covering the surface which is not to be enameled with borax flux or yellow ochre. A sample firing will show whether the small amount of enamel discoloration is objectionable or not. Sterling possesses more strength than fine silver and can be used to advantage if color change presents no problem.

Enamels are carried in stock by craft suppliers and may be purchased in lump or graded-size frit ready for use. It is best to get the prepared enamel unless the worker is experimenting or doing extensive enameling. Grinding, screening, and washing enamels take much time and effort.

The equipment needed is simple: a couple of small spatulas for placing the enamel, a small sieve to apply enamel by shaking, a small piece of monel or stainless steel metal screen, a few stainless steel stilts for holding work being fired, gum tragacanth or similar commercial product for holding the enamel in place, ochre for holding findings in place, a small bottle of Scale-Off or a similar coating to prevent fire scale, and a source of heat.

Enameling may be done by using a torch directed on the bottom of a piece resting on a screen. Direct flame on the enamel should be avoided. A more satisfactory means of firing is in a small kiln. Kilns are made similar to the household hot plate and have a simple silvered Pyrex dish for a cover. They work well when the work is small, and the kilns are inexpensive. Larger electric firing kilns with rheostat control and pyrometer are the best, but they are quite expensive for a worker who only occasionally uses the enameling process.

Before starting to enamel, all metalwork must be thoroughly cleaned and kept that way. It should either be freshly sanded cleaned with steel wool, pickled, or buffed. Finally, it should be washed prior to applying enamel; no soldering flux, grease, or fingermarks should be left to spoil the work.

Findings, such as for pins, may be hard-soldered prior to firing, but must be wired in place or covered with ochre; the heat will melt the solder and otherwise the pins will drop off. Earwires will not stand this heat. In most cases it is best to soft-solder all findings after firing. The area where they are to be soldered can be brushed free of enamel before firing, or the enamel can be easily ground away after firing and the findings soft-soldered. The low heat of soft-soldering will do no harm to the enamel.

Following are the steps taken in enameling a flat copper or sterling silver disc on both sides for earrings. First, the front of the disc is painted with Scale-Off to protect it from the heat. (Silver picks up bothersome fire scale; copper turns black, pits, and drops large scales if not covered.) After the Scale-Off has dried, gum tragacanth is applied with a brush to the back of the disc to hold the enamel. The disc is placed on a screen or clean paper and the enamel is evenly sprinkled over the disc from a sieve. The depth of the enamel should be about $\frac{1}{32}$ inch. A spatula is then carefully slipped under the disc to avoid disturbing the enamel and the disc is transferred to the monel screen, which is then placed in a kiln preheated to about 1400° F. Careful watch will have to be made during firing. The enamel first turns a dark brown or black, regardless of the color applied. A few seconds later it looks like shining, sweating sand, and this is followed by an "orange peel" surface as the enamel starts to melt. Only a few more seconds of heat are needed to bring the enamel from orange peel stage to the smooth, molten, finished surface. There is danger of overfiring, and the screen and disc are next removed from the kiln and allowed to cool slowly at room temperature. The yellow-red hot disc gradually changes color until it is the color of the enamel as applied when cool. The Scale-Off flakes off during cooling, leaving a clean front surface. It will be noticed that the flat disc is now slightly domed on the enameled side, that is, the back. Gum solution is painted on the front side and enamel is sprinkled on the disc the same as before. The second firing requires the disc to be placed on a stilt; otherwise, it would stick to the screen and spoil the work. Stilt marks can be avoided if the piece rests only on the edges of the stilt.

If some do show they can be ground or stoned smooth. The second firing will take the dome out of the disc because the enamel is now placed on both sides. The edge of the disc is sanded and buffed to restore brightness. A small area in the enamel at the back of the disc is ground down to the metal, and an earring finding is soft-soldered onto it. A final buff on the edge and removal of the soft-solder flux—and the earring is finished. Many pieces are not counterenameled (enameled on the back), but when a piece is counterenameled, it should be fired first, and any ground-off stilt marks will be on the back rather than the front of the object.

To fill depressions, or cloisons, water is mixed with the enamel to make a paste, which is spooned into the depressions with a small spatula or a flat-ended wire. The enamel should be allowed to dry before firing. Enamel settles during firing, so three or four firings may have to be made to bring the enamel up to the level of the metal, as in cloisonné

Small stencils may be placed over fired enamel, enamel of another color sprinkled on, and the piece refired after careful removal of the stencil. This will leave a slightly higher design fused upon the surface. A sgraffito effect can be made by sprinkling another color over an enameled surface and then scratching through this enamel to the glazed surface below. Refiring shows the design in the lower colored enamel outlined by the last applied color. Chunks and threads of enamel, also available from craft supply companies, can be laid upon sprinkled frit and fired, or refired upon an enameled surface. The latter gives a better effect because it can be controlled so as not to become obscured by sinking too far into the enamel.

Cleanliness is the key to good enamel work. The metal must be clean for good, even adherence and to avoid discoloration. A clean paper should be used for each color of enamel. After sprinkling, the excess can be returned to its bottle. One grain of another enamel color mixed with the color desired can ruin an article. Any doubtful enamel should be kept for counterenameling. Experience is a great help in enameling. Sources of heat application vary with the different equipment used; kilns of the same make and size will even work differently. Thickness of enamel is also important. Too little burns out or has a washed out appearance, while too much causes excess warpage with cracking and chipping. Some slow, slight deterioration takes place in enamels over a period of time, especially the transparent ones.

The stock of enamels should be kept small unless considerable enameling is being done. Enameling is a craft in itself. Used here it is a supplemental work process for jewelry

82

of our time. *Figure 82* shows enamel used as background: it is a pre-Columbian stone mask fixed by prongs over turquoise enamel.

ENGRAVING

Modern handcrafted jewelry contains little of the intricate scrolled engraving found on older pieces. Engraving of this type is a craft in its own right. Most jewelers do not attempt their own engraving but send the work out to professional engravers. Graceful curves of graduated width, such as in monograms, may appear easy to do but are extremely hard to execute. In this book, engraving is considered to help the craftsman know how to maintain the tools of the engraver and how to use them in many ways other than making complicated inscriptions and flourishes of design.

    The tool of the engraver is the graver, or burin. It is a small, chisel-shaped, tempered steel tool having a small wooden knob for a palm-fitting handle. The steel shafts of gravers have different cross sections of various sizes, so that when sharpened each gives a different type of engraved line. The slim triangular shaft known as the knife will produce a very small narrow line with a V bottom. The chisel will produce a wider line with a flat bottom. The flat is rectangular in cross section and, among other uses, accounts for the wide, bright cuts. The diamond and

Jewelry Working Techniques 75

lozenge cut V sections in the metal, while the round and onglette produce lines having a round or oval bottom. A rectangular graver, known as a liner, has grooves in the lower surface. It is used to cut the parallel lines for Florentine texture (see *Figure 83*).

The wooden handles and steel shafts of gravers are purchased separately; the latter are seldom usable when received. They are purposely made long to fit even the largest hand, and most workers find that shortening is necessary. The shaft can easily be shortened to the correct length by placing the shaft in a vise with the excess amount of shaft showing; a sharp blow with a hammer will snap it off at the level of the vise. The graver is then resharpened for use. Graver tips are best sharpened at a 45° angle for most work (see *Figure 84A*). The flat graver can be ground on the bottom to give lift to the cut metal without changing the cut contour (*Figure 84B*). Other shapes (*Figure 84C* and *D*) will have to be heated, bent, and tempered to give the upturned point needed for lift, especially in concave areas of work. Sharpening is started by first grinding the point to the correct angle. (Avoid overheating by watching the point for any change in color.) Next the roughness is removed by using a fine stone, such as Arkansas oilstone, impregnated with light oil. Best results are achieved by sharpening the point across, rather than with, the direction of cutting. A sharp jab into a wooden block removes any small sharpening burr. Sharpness can be tested by lightly pressing the point at a flat angle on a fingernail; there should be no slippage.

The graver is a tool made to remove metal. Drilling, sanding, sawing, scraping, and filing also remove metal, but the graver allows the worker to remove metal in areas where other methods do not work. Settings for stones can be enlarged and refined; bezel tops trued and leveled after burnishing without damage to the stone. Bright cuts can be made on the top of stone-setting prongs to add sparkle. Small spurs can be raised by a knife graver to form prongs for setting small stones. Engraved triangular V-shaped depressions radiating out from faceted stones to add sparkle and make the stone look larger can only be done with a graver. The tool is invaluable for removing excess solder or rough areas in places inaccessible to all other tools. Depressed areas and lines in niello and enamel work are done with the graver, as well as many kinds of texturing, the best known of which is Florentine (*Figure 85*).

No design transfer is involved in the uses of the graver except for lines used in niello and enameling. Chinese white works well in these cases for transfer and engraving. Several methods of holding the work can be used. The engraving block

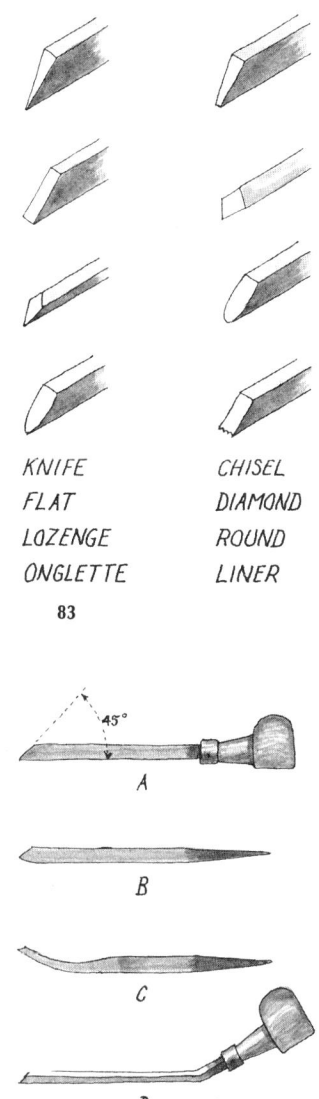

KNIFE   CHISEL
FLAT   DIAMOND
LOZENGE ROUND
ONGLETTE LINER

83

84

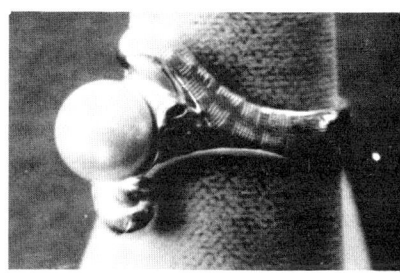

85

76   Jewelry: Queen of Crafts

or ball is the best holder but expensive and better left to the professional engraver. It is a heavy steel ball-shaped vise which rests on a leather ring, which allows the clamped article to be turned and tipped to any angle for ease and accuracy of cutting. Small articles can be held in a ring clamp, rotation being made by holding and turning against a bench pin for support. Metal pressed into warmed pitch in a pitch bowl or on a block of wood will hold flat work without slipping. A shellac stick—a small, flat, round wooden disk with shellac—is ideal for flat work, and the bench pin is used for support. *Figure 86* shows these three means of holding and supporting work.

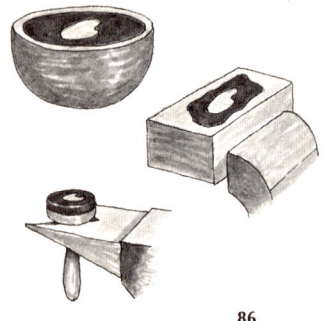

86

Cutting is done by holding the graver handle in the palm of the hand with the thumb resting beside the point. The thumb also rests on the work for guidance and support. The other hand holds the shellac stick, engraving ball, or ring clamp, and can also turn the work while carving. This thumb can also be placed beside the thumb supporting the graver tip to give still more control, but the thumb should never be placed in front of the graver where a slip would inflict a wound. Deep cuts should be done in stages, a little at a time; repeated cutting over the same line or area gives more control and the tool retains its sharpness longer. A light oil, such as oil of wintergreen, applied to the tip between cuts also keeps the tool sharp longer and leaves a smoother cut. Metal burrs left at the end of a stroke can be avoided by lowering the handle end of the graver to give lift to the point as it rises from the metal. Slow forward and downward pressure under complete control is the key to good engraving. One careless slip can ruin a piece of jewelry or require much time and effort in removing the error.

ETCHING

Removal of metal by chemicals rather than by the use of tools is known as etching. The action of acids upon metals can be controlled to produce unique effects obtainable in no other way. Etching can often make some jobs much easier.

Little equipment is needed for etching, and most of it may be found at home: a glass tray or Pyrex dish; a little string; paraffin, beeswax, or asphaltum varnish—all called resist; a small brush for application; a sharp knife for design scratching; and nitric acid, which can be purchased even in drugstores, completes the list. The design to be etched may be transferred to an unblemished surface by using Chinese white and carbon paper, followed by scratching the carbon lines into the metal. The piece is washed off, the light scratches leaving

Jewelry Working Techniques 77

guidelines for resist placement. The metal can be dipped into hot paraffin, brushed with hot beeswax, or simply painted with asphaltum varnish. Black asphaltum varnish has the advantage of showing up designs by contrast against shining metal, and it adheres well during the etching process. It should be given time to dry before being used in the acid—4 to 6 hours. All metal not covered by resist will be attacked by the acid, so it is necessary to cover the sides and bottom as well as the design parts not to be etched. Acid is mixed in the ratio of about one-third acid to two-thirds water; the acid is added to the water to avoid violent chemical reaction (*Figure 87*). A slightly higher acid content can be mixed for etching sterling silver.

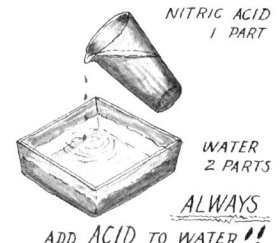

87

The resist-coated piece is laid on a couple of strings which act as slings to lower it into the Pyrex dish containing the acid. The exposed metal to be etched should be covered by acid while face upward so that the action may be observed and the bubbles being formed may be released (see *Figure 88*). In a few moments very minute bubbles will appear on the acid-covered bare metal. These should be watched carefully, but avoid breathing any fumes. For a smooth etch, small bubbles should form slowly, break away, and rise to the surface. Vapor indicates a violent reaction, which can be reduced by the addition of more water to the acid solution. Large bubbles should be forced to break loose and rise by disturbing them with a toothpick, cotton swab, or feather; otherwise a pit will result where they were located. Moderate action is preferable to fast action, as the latter is more likely to raise the resist, letting acid work upon areas not designed or intended to be etched. Since the acid works upon all exposed metal, it has a tendency to undercut the side walls of a design as the etching becomes deeper. If a deeper etch is desired, the piece should be washed and the resist removed; fresh resist is again applied as before, except that it is also painted on the side walls to prevent undercutting.

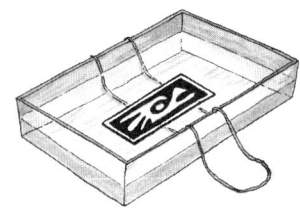

88

Bubbles appearing over the resist indicate a spot not covered. The piece should be flushed and dried, and resist should again be placed over the spot so that no etching will be done where it is not wanted.

Different depths of etching can be made by cleaning the piece after etching, painting on the resist as before, covering parts of the areas already etched, and again placing the piece into the acid for further action. Small, subtle variations in depth can be obtained in this manner, but a striking difference in relief should not be expected.

Temperature, strength of the acid solution, and length of

78 Jewelry: Queen of Crafts

time the piece is immersed in the acid determine etching depth. Conditions which will etch to about 1/32 inch in 2 to 4 hours will give satisfactory results. Work should be removed from the acid, flushed with water, and examined at intervals to determine the depth of the etch and the possible breakdown of bordering resist. Paraffin and beeswax can be removed by heating the metal and wiping it with a cloth dipped in paint thinner. Asphaltum varnish dissolves in turpentine or paint thinner. Scrubbing in hot soapy water will remove all traces of any type of resist.

Special mordants (corrosive compounds) for etching have been developed to replace nitric acid. These do not release poisonous gas fumes. Resists which do not chip at lower temperatures nor rise under long submersion have also been developed. Acids and mordant solutions for better work on different metals may be found in books devoted to the subject, but the nitric acid and asphaltum combination is adequate for most craftmen's needs.

A few last words. Etching leaves a surface with small pits similar to sandblasting, which makes a good contrast in texture to the shiny surrounding metal. Etching can also depress areas for the application of enamel; the texture of the etch makes a good ground for the enamel. This method was used for the tie clasp in *Figure 89* (bottom) and gives an entirely different appearance than the appliqué used on the clasp above it. Etching should not be used for piercing through metal; line control lessens as depth of the etching increases. About one third of the metal thickness should be regarded as maximum depth of an etch. As an antidote for spattered acid use soap and water, water and ammonia, or baking soda.

89

Jewelry Working Techniques 79

FILING

It is hard to imagine how any piece of jewelry can be made without the use of a file. Everyone knows what a file is and what it does, but not everyone knows how to use and take care of this simple, inexpensive, indispensable tool.

Filing should be considered as a smoothing rather than a forming process. Cutting metal to shape with a chisel, shears, or a saw is much faster than using a file. The file should be used in forming only to remove irregularities left by the other tools and to bring the work to a stage where abrasives should be employed. Conversely, to remove deep scratches and irregularities, much time and effort can be saved by filing before sanding.

Files are classified by length, shape, and cut. Regular tang-type files (those with a sharp point for insertion into handles) are measured from the tip to the beginning of the tang. Jeweler's files or needle files (*Figure 90*) are made from one piece of steel rod which includes the handle; they are measured by the entire length. Cross-section shapes include the barette, which is a low profile triangular file having two upper safe sides, with a cutting surface only on the broad base. Safe edges or sides are those having a smooth surface which do no cutting. Three-square is triangular in cross section; square, knife-edge, flat, round, oval, and half-round are all shaped as named and have cutting surfaces on all sides. Different companies produce slightly different shapes, which may also have safe sides on surfaces. Nearly all files vary in width from handle end to tip without changing cross section; some vary slightly, others end in a sharp point.

Cut refers to the type and coarseness of the teeth. Single-cut has parallel teeth cut diagonally across the file. Double-cut has shallower cuts at an angle over the first cuts. Jewelry files are made double-cut; larger files are cut single or double. The width and depth between lines determine the coarseness of a file whether single- or double-cut. It is possible to have a small file with large coarse teeth or a large file with small teeth.

Swiss files are numbered for progressive coarseness from 0 to 8; a #4 file gives a smooth finish without the excessive loading-up that plagues smoother files. American file coarseness is specified by name, such as rough, bastard, second-cut, smooth. Bastard gives a good degree of coarseness for the jewelry craftsman. It may appear that a vast collection of files is necessary. This is not true, as nearly all filing required for jewelry can be done with a 6- or 8-inch single-cut flat bastard, a 6- or 8-inch

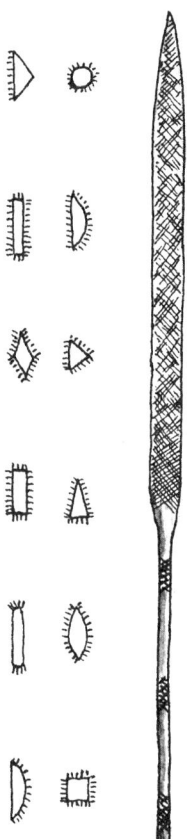

90

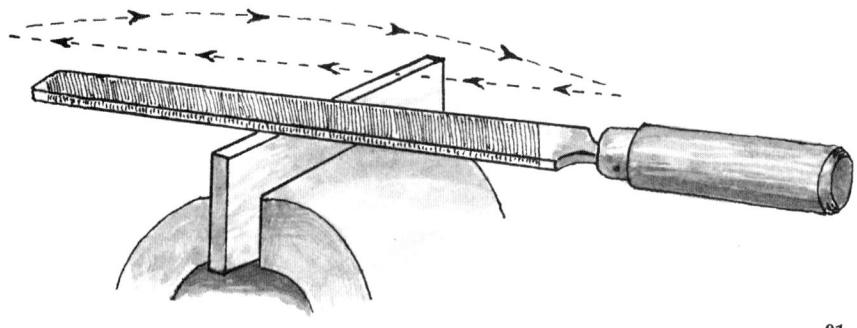

half-round-cut bastard or second-cut, and a set of needle files, which come in twelve different shapes in 5½- to 6-inch lengths. Other files may be added if desired.

Large pieces to be filed should be held in a vise, and both hands should be used to apply pressure and guide the file. Files cut in only one direction, on the forward stroke away from the body. Pressure should be applied when pushing the file; pressure should be relieved, or the file lifted off the work, on the return stroke, as shown in *Figure 91*. Forward with sideward movement in the same stroke produces smoother curves and keeps flat areas more level. Small work can be held with a hand vise, ring clamp, or in the hand, but additional support should be given by holding the work against the bench or bench pin.

Filing is usually done diagonally or nearly diagonally across a piece. Drawfiling, which leaves a smooth surface, is done by holding the file as in regular filing but pulling it along the length of the metal rather than across it. This is done where a smooth, level surface is required; it also leaves a smooth, uniform texture on the edges of small pierced holes or other inaccessible places which cannot be smoothed or buffed after filing.

Files are hard and brittle. Hard banging of a file against a metal or wood bench to loosen filings should be avoided. A file card or a stiff brush serves for this purpose and does not injure the teeth. Buildup of filings can be held to a minimum by rubbing chalk over the file before using on metal. *Do not oil*—this only increases chip buildup. One file is as hard and brittle as another, so files should be stored separately and not tossed together. Use the proper file for the job. On a large surface a small file instead of a larger one will tend to groove the filed areas, leaving uneven work. It is best to clean a file after use, especially after filing lead or steel. Lead chips may cling to silver and imbed themselves later in the silver when soldering is being done. Steel and lead chips included in filings and scrap gold reduce the value considerably when sent in for refining. Save old files if a flex-shaft tool is part of the shop equipment; they make excellent wheel dressers for truing or changing the shape of all the small abrasive wheels used with the machine.

Jewelry Working Techniques 81

FINDING APPLICATION

Findings are small parts needed to attach jewelry to the clothes or person. A finger holds a ring, but other jewelry requires clasps, screws, pins, bails, and so on, to hold them for wearing. Findings are small, sometimes have intricate parts, and are tedious to make. It is best to buy them rather than to attempt their manufacture, except on the very rare occasions when a handcrafted finding is needed because it forms an integral part of the design. As a rule, jewelry is only as good as the finding and its application. Findings from "junk" jewelry or "dime store" articles should not be used on handcrafted pieces regardless of the materials. Good findings, when findings are necessary, attached with hard silver solder or gold solder are the marks of a good craftsman and of well-executed work. A beautiful pin is useless if it has a clumsy clasp that does not hold or a pin stem that flaps and bends. Robbery and dropoff due to poor findings probably account for most jewelry losses. The worker cannot control robbery, but he can select the best findings and attach them strongly and properly.

Good findings are made from nickel-silver alloy, sterling silver, and karat gold in various colors. Prices vary and small design differences are made by suppliers; shopping will locate what is needed and what looks best at the right price. Findings which are most used include: earwires, cuff link backs, tie clips, tie tacks, scarf pins, spring rings and sisterhooks, necklace and bracelet box clasps, foldover catches, pendant loops, bails and bell caps, hinges, joints, catches and pin stems for pins and brooches, button eyes or pad eyes, jump rings, beads and balls, key rings, monogram letters, coin mounts, chain, decorated ring shanks, and pearl and stone prong settings.

Earwires

Earwires are made with large and small pads or with no pad on the end for soldering to the back of earrings. Large pads are used with soft solder, while the others are used with hard solder. An earwire for drop earrings has an attached ring in front to hold the drop, and a small ball is commonly fixed to the end of the wire, furnishing decoration next to the ear. Others have a pegged cup for pearl attachment or a prong setting for stones. Combinations of the above are also made. Earwires are made with wire loops for pierced ears or are held in place by a screw or clip. *Figure 92* shows a variety of earring findings.

Drops are easily attached to earwires by simply opening the small ring with pliers on the earwire, or drop, and reclos-

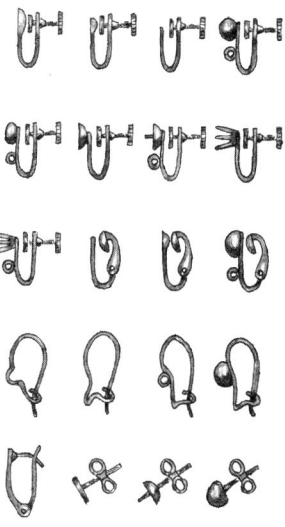

92

ing. Rings should be opened by turning the ends crosswise instead of spreading, which distorts the ring and makes it more difficult to close. Earwires which are to be soldered as well as the piece which is to be attached should be cleaned. Hand-held tweezers can be used to hold the earwire, but a third hand, (a base with a ball-socket joint which holds a pair of cross-locking tweezers at any angle) is of great use. The earring should be placed as level as possible with a screw-type earwire rested upon it. If hard solder is to be used, borax flux should be applied and a couple of snippets of solder should be laid alongside the earwire. Heat should be directed on and over the earring until the solder just starts to melt, then the flame is also played over the earwire base to bring both pieces up to soldering temperature to complete the joint. Clip earwires must be disassembled before hard-soldering or the heat will destroy the spring. Soft-soldering screw earwires is best done by first fluxing with soft-solder flux and melting a small snippet of solder in the cup or pad. After cooling, the earwire is placed onto the fluxed earring and sweated on; most of the heat should be directed onto the earring as mentioned before. Clip earrings do not have to be disassembled for sweating with soft solder, as the temperature is not enough to spoil the spring. Soft solder is slippery when melted, and unless the earwire and earring are held stationary, the pieces will slide out of position. Binding wire, clips, tweezers, or hand pressure should be used to hold the pieces together until the solder has solidified. Soldering should be done after all work on the earring has been completed and before any pearls or stones are set. Earrings with enamel work should have earwires soft-soldered to avoid damage to the enamel.

Pins, Brooches, and Cuff Links

The small hinges used to hold cuff link backs and pin stems and the small safety catches on pins and brooches (*Figure 93*) are all applied in the same manner. These small findings are

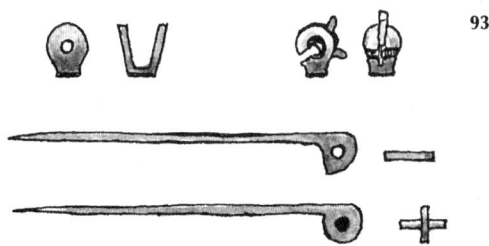
93

cleaned on the bottom as well as at the location of the joint on the article. It is best to file or rub on emery any finding before soldering, even though it is new and shiny; oil or oxides may still be present. The location of the hinge or catch is scratched into the piece. Placement is a very important factor, especially for pins. The weight and shape have to be considered when placing the findings in order for the piece to look its best when worn. The findings should be placed above the center of weight to prevent the top of the pin from tipping forward when it is worn.

Safety catches should be placed so that the side opening for the stem faces downward when wearing, as shown in *Figure 94*. This will sometimes help to hold a pin that has not had the safety catch properly closed. Also, the hinge finding is best set at a slightly horizontal angle, not quite in line with the safety catch opening but behind it. Constant pressure into the catch helps hold the pin if the catch comes open.

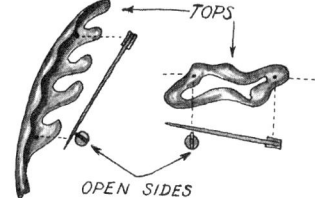

94

Better results are obtained if a flat snippet of hard solder is placed underneath the findings instead of alongside them, the joint area being very small, and this method avoids getting solder into the moving joint of the catch. To solder, place the hinge or catch in a third-hand tweezer, in the correct place at the correct angle touching the metal. Flux between the two surfaces only, and then insert the solder snippet. This causes a small pressure between finding and pin or cuff link if the two pieces touched firmly before insertion. Heat from the torch is then directed first over the pin or cuff link and then over the hinge when the temperature for solder melting is reached. When the solder melts the finding sinks to the other metal for a good, firm joint. Some craftsmen prefer soldering in two steps by applying solder to the finding or pin first and then locating and soldering the two together. Soft-soldering is done in the same way as hard-soldering, except that a different flux is used and less heat is needed.

After soldering and cleaning, the rest of the finding of a cuff link is inserted in the hinge and a wire rivet is fixed by peening or by using a pair of rivet pliers. Hinge pin wire is usually included with the finding, and it is scored at the proper length for breakoff. If these are not included, wire of the right diameter to form a rivet can be cut slightly longer than the width of the hinge. If a safety catch sticks after soldering and pickling, a drop of oil with a little heat will usually correct the trouble. More stubborn problems may require slight spreading of the sides to get movement started, followed by squeezing together again. If solder has entered the catch, a fresh start must be made with a new catch.

84 Jewelry: Queen of Crafts

There is a temptation to use the stem of a pin to hold and space the catch and hinge while soldering. Do not do this, for the stem will be spoiled. Catches and hinges can stand the heat, but temper is removed from stems. To complete the pin assembly the stem is measured so that only about 1/16 to 1/8 inch protrudes from the catch end. Snip to length, file sharp, and remove file marks by sanding and buffing. Test the point for sharpness and roughness and make sure that no cloth fibers will be snagged.

Stems are of two types: those with pre-fixed rivets and those with only a hole for rivet insertion. The latter is the same as those used for cuff links and are riveted in the same manner. The hinge frequently needs a little spreading for insertion of the pre-fixed-rivet-type stem. To complete the job the sides of the hinge are squeezed together after the rivet ends are aligned with the hinge holes.

Tie Tacks

Tie tacks are made in two parts: a sharpened pin much like an old phonograph needle fastens into a small clutch back. The pin has a flat, broadened base for soft-soldering or is made without a base for hard-soldering (*Figure 95A*). The pins can be held and soldered in the same way as hinges and catches. Pins without a base have such a small area of soldered joint, less than 1/16 inch square, that the strongest silver solder should be used. Of the three solders available—easy, medium, and hard—the hard should be used because it has the most strength. The same application method is used for scarf pins.

Tie Clips

Tie clips are made in two different styles: the alligator clip, which has a small spring to operate the movable jaws, and a tempered metal strip, which is bent back on itself to form the clip (*Figure 95B*). The alligator clip has to be disassembled when using the high heat necessary for hard solder. It may be left intact when soft-soldered. The metal strip clip sometimes loses temper during hard-soldering, but it can be easily soft-soldered. It presents a large area for strength and always appears on the back of the clip.

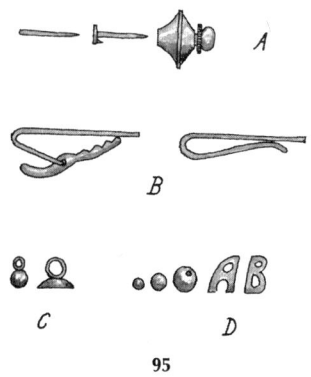

95

Button Eyes or Pad Eyes

These are small findings which have fixed rings on a base. The fixed ring is used for a chain, a jump ring, or bail to hold two parts of a work together, such as a pendant to chain or suspended parts of a necklace or charm bracelet. Regular soldering procedure is used for their application (*Figure 95C*).

Beads, Balls, and Monogram Letters

These are usually considered decorative pieces rather than findings but are listed in suppliers' catalogues under findings perhaps because of their size and miscellaneous nature. Beads and balls can be more easily held in place if a small flat area is filed where they are to be soldered. A small dapped depression will also hold them. A minimum of solder should be used with the letters; excess solder is hard to remove around these small pieces. Otherwise, the application is the same as for other findings (*Figure 95D*).

Decorated Ring Shanks

These are also listed under findings in catalogues. They have no place in handcrafted jewelry and should not be used by the craftsman. A ring should be designed and made as an integrated work, without relying upon prefabricated parts which can only cheapen its appearance (*Figure 96A*).

Pearl and Stone Prong Settings

These findings may be made, but the manufactured ones save time and work and are worth their cost. A prong setting is a prong setting whether made by hand or turned out by machine. The prongs on both settings are small and therefore extremely vulnerable to any excess heat during soldering. When soldering, heat should be applied to the underside of an article whenever possible. This prevents the tips of the prongs from melting. Cleaning, fluxing, soldering, placement, and holding are the same as for other findings. *Figure 96B* shows pearl settings, both pronged and pegged. *Figure 96C* represents settings for octagonal and round stones.

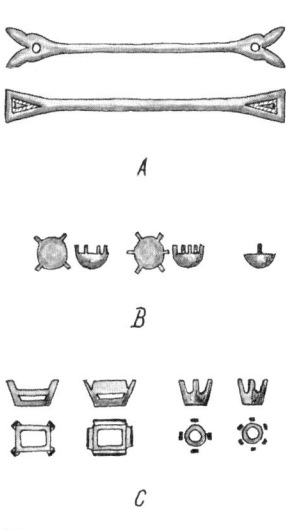

96

Spring Rings, Key Rings, Coin Mounts, Bails, Box and Foldover Catches, Pendant Loops

These findings are attached to other parts by the use of jump rings. Since their names are self-explanatory, no description is given. No soldering is involved with these findings, except for the soldering of the attaching jump ring as next described.

Jump Rings

Jump rings are the little split rings used frequently for connecting parts: drops to earrings and necklaces, pendants and drops to chains, small objects to charm bracelets, and as the last link in a chain to fit into the spring ring. These can be made by tightly wrapping wire around a rod the diameter of the desired size and sawing lengthwise across the coil to form individual rings. The coil is best held in a ring clamp for sawing. Jewelry supply firms carry a vast assortment of jump rings for those who do not wish to make their own. They are made from all the jewelry metals, in many sizes, out of many gauges of wire, and are shaped either round or oval.

Jump rings are used in two ways: either soldered to form a rigid part of a piece or to connect parts together as mentioned earlier. Before soldering a ring to another piece, see that the ends of the ring are tight together and in line with each other. A small flat spot can be filed on the outside where the ends meet. This gives more area for the soldered joint. The ring can be laid over a snippe of solder and the ends soldered first, or the ring can be positioned on or next to the work and soldered in one operation (*Figure 97*).

In either method the jump ring is best held by the third-hand tweezers and placed against the other metal. This is a very delicate soldering operation because of the great difference between the small amount of metal in the ring as compared with the part to which it is being soldered; both have to reach soldering temperature at the same time. Practically all heat must be directed onto the heavier part or else the solder will flow around the jump ring instead of filling the joint. The end of a piece of wire solder or a small ball of solder picked up on a sharp pointed steel wire is better than snippets for this type of soldering. When the metal has reached soldering temperature the end of the wire solder or the ball of solder is placed on the large metal surface next to the ring to flow and make the joint. The pointed wire is helpful to "steer" the melted solder into place if it does not immediately connect the two parts. Soft solder should never be used in this method.

A jump ring that is to hold two or more parts together or act as the last link in a chain is first spread open and threaded through the holes, rings, or chain links which it will connect, and then reclosed. A steel wire with a short 90° bend is stuck into the soldering block, and the short horizontal section is used for support while soldering (*Figure 97*). The jump ring is placed on this wire with the ends on top, letting the connected parts fall on either side. Wire solder or a small ball on a steel tip works best here. Use a small tip on the torch;

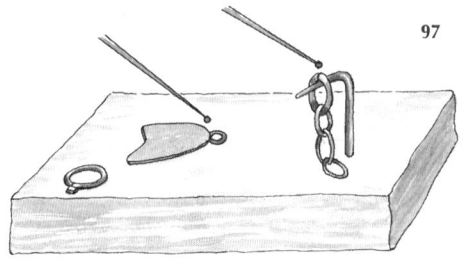

97

Jewelry Working Techniques 87

the amount of heat required is very small even though the temperature is the same as for heavy pieces. Flux the joint and solder, using the bottom of the torch flame to heat to soldering temperature. The steel support will draw some of the heat away and help to keep the jump ring from melting, but careful watch and quick removal of heat are necessary. Soft solder again should be avoided. *Figure 98* illustrates the proper way to spread a jump ring.

Some general remarks on the application of findings. Binding wire must be used in situations where soldered joints have been made on the opposite side from the finding to prevent it from falling off. Tweezers are preferable in other cases, and the article can be plunged into the pickle solution without having to remove binding wire. Ochre or asbestos fiber paste can be used to protect previously soldered joints and to help keep them in place. If more than one soldering operation is done on one piece, it is best to use hard solder first, medium next, and easy last. Also, if both soft and hard solder are used on the same piece, the soft-soldering is done last. Use silver solder in any place where gold and silver are to be soldered together. Gold solder melts at a temperature which could harm the silver. It was stated under ENAMELING that findings should be soft-soldered to enameled pieces. This is generally true, but small finding pieces, such as small hinges and catches, can be soldered prior to enameling; they must be protected and held in place with binding wire during enameling.

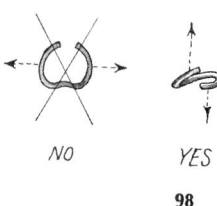

98

FORMING

Forming is not a working technique in itself but a combination of all techniques that change a two-dimensional shape into a three-dimensional form. Forming is done by bending, carving, chasing, repoussé, dapping, drawing metal strips through a drawplate, filing and sanding to some extent, fusing, hammering with and without stakes, using stamps and dies, and by combining different shapes together to create a form (appliqué). All these methods of forming, except hammering with or without stakes, are listed alphabetically at the beginning of this chapter (page 40).

Direct hammering on metal has limited use in jewelry making. A piece of metal can be placed in a vise or pair of pliers and bent by hammering; a section can be slightly domed, as shown in *Figure 99,* stretched, twisted, or flattened; round wire can be made square; articles can be peened for texture; or a heavy piece, such as a ring shank to a ring mandrel, can be made to stretch or conform. Other forming methods require

99

100

tools next to the metal, and the hammer furnishes only the power. Dapping punches and dies, chasing-repoussé liners and punches, and stamps are the tools used for jewelry forming. Stakes are horn-shaped tools held in a vise or hole in the bench, which furnish backing for metal that is hammered and stretched. These stakes and hammers are important and necessary to the silversmith in making formed pieces from ashtrays to chalices. They are expensive and seldom used for jewelry. Jewelers are sometimes silversmiths and vice versa, but this book will leave the silversmith's trade to itself and deal only with methods used in jewelry making.

Forming any kind of metal except appliqué changes the structure of the metal, making it brittle. Deep or drastic forming should be done in stages rather than all at once. Frequent annealing should be done to keep the metal malleable and easier to work.

FUSING

The use of heat to connect different pieces of metal without the use of solder is called fusing. Metal is kept below its melting point in soldering, only the solder being melted. In fusing, actual melting of the metal occurs and the liquid parts join each other.

Jewelry Working Techniques 89

Fusing has a limited use in jewelry, but the effects obtained by this method of joining are unique when planned and done with sensitivity. The finished article can be very distinctive and beautiful, possessing a natural "happy accident" quality. All too frequently fused work is done haphazardly and appears to be exactly what it is—blobs of metal connected without plan or technique.

To fuse a pin or pendant similar to the one shown in *Figure 100*, dip small pieces of scrap metal into flux and lay them on a charcoal or asbestos soldering block (*Figure 101*). These pieces should be placed to form a general outline of the desired piece. They will retain some planned design qualities, even though the process can be only partially controlled. Other fluxed pieces can be put on top of this bottom layer, joining and overlapping at different angles and in varying amounts. It is best to leave open spaces at intervals in the placement for two reasons: First, metal draws or balls up when melted and could become a solid mass of metal if too much heat is applied. Second, the piece is more interesting when it has an irregular outline and some openings to prevent a heavy, bulky appearance. The torch is then played over the whole assembly of pieces to bring them up to soldering heat, and finally concentrated on two or more pieces to cause them to melt, or partially melt, and join together.

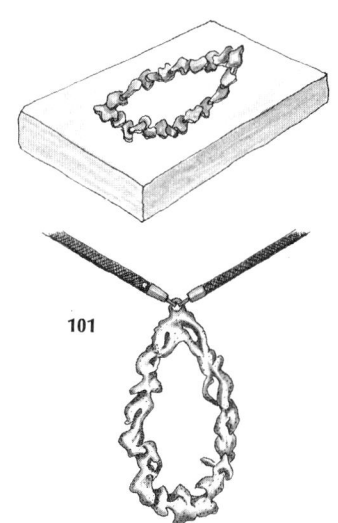

101

More control is possible with this careful fusing than melting all the parts at once. Some juggling and steering of metal can be done with a steel wire while the metal is soft. Melting temperature is reached when the metal starts to sweat and small bubbles rise on the surface; pieces will join each other at this stage if pressure is applied to them, and the pieces will retain part of their shape. More heat is applied if it is desired to have the pieces rounded by complete melting.

Very small pieces of sheet metal, shot, wire, or filings of the same or different metal can be dropped onto partially melted metal to add a different effect, texture, or dimension. Precut shapes can be used alone or with scrap pieces to give a more predictable outcome to fused articles. Filing, sanding, and buffing can be done with restraint; small areas can be smoother and unwanted projections removed without losing the unique effect of fusion. Odd and different metal forms can be made by melting scraps in a crucible and pouring into water. A silver or gold "nugget" can be made this way and used alone as a tie tack or soldered to other articles to become a contrasting element in a planned design.

Here is a small trick of the trade. Small shot or balls can be made for decorative purposes from small sheet scraps or short lengths of wire. If wire is used the size can be exactly controlled by the length of wire and gauge. It might seem to be a very simple operation: flux a short piece of wire and heat it until it melts and balls up on itself. Many times, however, the small shot will cool lopsided, have blisters, or will look like a wrinkled prune. The trick to avoid these troubles is in the removal of heat after fusion. The torch should be moved slowly away from the shot, allowing only the side of the flame to provide heat until the metal has solidified. Shot can be made perfectly round by making a half-round depression in an asbestos block for the metal to be melted in, or a flat area may be left if the shot is melted on a flat backing. A flattened ball gives a good soldering area and is preferable where a full sphere is not needed.

So much care is taken to avoid melting at all other times when heating metal that it is best to experiment with the fusion treatment, which gives a desired result under conditions that would ruin all other work.

GRANULATION

Granulation is a refined method of fusion: it is similar because heat without solder is used to connect metal to metal, but it differs in the refined and delicate nature of metal attachment without regular fusion. The joint is made by molecular exchange of metals, which can be like small entwined "roots" extending from one piece into the other at the point of contact. This is known as colloid hard-soldering.

Granulation is an ancient process extending back to Europe's Bronze Age, or about 2000 B.C. The Etruscans produced the most delicate and complicated work and brought granulation to its point of perfection about 600 to 500 B.C. From that time onward the granules used, by the Etruscans and others, became more coarse, and filigree tended to replace granulation as a decorative process. The secret of granule attachment was lost some ten to fifteen hundred years later. A craftsman attempting to duplicate the work of the early Etruscans in A.D. 1932 would have had to rediscover the nearly one-thousand-year-old lost secret by himself, because it was not until the following year that it was discovered, through design or accident, and patented by an Englishman.

Small granules or balls of metal with diameters as small as $1/100$ to $1/180$ inch are attached as design patterns or to form a mat covering on jewelry pieces. The play of light over these small balls gives a sheen not matched by any other texture nor accomplished by any other technique. The effect is much like that seen in microphotographs of the compound eye lenses of insects.

The small balls or granules are easily made. Very fine wire is cut to measured lengths to form coarse balls; filings from files of varied coarseness are used to form the smaller round granules. A torch cannot be used to melt and form these small grains of metal; the torch would blow them away or fuse them together. If a few should be melted, they would be covered with oxides or fire scale. The granules are best melted by sprinkling them over a bed of powdered charcoal in a crucible or ceramic container which can withstand high heat. Several alternate layers of filings and charcoal can be placed in the same container. The container is placed in a kiln and heated to 1900 to 2000° F. This ensures the melting of the gold throughout the entire mixture. The granules are recovered by carefully washing away the charcoal residue and then sized by screening them through a wire mesh sieve. The granules are free of fire scale or oxides because they were protected from the air by surrounding charcoal. Although other metals, such as silver, can be used, gold is recommended here as the wearing qualities of karat gold are much superior to silver. The work required for granulation would seem to preclude the use of a less valuable metal, as even slight wear on granulated parts takes away the distinctive light reflections of granulation.

A drop of solder, no matter how thinly applied, would swamp and nearly cover hundreds of small granules. *Figure 102A* shows how solder surrounds the granules, covering the fine detail of granulation. Colloid soldering, as shown in *Figure 102B*, retains the sharp outline of the individual granules for light reflection. Chemical change and a "happy circumstance" provide the answer: it is attached only at the point of contact. The "happy circumstance" in this case is the fact that some metals have an affinity for each other, and when heated together melt at a temperature below the melting point of either. An example is common soft solder made from lead and tin: tin melts at 455° F, lead at 633° F; together as solder the melting point is about 370° F. Copper and gold react the same way, but at higher temperatures.

In the granulation process, powdered copper carbonate is mixed with glue in equal parts and diluted with water to form a thin paste. Vegetable, fish, or animal glue is used instead of the modern plastic or epoxy glues. This mixture will hold the granules in place for the heating process, which will solder them to the article and to each other. The article with granules glued in place is put on a bed of charcoal in a crucible or ceramic container without covering. Heat is gradually raised

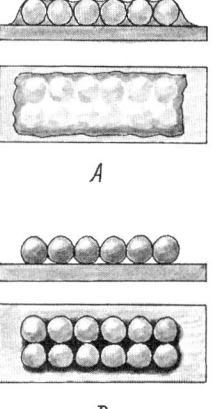

102

in the kiln and chemical reactions progress in this order: the copper carbonate in the glue changes to copper oxide and the glue burns, leaving carbon; this carbon combines with the oxygen in the copper oxide and is released as carbon dioxide, leaving only the copper between the joint. This copper covering starts to alloy with the gold to form a joint at contact at about 1650° F (cherry red to orange in color). A few more degrees and a little more time allow the copper covering the article and granules to further alloy and disappear from the surface to expose the gold. There is a safe range of nearly 300° F if fine gold is used for both article and granules: gold melts at 1945° F, and the joint is formed at 1650° F. Karat golds of different colors have different melting points, and some of them are very close or even below the heat necessary for granule soldering. It is wise to choose a gold, by karat and color, which will give a margin of safety for this work. Melting points of metals and alloys are given in the Appendix.

LAMINATING

The definition of laminating is "to roll, beat, or press into thin sheets; to cover with plates; or to become divided into laminae or plates." Metal lamination here follows the definition given, while also taking advantage of various metal colors for some striking results. Everyone knows what plywood is: a wooden sandwich. Metal lamination is the same, but metals of different thickness, color, and composition are used instead of wood.

In the small town of Taxco in central Mexico is a lovely church which dominates the central plaza. It was built and donated to the town by a miner who made his fortune there in the early eighteenth century. The base of the dome is decoratively lettered in blue and white mosaic tile, the message being, as the writer remembers: "God gave to Borda—Borda gives to God." Giving seems to be prevalent in Taxco, because the *platerias* (silver shops) around the plaza there have given a new usage for lamination to the world. This is known as "Marriage of Metals."

Lamination is not new. The Chinese, among others, have been very proficient for centuries in splitting and plugging holes in gold and silver coins and replacing the precious metal with lead. Nor does it appear to be a dying technique. The more recent introduction of laminated silver and copper 25-cent pieces by the United States Government is lamination on a grand scale. Appliqué, too, is a kind of lamination. But recent lamination has produced effects quite different from simple appliqué and tampered coins.

Jewelry Working Techniques 93

"Marriage of Metals" is lamination of sheets of different metals of different colors and different thicknesses to make up the basic metal to work. Metal sheets can be first soldered together and then a design cut out, or the sheets can be clamped together and all pieces sawed to shape at the same time and later soldered. The first method has an advantage: the sheets may be placed in rollers or hammered more easily to reduce the thickness when many different sheets are placed together. It also has a disadvantage: all the left-over metal after the design has been cut out is a layered mixture of different metals which cannot be used again and is not worth refining for a small shop.

Soldering should be done in stages instead of stacking all the pieces upon each other and attempting to do the job in one operation. Silver or gold should be used for the outside layers because they tarnish less than the other metals. A piece of silver should be placed level on a wire mesh screen, fluxed, and hard-solder snippets placed about ¼ inch apart over the entire surface. A little more than the usual amount of solder is required, more than most workers expect. Considerable heat is necessary, and soldering on a screen allows the lower piece to be heated as well as the top. A piece of metal of contrasting color, such as brass or copper, is fluxed on top of the first piece and heated to soldering temperature. While the solder is melted slight pressure ensures a closely soldered joint. After pickling, followed by cleaning the copper side of the piece, the process is repeated by soldering silver, brass, bronze, or gold to the copper side. The further addition of silver gives a solid piece of four contrasting colors. If more laminations are wanted, the piece can be cut in halves, thirds, or more sections, and soldered together as the single sheets were after hammering, or better rolling, the laminated block to usable thickness. The edges can be filed at different angles to reveal the different layers of color; wide angles leave broad stripes of color, which can be narrowed by lessening the angle of filing.

The inner portions of a laminated design can be made to show the colors in two ways. The metal can be raised from the back by using a dapping punch, a chasing tool, or a peen hammer. The raised front areas are then filed down to the level portion, uncovering the different layers as the filing progresses. A single round dapped dome, such as the one illustrated in *Figure 103*, will produce concentric rings of varied color when filed; peened work and overlapping or uneven doming in raised areas give designs of varied shapes, sizes, and colors. The other means of bringing out the inner metal colors is to carve or grind the flat lamination down from the front. This is similar to grinding

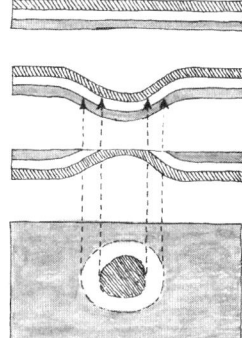

103

94   Jewelry: Queen of Crafts

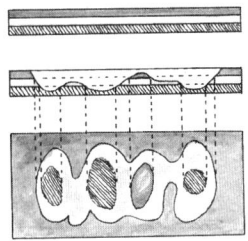

104

a stone intaglio and can be controlled to a much greater extent than the other method (*Figure 104*).

Finishing processes and finding application are a little different on laminated jewelry. A bright, shiny, glossy finish fails to show the different colors and defeats the purpose of lamination. A matte finish, such as that made by fine steel wool or very fine emery cloth, is ideal. Finding application should be done prior to the final filing or grinding of the work. Solder in the laminated joints will shrink and show the joints if findings are soldered after the joints have been smoothed to an unbroken surface.

To avoid heaviness in articles where many laminations are made, it is better to solder together overlapping rings instead of solid sheet; the stepped joints on the convex side are then filed off and the concave side ground down even with the start of the joint.

Metal inlay can be used alone or with the lamination process. Lines can be sawed in sheets, and flattened wire of another color metal can be inserted and soldered. Small round inlays of different sizes are made by drilling and soldering round wire of another metal into place.

Oxidation acts differently on different metals and can be used to advantage in some designs. Various metals react differently to acid; etched work on lamination gives a stratified appearance. This accounts for one objectionable feature of lamination: the baser metals, such as brass, bronze, and copper, quickly oxidize and cause the article to lose some of its brilliance. The application of a thin layer of lacquer by brushing or spraying will prevent oxidation for a long time on pieces which receive little wear. This is perhaps the only case where lacquer may be permitted on a good piece of jewelry, but even on laminated work, it detracts to some extent.

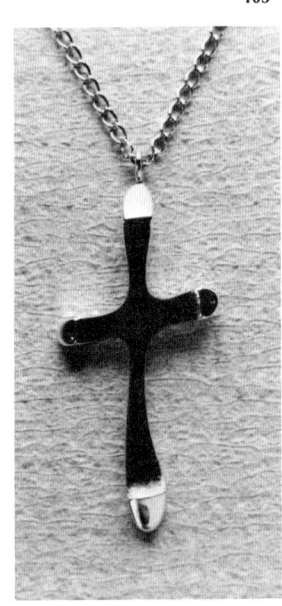

105

OXIDIZING

This is the term for coloring jewelry by a chemical process. Oxidizing usually forms dark sulphides on the metal surface to antique or otherwise enhance a jewelry piece, making strong contrasts between parts of a design (*Figure 105*).

Oxidizing is included in this chapter under the broader working technique of COLORING.

PEENING

Peening is a method used to stretch, broaden, texture, or fold metal over, as in riveting. There are various types of peen

Jewelry Working Techniques 95

hammers. The most common one used by the craftsman is the ball peen, which has a flat face on one end of the hammer head and a half-sphere shape on the other. Two other types of peen hammers are used mostly by silversmiths and blacksmiths: the straight and cross peen. They are seldom used by jewelry makers, as their function is to roughly stretch and spread metal.

Most jewelry craftsmen buy metal sheets according to gauge thickness—and reduce them to a thinner gauge by rolling, but metal can also be thinned and stretched using a peening hammer. A straight peen hammer, besides having one flat face, has a dull chisel-shaped end with the long axis running the same direction as the handle for stretching the metal outward in a sidewise direction. The cross peen differs by stretching the metal up and down in relation to the handle. These two hammers are of little use to the jeweler except for riveting in hard-to-reach places or to create an elongated type of peened texture.

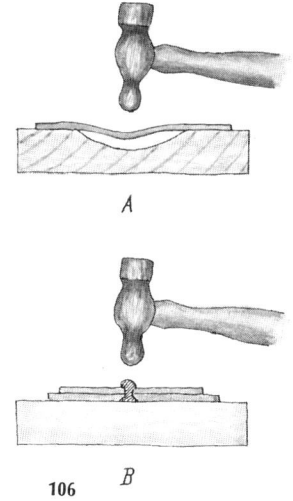

106

When the ball peen hammer is used for roughly bumping down concave areas, the metal should be backed by solid wood, lead, or pitch (as in chasing) for shallow forming, or placed over a wooden depression made to receive the metal in a specific form (*Figure 106A*). It is also used to spread the metal to form a rivet head (*Figure 106B*).

The other use for the ball peen hammer is to create a texture. The round-headed peen leaves round depressions in the metal, and when these are numerous and overlap, the texture is very distinctive: there is a great play of light reflections and a similar pattern with endless variations (*Figure 107*). A well-peened area is distinctive and easily recognized as handcrafted. The texture produced by the ball peen is a very good one, but unfortunately it has been overworked. It may be used when it especially enhances the design, but it should be avoided if only a "let's do something here" attitude is taken. The intricacy of a peened surface should not cover the inadequacy of poor workmanship *Figures 108* and *109* show different peening effects.

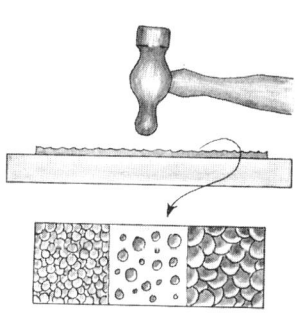

107

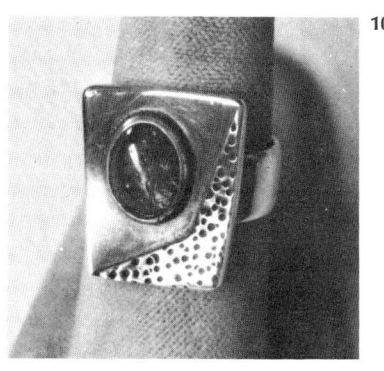

108

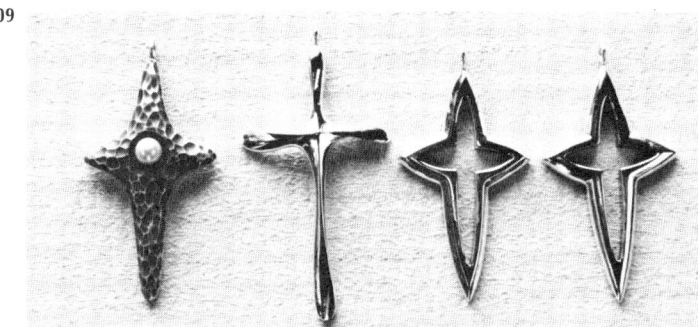

109

PICKLING

Pickling should always follow hard-soldering as a sure means of removing flux, discoloration, and surface oxides left after any soldering operation. Metal which has been heated for annealing should also be pickled.

The liquid pickle into which the metal is submerged is best contained in a Pyrex dish so that it may be used either hot or cold. Copper pans are made for pickling, but acid affects them to a limited degree, while Pyrex is not affected by acid or heat. The acid solution can be made by adding 1 part sulphuric acid to between 5 and 10 parts of water; the acid should be added to the water to avoid violent chemical reaction and acid sputter. This solution will work well on copper, brass, bronze, silver, and gold, either hot or cold. When it is used hot (below boiling), fluxes and oxides are usually dissolved in 3 to 5 minutes. Action is much slower in a cool pickle; 30 minutes might be necessary to free an article of flux.

Discoloration of gold, brass, and nickel alloys in findings is not removed as well by this pickle. This seldom presents a problem, however, because a buffing can remove all color. A pickle can be made from 1 part nitric acid to 8 parts water and used cold with these metals to restore color. In the few cases where buffing cannot be done after soldering because small detail would be lost, a much stronger acid solution called bright dip is made by combining equal parts of nitric acid and water. This solution should be used cold, and the metal should not be left in it more than a second or two because the action is very fast.

Sparex No. 2 is a commercial product which does the work of the usual sulphuric acid pickle and does not have the objectionable features of acid. It is supplied in granulated form in cans, so there is no danger of breakage. It does not give off noxious fumes while being heated in solution and does not affect clothing. Only a mild smarting is felt should it come in contact with the skin, and soap and water will easily remove it. A small can costing less than a dollar will last for months. It is highly recommended for use in the shop, and it is almost a necessity where many people are working together.

Rinsing should always follow pickling to stop the action of the pickle regardless of the solution used. Jewelry pieces which contain areas that might trap the pickle should be soaked in a solution of baking soda and water to neutralize the acid.

Most articles can be dropped into the pickle right after soldering; the time taken to pick them up allows them to cool somewhat from the soldering temperature. Heavy gold, brass, or bronze pieces should be left to cool a little before pickling to prevent them from becoming brittle. Clips and binding wire should be removed before pickling to avoid discoloring the metal which is held together. Pieces that have ochre applied to them should be allowed to cool and should then be washed to avoid contaminating the pickle. Only copper, brass, or wood tongs or tweezers should be placed in the solution, as iron or steel tools will discolor the metal being pickled and eventually ruin the pickle. Enamels are not affected by pickling, but to avoid cracking the enamel, pieces should be allowed to cool to room temperature before pickling.

Copper is removed from the surface of sterling silver while in the pickle, leaving a very thin layer of bloom on the article composed of pure silver. If no further work is needed on an article, it can be left in this state; filigree is often left this way without a final buffing.

Pickling does not remove underlying fire scale. This must be removed with abrasives or placed in the strong, fast-working bright dip. Pickling is not needed after soft-soldering. Scrubbing with soap and water removes the flux, and oxides are not formed on the metal at low temperatures.

PIERCING

Piercing is the cutting out of shapes from a piece of metal to form negative areas without breaking the outside edge (*Figure 110*). Jewelry with pierced designs became very popular with the Romans about A.D. 200. Up to that time decoration had depended mostly upon chasing, repoussé, appliqué, and the use of stones. Piercing alone or with other techniques added more interest to pieces which, up to that time, had mostly been solid, the exception being filigree. Piercing became more refined

110

and delicate, until it reached the lacy appearance typical of Byzantine jewelry.

Thought should be given in designing pierced work, not only to appearance, but to practicability of structure. Pieces which need a certain amount of strength should have sufficient metal left so that they will not break or bend. If the design is intricate, with many cutouts, a heavy-gauge metal will provide strength while the many cutouts will keep the piece from appearing heavy and clumsy. Sections should be left unpierced that are large enough for finding application. This might mean modifying the design a little, but findings are necessary and the less they show the better.

After a proper design has been worked out it is transferred to a sheet of metal with the cutout lines scratched in. In the cutout areas, which will be scrap metal, center-punch a small indentation for starting the drill. The punch mark should be made far enough away from the line so that the drill hole will not touch it. A small, #50 to #60, drill is used to drill the hole. One end of the blade of the jeweler's saw is loosened and the blade is threaded through the hole, with the design facing away from the handle of the saw. The blade is then fastened in the frame and the sawing is done by resting and holding the article on a bench pin as shown in *Figure 111*. The sawing should not be done on the line but close to it so that a little filing will be all that is necessary to smooth the cut to the line.

When a design demands a sharp narrow V, the cut is best made by sawing along one line to the bottom, then backing the saw out and sawing down the other side to meet the first cut. The point will then be as sharp as the blade is wide. The saw can be made to cut in a very small arc if short, fast strokes are used without forward pressure. A taut blade and beeswax rubbed over the teeth help prevent breakage. For more information see SAWING.

111

POLISHING

Polishing is usually the last working procedure needed to complete a jewelry piece. It follows any sawing, filing, sanding, soldering, or pickling process and imparts the final shining, glossy finish to the metal. Stones are set after polishing. Pieces which are left with a matte finish do not receive the final high polish. Before polishing is attempted the metal should have been made progressively smoother and have all scratches removed by filing followed by the use of coarse and then finer emery cloth or steel wool. Impregnated rubber abrasive wheels of varied coarseness can be substituted after filing if a flex-shaft tool is used. A smooth planishing hammer or a peen hammer and burnishing tools give texture but also give a polish to a surface if the tools are in good condition. The usual polishing techniques should not be used after polishing with hammers or burnishing tools; it is not only unnecessary but detracts from the texture.

Polishing can be done by hand (other than by planishing, peening, and burnishing) by rubbing tripoli over the metal to remove minute scratches. The piece is finally rubbed with rouge. A soft cloth can be placed over a stick or around a finger, rubbed over the tripoli or rouge bars, and then worked over the metal. Small holes and inaccessible angles can be polished by using a piece of string instead of cloth, threading the string through the hole and sliding the article back and forth over the tripoli- or rouge-charged string. All this is hard work and time consuming. There is nothing wrong in polishing by hand if power equipment is not available to the worker, but electrical power is available to almost everyone and should be used to buff and polish work better and more quickly.

The cost of a small electric motor of $\frac{1}{3}$ to $\frac{1}{2}$ HP, tapered spindles to hold the buffing wheels, and the buffs is not that great, and they should be included in all but the smallest workshops. Polishing by power has been covered under BUFFING in this chapter, except for work done with the flex-shaft machine. This is a very versatile electric tool which can be used not only with the rubber wheels, as mentioned earlier, to replace sanding and bring metal up to the point of polishing, but for buffing operations on small pieces. The small brushes and muslin and flannel buffs reach areas that are difficult or impossible to polish either by hand or by using the larger motor-driven buffing wheels. They are ideal for polishing the inside surface of rings.

Care should be taken with the cloth buffing wheels; use one buff only with tripoli, another only with rouge. A rouge-charged buff that has tripoli on it will leave a dull finish until all the tripoli has been worn off. There are many kinds of buffing compounds besides tripoli and rouge: bobbing compounds for faster cutting, different-colored rouges for special metals, such as platinum, and so on. Besides the cloth buffs, wood, felt, and leather buffing wheels are made for special purposes. Unless the amount of work done by the craftsman reaches a production level, all work can be satisfactorily done with no more than the tripoli-flannel buff and rouge-muslin combinations. (Some workers prefer to switch the combination of buffs and compounds. Whichever choice is made, stitched

100 Jewelry: Queen of Crafts

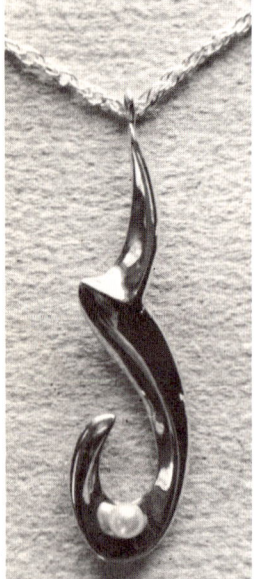

112

buffs for use with tripoli give better control for this more abrasive polishing compound.)

Polish is a texture or the ultimate in lack of texture (see the pendant in *Figure 112*), whichever the reader prefers. Polishing should be done with discretion; not all jewelry requires a high gloss nor do all the parts or areas of a single piece have to be highly polished. Variation in texture is an effective means of creating and holding interest.

Polishing stones is quite different from polishing metal and is described in Chapter 10, Simple Lapidary. However, the polishing of stones and metal do share several common operations. Both materials are polished by using a coarse abrasive wheel or compound first and progressively less coarse and slower material later. Also, both can be tumbled to give a polish. Tumbling is done by placing objects in a sealed rubber-lined steel drum that rotates and tumbles everything. Stones are polished by the action of various-sized silicon carbide grit and water over which they tumble, and metal is polished by substituting small steel shot or needles for abrasive grit. This method is mentioned for interest and information only. Tumbled baroque stones are used for cheap costume and souvenir jewelry, and tumbled metal pieces are seen in cheap, mass-produced cast objects.

REPOUSSE

Repoussé and chasing, shown in *Figures 113* and *114,* are working methods used together to form designs, patterns, or bas-relief on sheet metal. Chasing is depressing a line in metal from the front to the back, as in outlining a design. Repoussé is work done on the back to bump and form metal toward the

113

114

Jewelry Working Techniques 101

front. Since all but the most simple work involves the use of both methods, and it is difficult to describe one without the other, the repoussé work is described and illustrated under CHASING, this chapter.

RIVETING

Riveting is seldom used in jewelry to hold together metal parts which can be soldered. It is usually done to give an acceptable primitive effect which might fit an overall design. Appliqué and inlay of materials such as metals which cannot withstand soldering heat and wood, bone, and ivory must be riveted and/or glued into position unless they are held by prongs or bezels (see *Figure 115*).

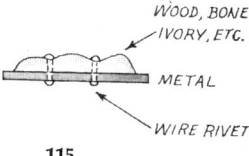
115

Riveting is perhaps most used to hold pin stems and cuff links to previously soldered hinge findings. These pins are either prefixed in a pin stem or are supplied with the hinges separately for pins and cuff links. A pin is riveted either by squeezing with small riveting pliers, which expand and form small heads on both ends of the pin simultaneously to make a rivet, or one end of the pin is supported on a steel block and the other end is peened to make it fast. Care should be taken in peening to ensure that the pin stays in the center of the hinge so that metal is left on each end to form a head. If pins are made, the wire should be of the largest gauge which will go through the hinge for a close fit. Very little metal needs to protrude from the ends of the hinge; as little as one sixth of the wire diameter on each end will be enough if the wire is tight fitting. If the wire is cut too long or fits loosely, the pin will have a tendency to bend rather than to spread to form a rivet head. Separate pieces of a bracelet or necklace can be riveted in the same manner if rivet heads are compatible with the design.

Heads of rivets can be made level with the metal or other material being riveted by using a larger drill to countersink the hole before riveting is started. Sanding and buffing will leave the rivet smooth and hardly noticeable. Bracelet and necklace pieces are items which can use countersunk rivet heads if they cannot have soldered hinge pins or if rivet heads would detract from their appearance.

Hollow rivets made from very small tubing are used to fasten metal to stones or to enameled areas. Metal initials and fraternity and school insignias for rings and pins have small lengths of this tubing soldered to their backs. The hollow rivets are pushed through drilled holes in the stones or enamel, and a round tapered punch is used to squeeze or gently tap the

102   Jewelry: Queen of Crafts

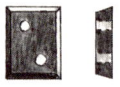

116

tubing over and down to form the heads (see *Figure 116*). These rivets hold well and are used where regular riveting cannot be done because of possible damage to the parts. Appliqué can be carried out in this manner by soldering these rivets to the back of a piece, so that the only evidence of their being riveted is on the back, where it does not show.

SANDING

The term "sanding" here is a misnomer to some degree, because sandpaper has little if any use in jewelry making. The abrasives used for jewelry work are not sand, and the backing for abrasive grains is usually cloth rather than paper, because cloth does not tear as easily. Sanding is a method of working regardless of abrasives, a method understood by everyone, and "sanding" is a less cumbersome term than "working with emery cloth or aluminum oxide cloth."

Abrasive cloth can be purchased at hardware stores in sheets or strips. It can be chosen by feel and sight to fulfill the worker's needs. Confusion sometimes arises when it is ordered by catalogue from different supply firms, as trade names and numbering systems vary. A short explanation of the abrasives and their numbering for degree of coarseness should be of help. Rubies and sapphires are composed of aluminum oxide when in a pure state and are colored red or blue, respectively. They are also known as corundum stones. An impure gray-black form of corundum called emery is also a natural product, crushed and graded for size for sanding and smoothing. In 1891 an American, George Acheson, invented and patented a process which produced silicon carbide by fusing sand, coke, sawdust, and salt to form a product slightly superior to the natural emery. This was given the trade name "Carborundum." There is little difference other than name between paper or cloth charged with the natural emery or corundum and the synthetic grit of silicon carbide called by such names as "Carborundum," "Natrolon," and "Crystalon" by different manufacturers. In common usage all of these when attached to flexible backing are known as emery cloth or emery paper. Crocus cloth is a cloth impregnated with rouge or iron oxide and is used after the finest emery cloth for polishing. Emery cloth is also classified as wet or dry. Either will work well with metal, although wet cloth is made especially for sanding stones while wet so as to avoid injurious heat. It is a little more expensive than the dry type and is unnecessary for metalwork.

Emery sheets usually measure 9 by 11 inches. Grit size for metalwork is numbered by zeros from 0 to 000; by number

Jewelry Working Techniques 103

and zeros from 3 to 3/0; by the names, coarse, medium, and fine; and by screen mesh per inch size, 80, 100, 220, 280, 320, 400. All the above systems indicate a sequence from coarse to fine. Only medium and fine grades are needed in jewelry working. After it is worn, a medium-grit cloth does the work of grit between medium and fine, and fine becomes finer with use. Some worn cloth should always be saved to provide distinctions of coarseness and fineness.

Sanding should be done to remove deep scratches, file marks, or small irregularities. It is not always necessary to use the coarse emery first. If irregularities are small, fine cloth will remove them without leaving the deeper scratches made by coarse cloth. Sanding is slow and should not replace, but follow, filing. Coarse sanding is then followed by fine sanding. Filing cuts the surface in only one direction, but sanding cuts on both the forward and backward strokes. It is best to make the sanding strokes all in one direction so that buffing can be done directly across the small scratches.

Emery sheets of 9 x 11 inches are too large for use on jewelry work and should be torn into smaller pieces about 2 by 3 inches. These pieces can be used flat or doubled over to sand with the fingers, folded over flat sticks for use on flat surfaces, or wrapped around dowels to reach rounded areas. Some articles can be clamped in a vise and a strip of emery cloth used like a shoeshine cloth on them. Under the pressure needed for sanding, a bench pin gives support and, if notched, will help hold the article firmly in various positions. Small metal pieces are better held in a ring clamp or hand vise than in the fingers.

There is an inexpensive little tool on the market for hand sanding which should be included in everyone's toolbox: a plastic emery-cloth holder, which does away with tacking or gluing emery cloth to a stick (see *Figure 117*). A 1-inch strip of emery cloth is folded over the tip and both ends are slipped under the edges of a clamp which is tightened by a thumbscrew at the base of the handle. Emery cloth, which can be purchased in 1-inch widths or 1-inch strips the length of a sheet, will fit the tool. The cloth can be changed in seconds, but having two sticks, one for coarse and one for fine cloth, makes them available at all times during sanding operations.

SAWING

Carpenters and machinists use saws with the teeth pointing forward, or away from the handle, so that the teeth cut on the push, or forward, stroke; jewelers place the blade with the

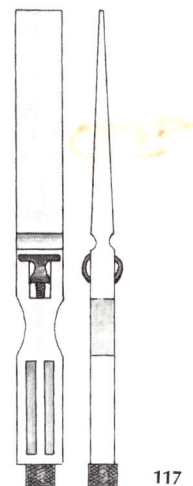

117

104   Jewelry: Queen of Crafts

teeth facing the handle, and the cutting stroke is made when the saw is pulled downward. This method is used because of the way small metalwork is held and supported best for sawing. Most sawing and piercing done by the jewelry craftsman is along curved lines, and the jeweler's saw blade is purposely made very thin.

One hand operates to move the saw downward while the other rotates the metal being sawed for a smoother flow of curved lines; this would not be possible if the metal were clamped in a vise and the work continually stopped to change position in the vise. The principle is the same for power-driven band saws and jigsaws, where a narrow blade cuts on a downward stroke, with the work supported on a table, while the work is fed and rotated into a blade that does not change its relative position.

The best platform or table for support while sawing is the combination bench pin and anvil shown under Tools, Chapter 4, and in *Figure 118*. The bench pin with a V notch gives rigid support to the metal on three sides while sawing. A V-notched board can be attached by a C clamp and will furnish support for sawing, but the combination is recommended for its versatility. It is easily clamped to the bench, has nothing extending above the pin surface, such as the top of a C clamp,

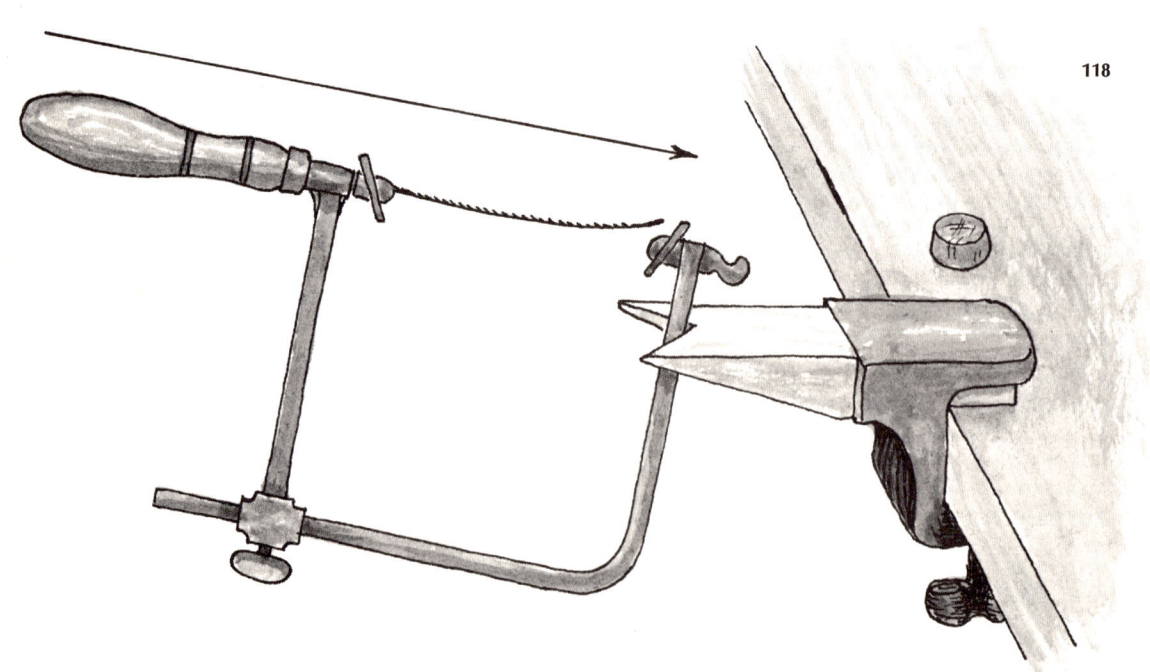

118

Jewelry Working Techniques   105

and has a smooth steel surface for center-punching, stamping, or straightening metal. Small work to be sawed is placed in a ring or hand clamp and braced against the bench pin for support.

Sawing is one of the most often-used methods of shaping jewelry metals, so the choice of saw frame and blades is important. Frames are like coping saws; they are C-shaped with attached handles and are adjustable for blade length across the opening. Frames differ in size according to the distance between the saw blade and the throat of the frame. This measurement varies from 2¼ up to 12 inches. A 5½-inch saw is a good general-purpose saw for jewelry work. The larger-throated saws are more useful for metalwork on large flat work, such as trays, plates, and some silverware. The 5½-inch saw can also handle smaller work, but a smaller, 2¼-inch frame is easier to handle and has better balance where the deeper throat is not needed. There is little difference in price between a good frame and a cheap one, so the best quality should be bought. Tension is necessary at all times while sawing, and so the frame should be of good steel with a spring to it. Blades are changed or loosened frequently because of breakage or for insertion into holes for pierced work, so the tightening thumbscrews to clamp the blade in place should work easily and positively.

Saw blades are furnished in 5-inch lengths to fit all frames and are numbered by a system which varies with thickness and number and size of teeth, allowing for various degrees of intricacy of work and metal thickness. These numbers go from a medium size, satisfactory for all work for two reasons: First, coarse to fine: 4, 3, 2, 1, 0, 2/0, 3/0. The author has found #2, this blade can be used satisfactorily on 24-gauge metal and all thicker gauges. Second, thinner gauges are seldom sawed but are usually cut with shears. A #2 blade can be manipulated to give intricate cuts and angles; it leaves a cut only as wide as an average pencil or ball-point pen line and has a strength against breakage not found in finer blades. There is a reason for the manufacture of coarser and finer blades, but until the need arises, it is useless for the craftsman to stock up on an assortment of blade sizes. Blades are made from high-grade tempered steel and their cost is only about a cent each for the best when purchased by the gross. Frames are made adjustable to permit the use of the longer pieces of a broken blade, but this is usually not satisfactory because the temper of the blade is higher in the toothed section.

A blade is first inserted and tightened into the frame at one end with the teeth pointing out from the frame and toward the handle. The frame is next adjusted and fastened so that the blade is just short of reaching across the frame opening. The frame is then compressed against the bench to shorten the opening so that the loose end of the blade can be inserted into the frame and clamped into position (*Figure 118*). This should give the blade sufficient tension to make the blade taut and produce a "ping" sound when picked. The saw and blade are now ready for outside sawing work. For pierced work the saw is loosened on one end and the blade is threaded through a hole in the work and again fastened in place as just described.

The first stroke of the saw is likely to creep over the work unless a notch is first made for the cut. This can be made by a small file or by moving the saw upward a stroke or two before the downward strokes are started. The piece to be cut should be firmly held down on the bench pin while sawing, and the strokes of the saw should be perpendicular to the work. Little if any pressure is needed to move the blade forward. Long and even downward cutting strokes are best for cuts which are rather straight; tight circles and angles are best made by short and more rapid strokes taken while turning the metal. Sticking and cramping of the saw blade usually occurs on these short turns. For lubrication and smooth cutting, partially fill the teeth with beeswax. An additional rubbing just before a sharp turn is started helps make sawing without breaking the blade easier. This also applies when backing out of a cut, as it is sometimes difficult to guide the saw backward through many intricate curves. All saws have a "set" to them: the points of the teeth are alternately bent slightly to each side to lessen drag and to make turning possible. The set, or the points of the teeth, naturally wear first, and care should be taken to use a sharp saw blade for the more difficult curved work.

As a rule cutting strokes should be perpendicular to the work, with two or more teeth in contact with the metal at all times; that is, the metal thickness should be at least the thickness of the space between two teeth. If it is necessary to saw very thin metal along a straight line or gentle curve with a blade too coarse for it, the saw frame can be tilted top forward to make a sloping cut across the metal to give a thicker cutting area. The saw can be used to "file" in some very difficult places where even jewelry files cannot reach by gently using the saw blade on one side. After use, blades should be cleaned of all beeswax and metal chips with a bristle brush, and one end of the blade should be loosened to release tension on the blade and frame.

Figure 119 shows four pairs of earrings which all required sawing for their outline shapes. The pairs on the left and bottom are also pierced. When sawing or piercing thin sheet metal

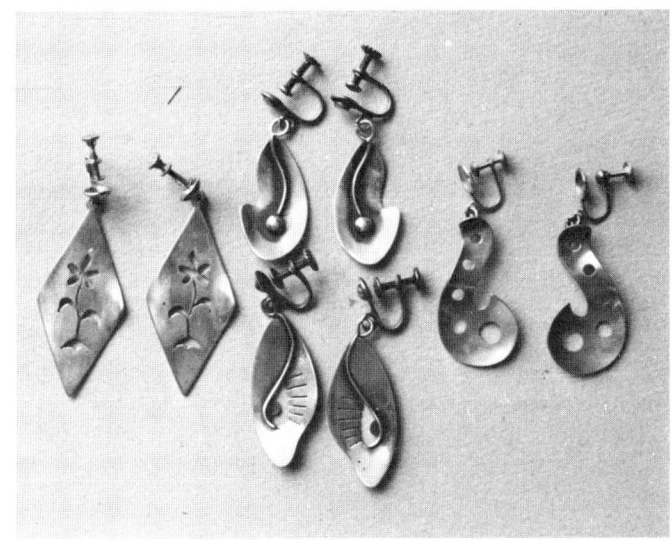

119

120

where an opposite, or a left and right, design is to be made, it is best to clamp both sheets together and saw them both at the same time. Even the slightest difference between the two becomes quite apparent on small intricate work. If the saw is perpendicular to the work at all times, sawing the two sheets together will make an exact duplicate.

Figure 120 is also an example of outline and pierced sawing. Thirteen separate cutouts are needed for this design, which includes the one behind the mounted translucent opal stone. Each must be center-punched, drilled, and sawed separately for pierced work.

SOLDERING

Among all the jewelry working techniques, soldering is first in importance and required skill. It can be truly said that a piece of jewelry is only as good as its soldering. Hard solder (silver or gold solder) has a tensile strength of more than 20 tons per square inch, and although the soldered base of small findings is but a small fraction of a square inch, if properly soldered it is not likely to be pulled away.

Soldering has been mentioned in this chapter under ENAMELING, FINDING APPLICATION, FUSING, GRANULATION, LAMINATING, and PICKLING. Its use under these working techniques was specific rather than general. Types of soldering, sources of heat, fluxes, solders, methods of holding work for soldering, pickling, and cleanup will be described or mentioned again for easy reference to general soldering.

Two types of soldering are performed on jewelry: (1) soft-soldering or low-heat soldering, for articles which cannot be otherwise soldered because high temperatures would affect them; and (2) hard-soldering, or high-heat soldering, where the temperature required for soldering is just below the melting point of the metals to be joined. Soft-soldering should be avoided whenever possible: it has very little strength compared with hard-soldering and the soldered joint is much more visible.

Successful soldering depends upon a few simple rules. All metal parts should be cleaned by sanding or pickling just before soldering. They should also fit closely, touching each other at the point of contact. This is necessary because solder, especially hard solder, will not flow to fill gaps in the work. The joint is also stronger when less solder is used. Fluxes are different for hard and soft solder, but flux is necessary for all soldering jobs to absorb any oxides present and to prevent metal parts from forming oxides during heating. All parts have to be heated sufficiently to melt the solder. If this is not done, the solder will ball up on itself or adhere only to the hottest section being soldered. Heavier or thicker sections should have more heat directed on them so that large and small pieces are equally heated at the same time. All flux must be removed, by scrubbing with soap and water for soft-solder flux or by pickling and rinsing for hard-solder flux. Excess solder can be removed by scraping, sanding, or filing, and the joint can be completed by buffing.

The source of heat can be the same for soft- and hard-soldering, except for the soldering iron and Bunsen burner, which are good only for soft-soldering. A small bottled propane gas torch, such as the Bernz-O-Matic, or a torch which uses household gas and air, or an acetylene tank and torch, such as the Prest-O-Lite, can supply heat for both hard- and soft-soldering. All these and the acetylene-oxygen torch can be carefully regulated, but the acetylene-oxygen type is more expensive. A fuller description of these torches can be found under Tools, Chapter 4.

Soft solder can be purchased at hardware stores in bar or wire form. The wire is handier for jewelry work. It is an alloy of tin and lead and is supplied in three grades which have different melting points. The most common solder is 50 tin/50 lead, which melts at about 440° F. This will fulfill most needs of the jewelry worker. If solder with a lower melting point is desired, there is the 60 tin/40 lead solder, which melts at about 370° F. A 40 tin/60 lead alloy has a higher melting point, about 460° F, and gives a little more strength to a joint. If for some reason solder with an especially low melting point is needed, such as in repair work, there is a tin-lead-bismuth solder, which melts at below 300° F.

The best fluxes for all soft solders used in jewelry work are the commercial preparations. They are not corrosive like the acid fluxes, and when in the rosin paste form, they are

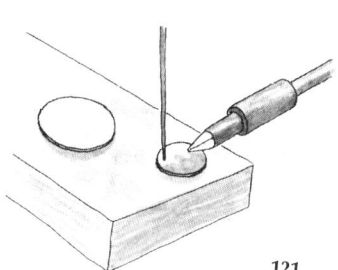
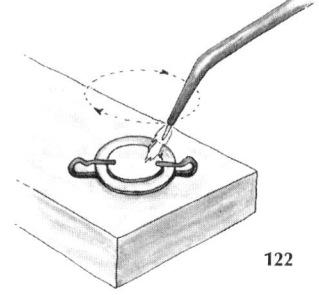
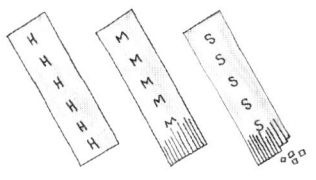

121 122 123

easily applied. They may be stored for years without deteriorating.

If soft solder is used for appliqué work, one piece can be tinned (covered with solder) by first covering the back with flux and melting the solder over the entire area. In this case the soldering iron (*Figure 121*) is helpful, as it is used not only to apply the solder but to spread it evenly. After cooling and washing, flux is applied to both pieces of metal where they will join. Soft solder is extremely slippery when melted; pieces should be held firmly in place by wire, tweezers, or clips so that no slippage will occur. The torch is then applied over all areas of all pieces, as shown in *Figure 122*, until the solder melts and fuses the joint. This is called sweat-soldering. Allow plenty of time for the solder to harden before removing the holding devices; soft solder takes longer than hard solder to solidify. Soap and water and a small brush will remove all flux.

Small pieces, such as findings, can be tinned by holding them in tweezers and rubbing them over a hot soldering-iron tip or by placing them on a piece of copper that has been tinned and heated. The copper piece is heated so that the solder is melted onto the finding, and the finding is lifted off while the solder is still in a liquid state. These are then refluxed, placed in position, and sweat-soldered to the article.

Hard solders are the silver and karat gold used on most well-made jewelry. These are furnished in sheets, small square snippets, or wire form, and gold solders are made in different colors. *Figure 123* illustrates the method of cutting sheet solder into snippets about 1/16-inch square and also the scratching of letters on the sheets to permanently identify hard, medium, and soft, or easy, solders. Silver solder is an alloy of silver, copper, and zinc and is classified by melting temperatures as easy, medium, and hard; these melt and flow at 1325° F, 1390° F and 1450° F, respectively. Sterling silver is an alloy of 925 parts of silver and 75 parts copper, which melts and flows at 1640° F; this is considerably above the melting points of the solders used to join it.

Much has been written about the use of easy, medium, and hard grades of hard solder and the merits of taking advantage of their different melting points. It has been recommended that multiple soldering operations on a single article progress in the use of solder from the hard to medium to easy. This order of working is supposedly followed in order not to disturb or remelt joints soldered in a previous operation. This may be true under very controlled conditions, but in shop practice with a torch, the few degrees difference are almost negligible. In the first place a previously soldered joint of any grade takes more heat to remelt, and in the second place a joint can be better protected and held in place if necessary by the use of ochre or wet asbestos fiber. The author has found that one grade, easy or medium, is sufficient for nearly all work. The real advantage lies in the strength of the joint produced by the different grades. If a joint is subjected to considerable strain, medium hard solder or hard solder will provide more strength. The harder grade of solder sold by some suppliers is also better in color and more closely matches sterling silver.

Gold solders are listed by color and karat, and there is a rather wide range of melting points. Golds and solders of the same karat but different colors have different melting points because of the different metals used to alloy them. Suppliers have their own specifications showing the melting point of each, and these should be carefully consulted before ordering. A solder listed as 14K yellow does not mean that the solder itself is 14K yellow gold, but that it is a gold alloy which comes the closest to matching 14K yellow gold.

In buying silver solder, sheet solder is the best form to purchase, as it can easily be cleaned just before cutting the small snippets. The precut snippets cannot be easily cleaned and become tarnished if not quickly used or kept tightly sealed. Gold does not tarnish quickly, but both silver and gold pick up oil and grease from handling. Wire solder is more useful for work which requires considerable solder. Snippets of solder are handled and spotted more easily than poking the end of wire solder into the work because the wire tends to ball up on the end.

Flux used for hard-soldering can be the same whether used for copper, brass, silver, or gold work, or combinations of these metals. Borax has been used for years as the basis for hard-soldering flux. Household powdered borax mixed with water to a thin paste is still a very good flux. Commercial concerns prepare flux under various trade names; some as borax compounds, some contain fluorides. All are good and their choice is generally up to the individual. These commercial fluxes are recommended here because most are superior to the basic borax and many, specially the liquids, do little of the bubbling and sputtering that dislodges solder snippets.

As stated before, hard-soldering is used for strength and matching color. Pieces to be soldered should be cleaned just

Jewelry Working Techniques 111

before soldering; this is more important for hard-soldering because of the high heat necessary for fusing. This heat can extend old oxides and form new ones. The proper hard solder should be selected for the job; hard silver solder to join silver pieces subjected to strain, or the easy or medium solder for ordinary work. Gold solder should be matched by color and karat rating. The same principle of heat distribution is used for both hard-soldering and soft-soldering: most of the heat is directed upon the heavier parts so that they reach the heat of fusion at the same time as smaller pieces. This avoids the balling-up of solder or the fusion of solder to only one side of a joint. Parts to be joined (*Figure 124*) should be securely held in place by binding wire, clamps, or tweezers as described under FINDING APPLICATION in this chapter. Solder snippets can be placed on the side opposite from the torch flame so that they must absorb heat for melting from the metal rather than from the torch, and thus avoid ball-up. *Figure 125* shows examples of solder placement for best results. Small parts can be placed upon a snippet, or a melted snippet on the end of a wire poker can be used to place the solder when correct temperature has been reached. The flame is directed downward and in the direction of the small arrows shown in the same figure. Solder is placed outside tight curves because of the difficulty of dressing up the joint in case too much solder should flow upon the backing piece. Flux should be applied to the solder as well as to the areas to be joined. Slow heat at first allows evaporation of the water in the flux without displacing the snippets.

If the source of heat can be adjusted for mixture of gas and air, or gas and oxygen, a soft neutral flame should be used for soldering operations. The torch should be adjusted for proper combustion. A large yellow flame surrounding the small inner blue cone shows an excess of gas; a dark blue flame on the outside of the inner cone shows an excess of air, and this is also a noisy, hissing flame. Adjustment of the flame midway between the two will give a neutral flame for best soldering results (see *Figure 126*).

Pickling, as described in this chapter, can follow any soldering operation almost immediately. When cooled quickly hard solder has less tendency to crystallize than soft solder. A few seconds after heat has been withdrawn is sufficient; the metal only has to cool below the soldering color stage before quenching. A safe commercial pickling compound, such as Sparex No. 2, is recommended for removing flux and surface oxides.

A soldering operation which differs slightly from the others is employed for filigree work. Because of the fineness of the

124

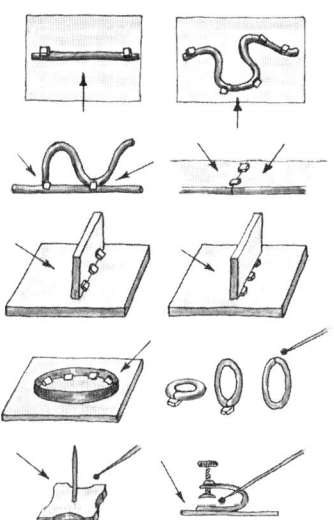

125

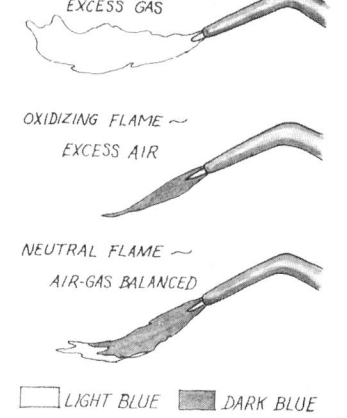

REDUCING FLAME — EXCESS GAS

OXIDIZING FLAME — EXCESS AIR

NEUTRAL FLAME — AIR-GAS BALANCED

☐ LIGHT BLUE ■ DARK BLUE
☐ YELLOW

126

112   Jewelry: Queen of Crafts

parts to be soldered, solder snippets are not employed. Filings of easy solder are mixed with flux, and the thin paste of flux and solder is applied to joints. Slow, careful heating will not dislodge these small solder filings. An assembly of small wire pieces for filigree is held in place for soldering by a method different from that used for soldering together one or two large pieces. It is best to solder the whole assembly of parts in one operation, because metal and flux expansion during heating would otherwise separate most of the joints. A film of beeswax is melted upon a flat surface or a sheet of casting wax is placed upon a backing, and the filigree wire is pressed into place about one-third the thickness of the wires. Plaster of paris or better, cristobalite is poured over the assembly of parts, and after hardening and drying, the wax is melted away and the partially imbedded metal parts are scrubbed and scraped clean. Flux with filings is applied to joints, and the soldering is done by bringing the plaster-metal piece gradually up to fusing temperature. Plaster or cristobalite will disintegrate if placed in water while still hot; pickling and scrubbing will finish the job. Gum tragacanth can be mixed with flux to act as a binder for small metal parts, but it is not as strong or as positive as the plaster method. Greek filigree is shown in *Figure 127*.

Borax, the bases of most fluxes, prevents the formation of oxides at soldered joints. Many workers develop the habit of dipping all pieces to be soldered into a saturated solution of borax and alcohol before placing them in position to be

127

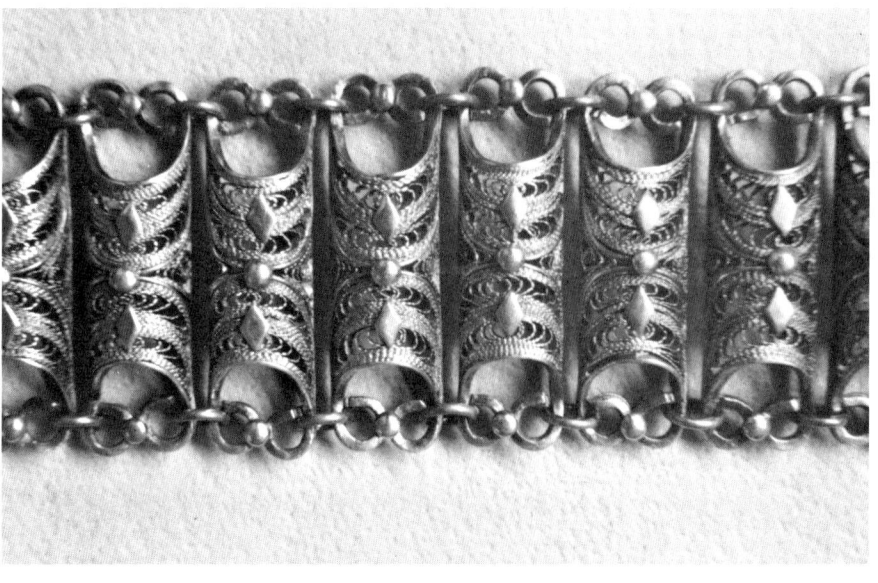

Jewelry Working Techniques 113

soldered. They do this to help protect all areas from excessive oxidation during hard-soldering. This is a good practice and leaves the work cleaner after pickling. The soldering torch ignites and burns off the alcohol, leaving a very thin white coating of borax as a protective film all over the work. Regular fluxing and soldering follow this burnoff of alcohol.

Describing soldering temperatures by color of metal is tricky at best because of the variable factors involved, such as surrounding light and individual interpretation of colors. This simple guide to temperatures is given only as a help; experience is the most valuable aid with soldering temperatures.

200 to 300° F	Water from flux evaporates.
900° F	First sign of color change to red.
1000 to 1100° F	A definite red but dull color.
1100° F plus	Flux melts.
1300 to 1400° F	Brighter red but not orange or pink. This is hard-soldering temperature, and further rise in temperature to any great extent will start to melt the basic metal pieces.
1600° F	Danger zone and close to trouble. Sterling silver melts at 1640° F.

STAMPING

Stamping is one of the oldest methods of decorating sheet metal. Punches with a device or design on one end can be hammered to press into the metal an exact replica of the punch face. A punch design can be repeated to form a border; it can repeat an element in a design; or it can be used with other punches of differently marked faces to form an overall design. Indian jewelry of the Southwest relies heavily upon stamping for decoration. The Navaho or Zuñi craftsman forms his own punches from scrap steel by first annealing it and filing and/or punching his own designs into the softened steel faces. The punches are then tempered and polished for use and become part of his most valued possessions. *Figure 128* shows the simple tool needed and various designs. Some have the same pattern but vary in size or curvature. Some punch patterns are made mostly of straight lines, while others are circles or arcs of varied curvature. Some are needed in pairs for right and left (*Figure 129*, right). The punches are usually used together in making a design, and so the variety of designs is almost endless. Many of the designs are decorative only, while others are symbolic and meaningful to anyone who can interpret Indian design. Because this type of jewelry frequently has areas formed by punches, it is difficult to say where chasing, repoussé, dapping, and punching end and strict stamping

128

129

130

begins. Stamping should be regarded, however, as only the impression left by the stamp. In order to get a clear-cut stamp impression the metal has to be placed on a steel block; this compresses and spreads the metal a small amount rather than forming it up or down as with chasing tools or dapping punches. For best results the tool should be held perpendicular to the work and hit a sharp blow with the hammer. Metal to be stamped should be free of scratches so that little buffing is needed after stamping is done. Buffing tends to soften the sharp outline of the stamp. Design transfer should be made with carbon paper, but the carbon lines should not be scratched in. The metal should be annealed when stamping is started to make the work easier, but frequent annealing while working is not required, as stamped areas do not usually overlap each other or stretch the metal enough to make it hard and brittle. Stamping should be done before close outline cutting because there is some stretching; this is especially true where a stamped border is made close to a metal outline or edge (*Figure 130*).

Jewelry and craft suppliers all carry stamping punches in stock, and the various designs can be chosen from a catalogue. Leathercraft companies have more recently developed stamps for metal, as they closely resemble the stamps used in leather carving. These have a harder temper than the regular leather tools. More satisfaction comes from making one's own individual stamps out of drill rod or tool steel. They are easily made and tempered or case-hardened; the cost is also much less than the manufactured stamps. Proper tempering instructions can be found later in this chapter under TEMPERING. The source of heat used for hard-soldering, files to form the design, and emery cloth for cleaning and polishing are all that is needed to make a stamping tool.

Stamping tools can be made for texturing as well as for forming a design. The face of the stamp can be filed with straight lines or crosshatched with lines to form small diamond shapes for texture. A texturing surface can also be placed on the tool face by driving it against an old file while red hot and later tempering it. Stamping has a limited use in handcrafted jewelry, because if much stamping is done the articles all seem to fit the Indian motif. This is permissible if that type of jewelry has been designed, but stamping, because of its close association with Indian pieces, can easily slip out of performing only accent work and can overpower other parts of a good design. Excellent stamping can be done easily with inexpensive equipment, and the variety of designs made by combining stamps is limited only by the worker's imagination.

Stamps can also be bought to inscribe pieces: sterling, 10K, 14K, 18K. These stamps are almost necessary for articles made for sale. There are regulations for their use and laws against their abuse, and so pieces stamped with these markings should come up to standard. Stamps can also be bought to inscribe the craftsman's initials or mark. They cost only two or three times the cost of regular prefabricated stamps and lend a personalized touch to the jewelry. It is not necessary to have a personal stamp on sterling, but it must accompany any gold stamp on a piece. All these stamps are made straight or with a curve in the shank to allow stamping the inside of a ring. The curved stamp is the more versatile, as it can be used on all pieces.

STONE AND PEARL SETTING

Stone Setting

Stones possessing brilliant color and a pleasing surface have been prized as adornment since before the dawn of man's history. The beauty of silver and gold and their easy adaptability for holding stones, as well as for forming wearable pieces of jewelry by themselves, have made precious metals and stones close and almost inseparable companions. Stones vary in hardness: some are transparent, while others are translucent or opaque; some are thin, and some are thick. Some stones are cut and polished to draw out and enhance their natural beauty, and others are left as they are found. Settings for stones are designed to hold them securely while displaying the stones to the best possible advantage. There are several ways of setting

131

stones to accomplish this, including stone piercing for wire insertion (*Figure 131*).

The easiest and simplest settings are made of wire wrapped around baroque stones (*Figure 132*). These are natural little stones of lapidary shop scraps which have been put through the tumbling machine for grinding and polishing. Usually copper or silver wire is bent to hold the stone and conform to its contours, or the wire is formed into a cage where the stone tumbles about freely. This type of stone setting is generally seen at county fairs, carnivals, and tourist centers, and its simple method of setting is often taught for therapeutic purposes in hospitals and at children's summer camps. Some good work has been produced by serious craftsmen using good materials, but a craftsman capable of setting stones in the better and more conventional ways will not need instruction on how to set tumbled stones if he wants to do so.

132

Cabochons are stones ground and polished in domed form. They have a flat, or nearly flat, lower surface (*Figure 133*). The sides of the stone start to slope from this flat bottom to form the dome, and this angle makes it possible to form metal over it to hold the stone in place. Although not flattering to a beautiful stone, the French term *en cabochon*, meaning a bald head, is expressive. The dome can vary from high to nearly flat, and the outline can have many shapes, the most common ones running from round to long, slender oval. Opaque stones are cut cabochon to show them to best advantage, since light is reflected only from their surface.

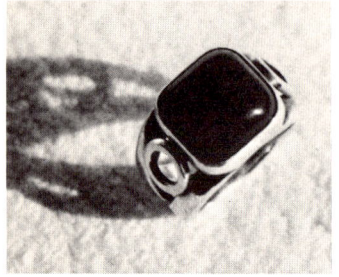

133

Bezel is the most common form of setting for cabochons. It consists of a small open-topped metal box into which the stone is placed. The sides of the box are bent over the sloping sides of the stone to hold it firmly (*see Figure 134*). The bezel is started by cutting a narrow strip of metal long enough to encircle the stone and about one-third the height of the domed top. Sterling silver or fine silver about 26 gauge can be used for this bezel strip, but fine silver is easier to work because there is no spring to the metal. The stone is placed on a flat surface and the strip is closely formed edgewise by hand around the stone and marked where the ends meet. The surplus is cut off, the ends are straightened and filed for a close fit, and the ends are soldered together.

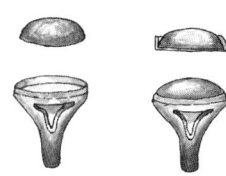

134

A note here. Karat golds are harder to work, so the forming of the strip around the stone may have to be done carefully with round or half-round ring pliers. Also, a better fit is made for round or oval stones if the strip is cut a little undersize, about $\frac{1}{32}$ inch short. After soldering the strip can be placed on a ring mandrel and tapped gently with a hammer or mallet to stretch it for a perfect fit. This alleviates cutting apart, shortening, and resoldering a strip that was cut too long. The strip does not have to be in a perfect shape for soldering. It can be flattened somewhat to make soldering easier and reshaped by slipping it over the stone later. The strip is bent smaller than the stone and then spread out so that the ends come together with pressure against each other. This is enough to hold the ends and makes binding with wire unnecessary. The strip is held by self-locking tweezers for soldering, with the joint resting on a soldering block. A snippet of solder is placed over this joint on the inside of the bezel and the joint is fluxed and soldered. The strip is very easily melted, so the torch should be set for a small neutral flame, with most of the heat directed onto the block close to the joint. A steel wire pick to guide the flow of solder from one side of the joint to the other is a great help in this delicate soldering operation. After soldering, the bezel should be pickled and excess solder filed away from the joint. Do not work this joint too much, as there is more soldering to be done; remember that solder shrinks when remelted, and a joint which is almost invisible is desirable. The bezel ring is now reshaped to fit the stone exactly, and the bottom is smoothed to a level surface by rubbing it over a fine, flat file and emery cloth. The ring is placed in position on the flat area, making sure that it touches the other metal all around. It is then fluxed, and solder snippets are placed against both metal and ring around the inside at intervals of about $\frac{3}{16}$ to $\frac{1}{4}$ inch and soldered. Here again care must be taken not to melt the fragile bezel ring. Resting the piece on a wire screen and directing the flame on the bottom helps in preheating the heavier part.

There are variations in bezel settings. One is made when it

118   Jewelry: Queen of Crafts

is desired to have a stone set higher than it would be if it rested upon its base. This requires a smaller inner ring soldered to the first bezel strip to act as a shoulder to support the stone (*Figure 135A*). The outer ring is cut wider than the inner strip so that it projects above the bottom of the stone and can be worked over the sides for holding. Two metal strips can be soldered together first and the bezel measured, formed, and soldered, or the rings can be made separately and soldered after being slipped one inside the other. Bezel wire can be purchased in straight strips in various widths either flat or with shoulders for higher setting, and many have decorative designs rolled or stamped into the side which is to be soldered to the base.

Another variation of the straight box bezel setting is made to hold cabochons which are not flat, but are rounded slightly on the bottom or are translucent or transparent. In these cases the backing metal is sawed away inside the bezel ring to leave only a shoulder for the stone to rest on, as illustrated in *Figure 135B*. This provides a space into which the rounded bottom of a cabochon can fit and a means to transmit light for transparent or translucent stones. Such stones as agate or amethyst look much better when mounted in a bezel setting with an open back. This cutout method is also useful to lighten the weight of an article, and in the case of gold, it can lower the cost of the jewelry piece.

If a stone is mounted on a curved surface, the bottom of the bezel will not, of course, be flat, so this requires another modification. The stone must be supported and held level, which requires the double-ring shoulder-type bezel, shown in *Figure 135C*. The bottom of the bezel has to be filed to fit the contour of the piece.

Square or rectangular cabochons (*Figure 136*), because of their sharp corners, are more difficult to fit than round or oval

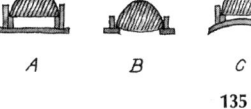

A   B   C

135

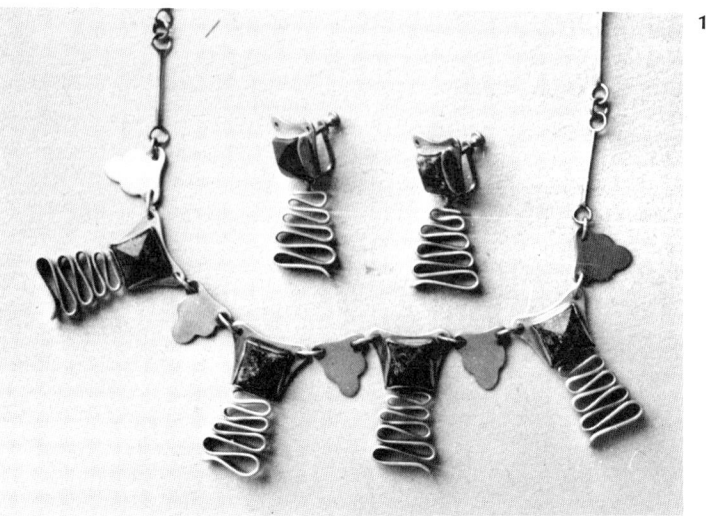

136

stones because the bezel wire cannot be tightly fitted at the corners. A V or miter joint can be made by using the corner angle of a square file to cut nearly through the metal where the bends are to be made. It is best to work one corner at a time. File a 45° angle on the end of the wire; mark, file, and bend the first corner; replace the stone and mark, file, bend again, and so on. This type of bezel can also be made from two pieces of bezel wire, both shaped in the form of an L. They require only one square flat end and one mitered corner bend each. The two pieces are then placed together to form the box of the bezel and soldered. The latter method has the advantage of being adjustable in one dimension (see *Figure 137*). In both methods all mitered corners should be soldered for strength.

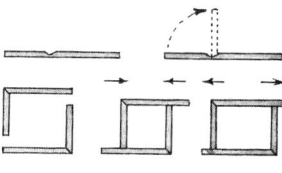

137

After all types of bezels have been soldered in place they should be filed and made smooth and level across their tops. The sides and the soldered joints should be dressed up, any burrs removed, and the whole jewelry piece buffed and polished before the stones are set. A polished burnishing tool is best for setting or bending the bezel top against and over the sloping side of a cabochon. The stone is placed in the bezel box and the tool is moved up under pressure at five or six separate places around the stone. Bending the bezel over shrinks the metal ring into a smaller diameter, so this preliminary spacing of a few bendovers serves two purposes: it holds the stone in place, and it distributes the extra metal evenly around the stone. The metal would wrinkle if the burnishing was done continuously around from start to finish. The bezel is forced down all around with an upward rolling stroke of the burnisher. The strokes later can go around the stone at the bezel top for smoothing the work. If the stone is not made tight this way, the bezel top can be pushed or gently tapped down from the top toward the stone, using a flat stone-setting tool. Tool marks on the bezel can be removed with a file. Do this carefully so as not to injure the stone, and finish the setting job by buffing and polishing.

All bezels do not have to be straight and level across their tops. Scallops or rounded points can be filed in the tops before they are burnished. A texture can be given to a bezel by running a millegrain tool along the top edge of the metal alongside the stone. This little wheel impresses the metal to form a continuous row of very small sparkling beads. Make certain that this will make the whole piece look better before using the millegrain tool. A plain, smooth bezel top always looks good, but the addition of this textured edge can detract from a handmade article by making it look machine finished.

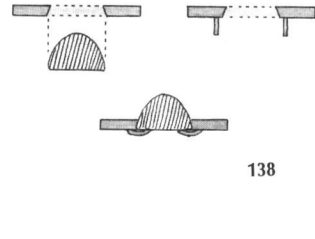

138

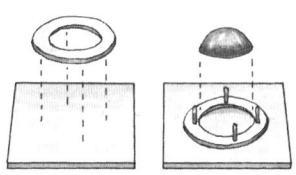

139

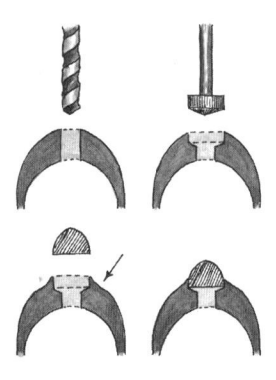

140

Cabochons can also be set by using prongs instead of a bezel. One way of doing this is to saw and file a slightly sloping hole in the metal which is to hold the stone so that the stone fits through from the back (see *Figure 138*). The bottom of the stone should be level, or nearly so, with the back of the metal; the sides of the hole which slope inward and upward keep the stone from going all the way through the metal from back to front. Three or four prongs are soldered upright around the hole at the back, the stone is inserted, and the prongs are bent over the stone to lock it in place. This is a good way to set a stone in an article which does not receive rough treatment and the back of which is never exposed while worn. A stone in a pin or brooch is often set this way.

Wire prongs can be used on the front or top of the stone in place of a bezel, but this method exposes the bottom edge of the stone, which may or may not be objectionable according to the design or the workman's choice of methods. *Figure 139* shows how the edge can easily be hidden by cutting a small ring out of metal into which the stone can be sunk; the ring is soldered in place; and the prongs are later soldered to the ring. The top piece of appliqué work should have the hole for the stone cut into it prior to soldering onto the underlying metal.

A gypsy setting, illustrated in *Figure 140*, has long been used to set cabochons firmly in places where they are exposed to shock, as when mounted in a ring. This setting also requires considerable thickness of metal, which is usually found only in the front section of a ring. There is much work involved in this setting, and it is used more often to mount small round stones than large or oval stones. A small hole is first drilled through the metal to act as a guide for a stone-setting burr. The type used is a flat or obtuse pointed burr just large enough to allow the stone to drop into the hole it makes. The depth of the hole does not have to be great; higher-domed stones should be set a little lower than more shallow ones, but as a rule the stone does not have to be deeper than half the amount that would be used for a bezel to set the same stone. The stone is placed in the hole and a flat stone pusher or chasing tool is used to tap the surrounding metal down against the sloping sides of the stone. The setting can be made more easily by removing metal with a file or graver at the point marked by an arrow in *Figure 140*. Both hands have to be free to use the tool and hammer while working, so the ring mandrel is held in a vise to give solid support. There are hammering attachments for flex-shaft machines which make this work easier, but they are expensive and are used mostly by professionals. A very handy and inexpensive tool that can be used for

Jewelry Working Techniques 121

this and other purposes is the spring-loaded center punch with demountable tips. A center punch point can be ground flat and polished for use as a small hammer; the tension is adjustable on this punch for heavy or soft blows. It is also a good substitute for the stone-setting tool in setting bezels and has the advantage of leaving a hand free for holding and manipulating the work.

A variation of the bezel setting is done with a round dapped piece for the supporting and holding metal. It gives the effect of a bubble, the top half of which is stone, the lower half metal. These stone-and-metal bubbles are made only with round stones, usually of small diameter (*Figure 141*), which cannot be mounted in any other manner. They form complete little units, such as stamens and pistils of a flower design or the eyes of an insect or animal (see *Figure 142*). A disc is cut and dapped, which, after dapping, is a little larger than the base of the round cabochon. A wire ring is then soldered inside the dapped piece to act as a supporting shoulder for the base of the stone. A small flat area should be filed on the bottom of the dapped piece on the outside for a bigger, stronger area for soldering to the rest of the jewelry piece. The stone is set in place and the edge of the dapped metal is worked over the stone and finished in the same manner as any bezel.

Transparent stones are cut with facets to bring out their sparkle. They are dependent upon light entering and reflecting back out of the top to show them to best advantage and bring out their full beauty of color and glitter. The setting of these stones must be done so as to interfere as little as possible with light reflection and still provide a secure and pleasing means of attachment. The prong setting best fulfills these requirements. The classic example of this setting is the engagement ring. Except for special cuts a faceted stone is cut in the following manner: A flat surface is ground and polished at the top (called the table; the widest cross section of the stone is called the girdle), and facets are placed between the table and the girdle to form the upper half of the gem (known as the crown). The lower half (called the pavilion) is ground with facets from the girdle downward and culminates in a point at the bottom (see *Figure 143*).

Jewelry supply firms provide these prong settings in various sizes, styles, and number of prongs, in different shapes for use with round, navette, cushion, octagon, or oval cut stones, and in different metals. These settings are classed as findings and in the majority of cases are best purchased rather than made by the home craftsman. Pronged settings are first soldered to the jewelry piece with the appropriate hard solder

141

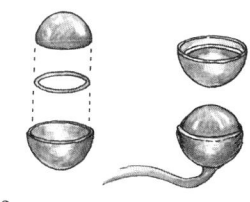

142

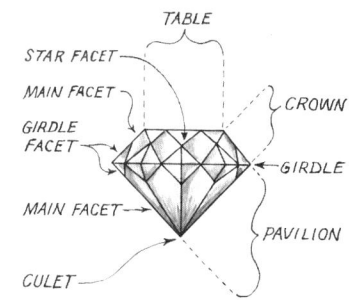

143

122   Jewelry: Queen of Crafts

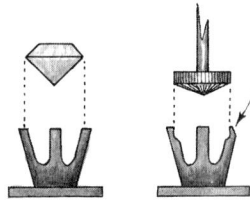

144

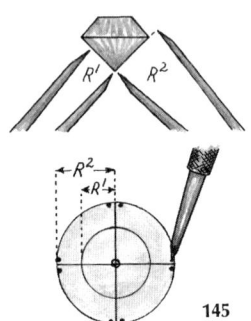

145

before any fitting of the stone is attempted. These findings, with their slender prongs, are delicate, and it might be well for the worker to review FINDING APPLICATION in this chapter before working. A shoulder for the stone to rest upon must be cut into the inner side of the prongs. For round stones this is accomplished by using a stone-setting burr the same size as the stone to be set (see *Figure 144*). The spread of the prongs and the depth of cut should allow the stone to set evenly when the shoulder has been completed; the cut extends about halfway through the prong. The tops of the prongs are then filed and sanded to a length which will allow them to extend above the supported stone girdle and table facet. The prongs are then filed to a point, as indicated by an arrow in *Figure 144*, and pressed tightly against the face of crown facets so that no snagging of fabric can occur. The inside shoulder notches on the prongs of settings which are not made for round stones must be made individually because a setting burr cannot do the job on all of them simultaneously. A file or a burr can be used for this, but frequent fittings are necessary to make sure that the stone remains level and rests evenly upon all prong shoulders. All stones are hard and most are also brittle; unless the stones have a level support they can be easily cracked when the prong tips are bent over them and pressure is exerted on the stone.

As stated before, in most cases it is better to buy prong settings rather than to attempt making them. There are, however, two simple prong settings which are easy to make and are quite effective. One is for round stones, and is made by dapping a single piece of sheet metal. With a pair of dividers measure about two thirds the distance from the lower point of the stone to the girdle and use this for a radius to scribe a circle. Open the dividers up so that they measure about 1/16 inch longer than the distance from stone point to girdle and scribe a circle using the same center as before. The inner circle will form the base of the prongs and the outer circle will form the tops. The circle is then equally divided into four parts for a four-prong setting by scratching two diameters across the piece at 90° to each other. (The circle can be equally divided into as many sections as desired, depending upon how many prongs are wanted.) On each side of the points where the lines intersect the outer circle, make small center punch marks on the circle about 1/32 to 1/16 inch away from the straight diameter lines. These four pairs of closely punched marks form the width of the prong tops (see *Figure 145*). Arcs are then marked which will touch the inner circle and pass through the outer center punch marks. The marked setting is sawed out, filed

Jewelry Working Techniques 123

smooth, and dapped into a hole in the dapping die which is slightly larger than the stone girdle, to allow for metal thickness. A small hole should also be drilled through the middle of the piece to receive the point of the stone so that it will not be broken off while setting. The stone should just fit between the prongs after dapping, as illustrated in *Figure 146*. Soldering the setting in place at this time makes further work and the setting of the stone easier. A shoulder is then cut into the prongs with a stone-setting burr or by filing. Prong tips will have to be shaped for width and length by filing; the setting and the rest of the piece should be buffed and polished before the stone is set in the regular manner by burnishing over the prongs (*Figure 147*). Prongs of any number can be made by following these same steps. This makes a strong setting which can be used wherever a prong setting is needed. The stone in *Figure 148* was set in this manner.

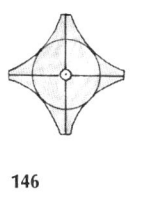
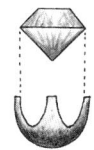

146

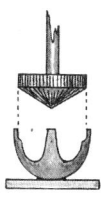

147

Another setting made out of sheet metal works well for round, oval, and emerald cut stones. *Figure 149* shows how this setting appears when an oval stone is used. The outline of the stone is lightly marked on the metal and another line is then marked about 1/16 inch inside the outline of the stone. At the corners mark the prongs which are to fold inward over the corner facets; these should extend an additional 1/16 to 1/8 inch past the inner line for length; larger stones take longer prongs. A hole is drilled in the center area for pierced sawing. The lines to be sawed are the ends of the prongs and the inner lines along the four sides. It should appear as a rectangular hole with four projections inward at the corners when sawed as drawn in *Figure 150*. The prongs are made by sawing outward alongside these projections to a depth of 3/16 inch; the

148

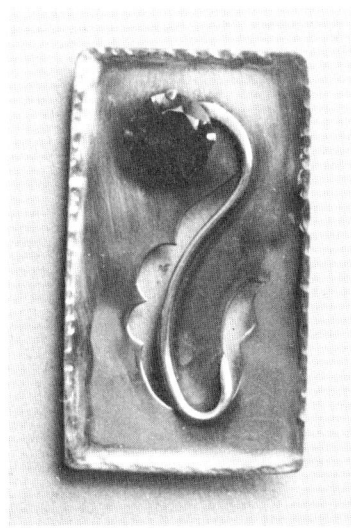

149

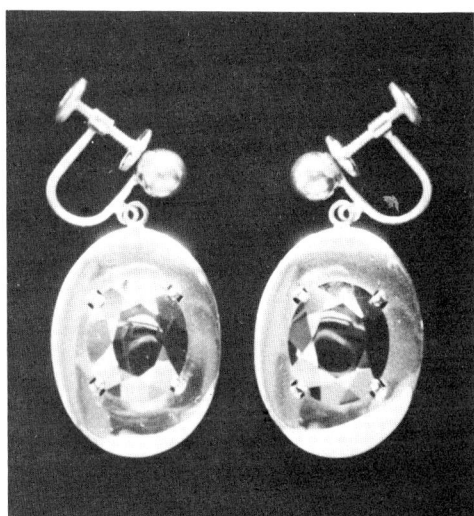

150

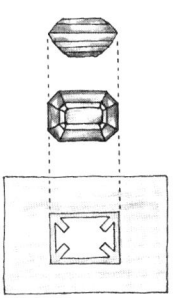

124   Jewelry: Queen of Crafts

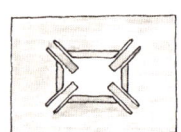

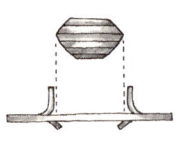

151

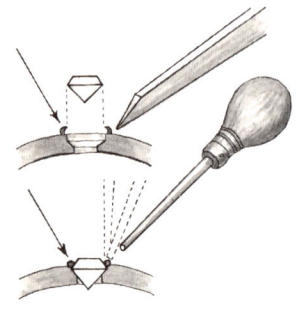

152

CUT SLOPING SIDES HERE

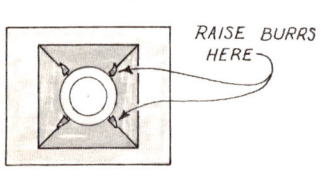
RAISE BURRS HERE

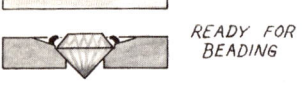
READY FOR BEADING

153

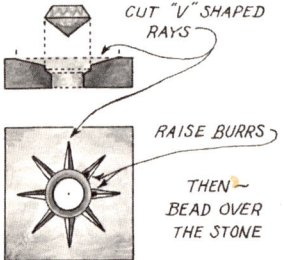
CUT "V" SHAPED RAYS

RAISE BURRS
THEN BEAD OVER THE STONE

154

⅛ inch margin past the stone outline allows for prong bending. The piece is trued and smoothed with a file and emery cloth. Prongs are bent up so that the stone can be fitted into place, as shown in *Figure 151*. The side areas between the two marked lines can be bent slightly down to make a better and lower shoulder for the stone to rest upon. The prongs are rounded, tapered, buffed, and burnished to complete the setting. This type of setting is not as strong as the dapped setting, but it can be used for pins or pendants to show a stone to good advantage.

For several reasons not all faceted stones are mounted in raised pronged settings. The upward projection of stones and setting takes space, and some do not lend themselves to prong mountings because of design restrictions. This is especially true of jewelry pieces designed for men. Methods have been devised for holding stones at a low level or flush with the metal to which they are mounted; these will hold stones securely and interfere little with light reflection. All these mountings require a shoulder for support below the girdle of the stone. In cast jewelry this can be provided for in the wax before casting; in handwrought metal the opening has to be cut out of the sheet metal by using a burring tool or graver. In either cast or sheet metal, the prongs must be formed by removing metal around the stones and leaving only enough metal to form prongs at various points. Metal burrs can also be gouged into the metal with a graver and pried up to form prongs, which can be turned over the stone with the beading tool (*Figure 152*). Many variations of this type of setting are made, the most common of which are known as diamond and star settings. The diamond setting (*Figure 153*) is made by first drilling a guide hole. This is followed by using a burring tool to form a shoulder for the stone in the sunken hole. A square area is then marked around the hole, and the sides are engraved sloping down to the hole on all four sides. A pointed graver then is pushed steeply into the metal a short distance away from the stone at the junctures of the four sloping cuts. This raises a burr, which can be turned over and down onto the stone with a beading tool. When done properly this makes a very good setting which is little affected by wear, as the prongs are below the surface of the surrounding metal. The star setting, shown in *Figure 154*, is similar. The engraving is made by cutting slender triangles toward the stone hole instead of a depressed square as for the diamond setting. This gives a radiating star-burst effect to the stone after it is mounted. Burrs are turned over with the beading tool in the same manner for holding.

Pearl Setting

Although pearls are not stones, they are so frequently mounted in jewelry that any description of stone setting would be incomplete without including methods for their attachment. Pearls are mounted by prongs or rivets, held in cups, or pegged; and combinations of these methods may be used.

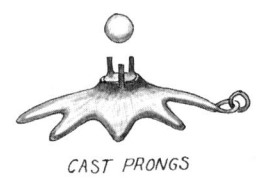

155 CAST PRONGS

Cast jewelry pieces can be made with an indentation for the pearl to set into and with three or more cast metal prongs long enough to extend upward and over the curve of the pearl for bending over and down to hold it tightly (see *Figure 155*). A cup with prongs to hold the pearl can be made from sheet metal by dapping. To determine the size of the disc, the pearl is fitted into a hole in the dapping die where it fits snugly after allowing for the metal thickness (20 or 22 gauge) on all sides. A scrap piece of metal can be dapped first for this purpose. *Figure 156A* shows soft wire bent over half the pearl and marked; this can also be used to measure the diameter of the disc. A circle of this diameter is then marked on the metal and a larger circle scribed around it; this circle should be large enough to form the prongs necessary for bending slightly over the curved top of the pearl. Three or more prongs are then spaced and marked between these two circles. The pattern should now resemble a cog wheel; the cogs, of course, will later form the prongs (*Figure 156B*). This piece is then sawed out, evened up by filing, and then dapped. This setting is held better to a jewelry piece if a small area on the bottom is filed flat to make a wider base for soldering. After it has been attached, the prongs can be filed to a better shape and set with a burnisher after all dressing and buffing has been done. *Figure 156C* illustrates the finished setting.

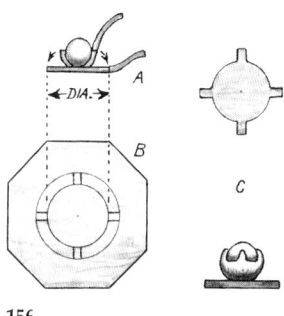

156

Pearls can be purchased which are drilled all the way through, only halfway through, or not drilled at all. Those having no holes are set by the above, prong method of mounting. Pearls which are drilled all the way through can be made fast by slipping them over a wire which has been soldered on one end to a pin or ring. The wire should fit the hole in the pearl snugly and extend 1/32 to 1/16 inch above the pearl. This metal tip is then riveted carefully by very light blows with a chasing tool, or it can be burnished and pressed into shape with a beading tool, as done in *Figure 157A*. Pearls are delicate and easily cracked or scratched, so this work should be performed very carefully.

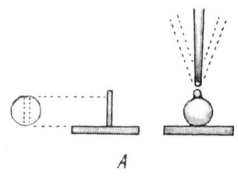

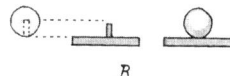

157

Half-drilled pearls are mounted by pegging them onto a wire base and fastening them with glue (see *Figure 157B*). The wire should be roughened a little with coarse emery cloth,

158

159

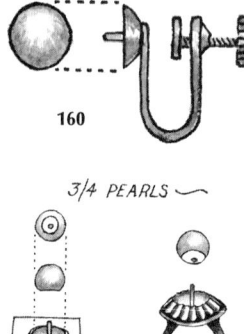
160

3/4 PEARLS

161

or a small notch or two should be put into the side by filing. Modern pearl cement or the newer epoxy cements will hold the pearl firmly. In fact these cements hold pearls so securely that it is difficult to get them off once the cement has set. There are solvents to accomplish this, but they are slow-acting. The easiest and fastest way to remove a pegged pearl is to heat the metal parts slightly and carefully twist and pull off the pearl before it becomes hot. The pearls in *Figures 158* and *159* were attached in this manner.

Small metal cups with a peg in the middle are used to hold the pearl where the base of the pearl looks better hidden and no prongs are desired. Earring findings for pearls are made in this manner and need only cementing to hold them in place

162

163

(*Figure 160*). Pearls can be purchased with a flat area ground on one side. This grinding is done to remove a blister or blemish on an otherwise good pearl. They are known as three-quarter pearls and are much cheaper than the perfectly round ones, although they may possess good texture and color. These pearls can be used to advantage in pegged cups or depressions where the pearl base cannot be seen from the side (see *Figures 161* and *162*).

The setting of baroque pearls, because of their odd and varied shapes, can tax the ingenuity of the worker. They can be drilled and pegged, or wire prongs can be spaced and soldered to fit and hold them. If the form is quite flat, like the pearl in *Figure 163*, a bezel can sometimes be used, or a partial bezel can hold down one end or side with prongs on the other side of the pearl to lock it in place. Baroques are seldom purchased already drilled. If drilling is necessary—on any pearl for that matter—an ordinary carbon drill is used. Pearls can be held in a ring clamp. It helps to file a very small flat spot on the pearl before starting the drill, which will otherwise tend to creep.

Blister pearls closely resemble stone cabochons, both round and oval. These may be set in the same manner as stones, by prongs or bezels.

STONING

Stoning is a process used for smoothing metal, enamel, and, in some cases, stones. To a great extent it has been replaced by better methods made possible by new tools and superior materials. The process of stoning follows filing and consists in rubbing the stone over the work to remove scratches or other irregularities on small surfaces which are difficult to reach. The common stone used for this work is Scotch stone, a natural stone of fine texture which is available in small, 5- or 6-inch lengths and in cross sections which vary from ⅛- to ½-inch squares. The stone is rather soft, so an end may be filed or ground to shape in order to reach and smooth different contours in a piece of work. During stoning both the work and the stone must be kept wet, preferably under running water, to avoid clogging and filling the stone with metal particles. Because of the slowness of this working method and the small size of the stones, other methods are recommended for large exposed areas. Stoning is an abrasive process, so buffing and polishing must follow for finishing.

The advent of the flex-shaft tool, with the many sizes and shapes of grinding wheels and silicon carbide impregnated

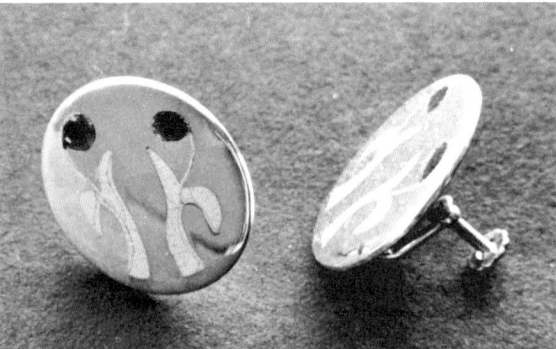

164

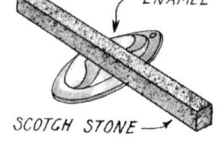

165

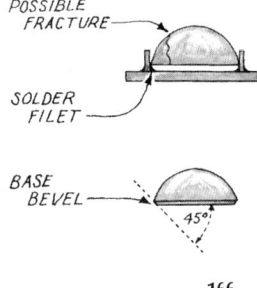

166

rubber wheels, has made stoning metal with the Scotch stone almost obsolete. These small wheels can be easily shaped on an old file so that they can be used in any area which has to be stoned. Neither the metal nor these wheels have to be wet while working, and they are much faster. The narrow cross section of the plastic emery-cloth holder, mentioned under SANDING, can reach places which would formerly have had to be stoned. It is also used dry, and when a fine, worn cloth is used, it produces a finish as smooth as the stone.

This does not mean that wet stoning has no use in today's working methods. The smoothing and leveling of enameled surfaces (*Figure 164*) is still done by wet stoning with either the Scotch stone or Carborundum stone. Carborundum stones are available in the same sizes and shapes as Scotch stones. They last longer but are not as easily shaped for particular job requirements. The flex-shaft grinding wheels tear up the enamel surface too much, and the rubber wheels have little effect. The wet type of emery cloth mounted on emery sticks does fine work on enameled surfaces if a stone is not available, but constant wetting of the work and cloth, or working under running water, is necessary for its use the same as for stones. *Figure 165* shows plique-à-jour enameled earrings after stoning and polishing.

Stoning can also be done on cabochon stones if the cabochons have a slight bevel ground and are polished where the base and sloping sides meet. This bevel is made on a cabochon by stoning or grinding a 45° bevel with a $\frac{1}{32}$- to $\frac{1}{16}$-inch face. If this is not done the sharp corner at the base of the cabochon rests upon the solder fillet at the bottom of the bezel and can be broken when it is pressed down for setting (see *Figure 166*). This stoning should be done only on a cabochon set in a bezel, which will hide the small stoned bevel.

TEMPERING

The three precious metals used in jewelry are silver, gold, and platinum. They are classed as precious not only for their appearance, workability, and wearability, but also for their relative rarity. A metal less valuable but found in great quantity

Jewelry Working Techniques 129

is iron. Iron in latin is *ferrum,* and a metal alloy with iron as its base is known as a ferrous metal. Metal of almost any kind, including silver, gold, and platinum, can be hardened by working, but a unique hardening process is required for ferrous metals. This hardening process is made possible by the combination of carbon with iron in proper proportions to form the alloy, steel. The treatment of steel by heat in a specific manner is tempering. Pure iron cannot be tempered. The importance of steel to our age cannot be overestimated; its importance to the jeweler is evidenced by his use of tempered steel tools almost exclusively for the forming of his jewelry. Steel was once used as jewelry metal, but it is now better used for tools to work other metals because of its unique qualities.

The percentage of carbon in steel for tools varies from slightly less than 1 to ½ percent, depending upon the desired qualities of the steel. This small amount of carbon is all that is necessary to change a very malleable metal into one that, after a heat treatment, is as brittle as glass. But a very brittle tool is of little use to anyone for hammering and forming metals. Therefore, the process of tempering this hardness to a more usable state is necessary (see *Figure 167*). Steel in an annealed condition is, like iron, malleable. Two heat processes are necessary to temper it so that the metal is hard but not too brittle. First it must be hardened, and later the hardness is decreased, or tempered.

Tempering is a very complicated subject when large and small objects and various alloys of steels are considered; but only a simple, rudimentary knowledge is needed for a craftsman to make and temper some simple tools, such as chasing tools, gravers, and punches.

Tool steel can be purchased in round or hexagonal rod form for making these small tools. The steel usually comes in an annealed state. If it is hard, it can be annealed by being heated to a red color and cooled slowly to room temperature, or it can be embedded in sand for still slower cooling. For small tools the rod is first cut into 5- to 6-inch lengths, and an end is filed and sanded to the desired shape and polished if the design requires it. It is then heated to a cherry red (approximately 1400° F) about one third its length from the finished end and then quickly submerged in water. It should be agitated while cooling to allow quicker and more even cooling. This sudden change in temperature alters the physical structure of the metal and makes the heated area very hard and brittle. After cooling, the piece is then polished along one side with emery cloth to reveal shiny metal. This is necessary because the proper temperature of reheating and cooling to

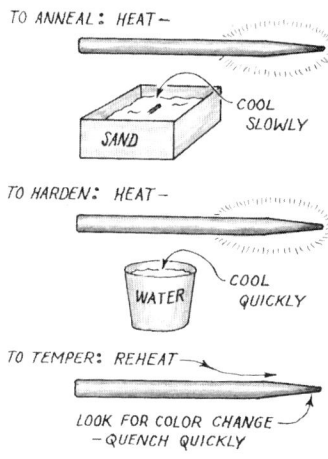

167

fix the temper is revealed by the color shown on this polished area. These colors are oxides in various stages of development. The steel is again heated by directing the flame just above the previously heated end section and observing the changes of color, which will progress from the source of heat to the tool tip. When the desired color has reached the tip, the metal is again plunged into water for quick cooling and "freezing" the temper at the desired degree of hardness. As a guide, the colors are listed here with approximate matching temperatures and the types of tools for which the temper is most appropriate:

Pale or light straw	420° F	Engraving tools, hard-edged tools required to stay sharp
Dark straw	450° F	Punches, such as chasing tools
Dark brown	500° F	Shop-fashioned drills
Purple	540° F	Hammerfaces, center punches, scribes
Blue	570° F	Screwdrivers, cold chisels

The above is a rule-of-thumb or shop-practice means of tempering, which will generally give good results. A tool can be made harder, so that it holds a sharp edge longer, or softer, so that it does not chip easily, by annealing and retempering to the degree of hardness desired by the worker. The rule is: the lower the heat for tempering, the harder the metal will be.

After tempering, the tools are shined and polished with emery cloth. Files should not be used on the tempered tools, since the tools will be as hard, or nearly as hard, as the files and will ruin them. Any irregularities or pits left by heating can be stoned away with a Carborundum stone and polished with fine emery cloth.

TEXTURING

Any work which changes a metal surface can be called texturing whether it is given a high gloss or a very rough and irregular surface, like that of the earrings in *Figure 168*. Textures can be made by the use of heat, abrasives, tools, or acids. Some textures appeal to the eye, others to the sense of touch. All of them afford contrast to each other or to surrounding materials. They are capable of giving a jewelry item interest and beauty, or if improperly used, they can also ruin it. All textures should be applied with forethought to the effect. Restrained or limited use should be made of textures, and they should never be used to cover shoddy workmanship.

Textures are most effective when they are honest and just textures rather than imitations of textures found in other materials, such as tree bark, wood grain, cloth, and so forth.

168

Many of the processes already described in this chapter create textures, either as their main purpose or as the result of other work. Each has been described under its particular heading, but it might be well to review them here under one heading as processes which impart textures.

Buffing
Buffing consists in using bobbing compound, tripoli, and rouge to remove scratches and to give a final high gloss to metal. Different textures, such as satin, dull, and matte finishes, can be made by stopping the buffing operation short of the final polish. Bristle brushes used with these compounds vary the matte finish a little, and brass and steel wire brushes make an entirely different texture.

Burnishing Tools
Burnishing tools leave small indentations in the metal and when not removed, leave a texture both pleasing and indicative of handmade work. Tools of different curvature vary the pattern.

Chasing Tools
Besides their common use to form metal up or down for repoussé work, chasing tools of all shapes can be used to impress different shapes into metal for texture. They can be used separately, in combination with each other, perpendicular to or at an angle with the work, or varied in depth of impression to give different effects.

Drilling

A "moon crater" texture can be made by drilling closely spaced holes only partially through the metal and sloping the sides of the partial holes with a stone-setting burr or a large drill. Small circular burrs or dentists' burr drills can be lightly worked over a surface while the work is in rotation; their forms and the angles of working make a wide selection of textures. Texturing is a very important part of a jewelry maker's craft. The worker should notice textures already made and experiment to develop new textures of his own.

Engraving

Engraving cuts rather than stamps a texture. The well-known Florentine texture is made with a lined graver. Small parallel lines, crosshatched lines at different angles, and basket-type engraving can all be done with this tool. Other gravers can be used to gouge out or chip flakes away, and flat gravers can be used at a steep angle and wiggled over the metal to change the surface.

Etching

Etching changes a surface by the action of acid on the metal and leaves a sandblasted look. A rougher pitted texture can be made if the bubbles which form on the metal during etching are not brushed away.

Fusing

Fusing changes the shape of metals as well as the texture. Heating metal to just below flowing temperature produces small surface bubbles which cannot be duplicated by mechanical working. Texture variations are subtle between melted areas and areas which have been kept just below melting point. Cold metal filings dropped on nearly molten metal make a sandpaper texture if the heat is enough to fuse without melting them.

Granulation

Granulation is a very distinctive texture formed by the addition of minute balls over the surface of the metal. The balls are attached by the colloid hard-soldering process.

Oxidizing

Oxidizing has a close relationship to texturing. Identically textured surfaces appear drastically changed if oxidized. For example, ground textures which shimmer with light reflections become nonreflective and velvety after oxidizing.

Peening

Peening is one of the most-used texturing methods. Indentations are made by using straight, cross, or ball peen hammers. The hammer face size, amount of peening, and force of blows vary the texture design. These markings can be left as a result of forming work or can be made just for texture. A craftsman should use this texture with discretion.

Polishing

Polishing operations such as the use of steel wool and emery cloth, which are usually done in preparation for buffing, furnish textures that can be used as a final finish. Flex-shaft grinding wheels and silicon carbide impregnated rubber wheels of assorted grit sizes make textures with a brushed effect. These are very attractive when oxidized.

Stamping

Stamping, done with a hammer and punches which have assorted texture ends, impresses a texture on the metal. The punches can also have figures and shapes filed into their ends and, after tempering, may be used separately or together to stamp a texture made up of repeated shapes. Indented nail punches of different sizes, center punches, leather tools, and chasing tools can all be used as texturing punches.

Stone Setting

Stone setting sometimes calls for the use of a millegrain tool on the top edge of a bezel-set stone. The small wheel leaves a texture of small beads when it is pushed or rolled over metal.

Stoning

Stoning to smooth the metal after filing and before buffing leaves a texture similar to the texture made by sanding with emery cloth. A Scotch stone or Carborundum stone can be used for this. Scotch stones can be shaped on one end by filing or grinding to give texture to areas that cannot be reached with emery cloth.

TRUMMING

This method of working has limited uses, but its effect in smoothing metal can be attained in no other way. Trumming is done by rubbing the metal piece back and forth over a string that has been rubbed over a buffing or polishing compound (*Figure 169*). One end of the string is held firmly in a vise and drawn taut with one hand while rubbing the metal over the

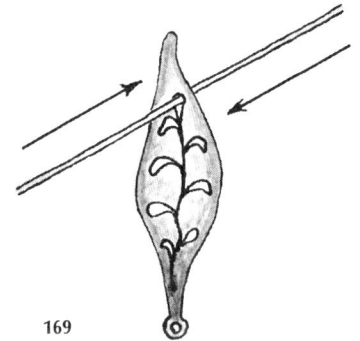
169

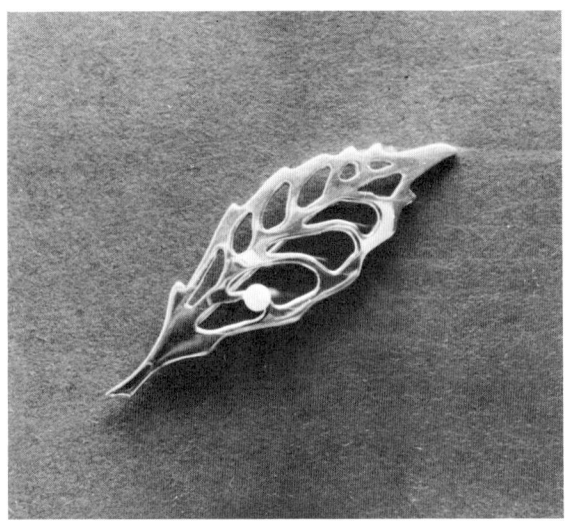

170

string with the other. A new string should be used for polishing with rouge.

Small areas of metal such as the side walls of pierced holes seldom have to be meticulously finished because they are small and are not likely to be inspected closely, and their protected position allows natural oxidation to form in a short period of time. Small areas do exist, however, which look better if trumming is used to smooth and polish. Bezels with pierced sides, intricate cutouts in metal pieces, and filigree joints can be polished in areas too small for finishing by filing and sanding (*Figure 170*).

CHAPTER 6
JEWELRY WITHOUT SOLDER

Silver pendant with a hole drilled through the top for chain attachment. The pearl was attached to a soldered peg.

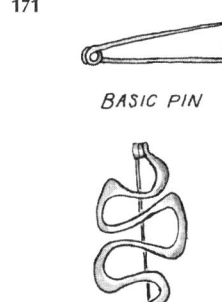

BASIC PIN

PIN WITHOUT SOLDER

Jewelry made without the use of solder can be very effective. The only important difference between nonsoldered and soldered pieces is that the former will necessarily tend toward greater simplicity. Earrings, buckles, rings, pins, tie clasps, bracelets, key chains, or other pieces of jewelry can be well designed and executed without the use of solder.

Five of the six tie clasps illustrated under DECORATION in Chapter 2 can be made without solder. The belt buckle in Chapter 2 illustrating UNITY needs only sawing, filing, and finishing. Pins are made with the simple safety-pin type catch and spring pin, as shown in *Figure 171*. Both ends of the wire which forms the catch and pin should be hammered before forming to work-harden them for necessary stiffness. Gold wire of 18 gauge or silver wire of 14 or 16 gauge will retain

171

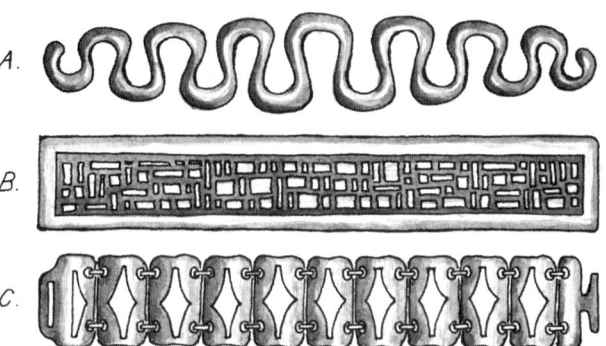

its shape for this type of pin. Flattening various areas after shaping the pin adds interest and also stiffens the pin. Both round and square wire may be used. The wire does not have to lie flat, as shown in the illustration, but can twist around, over, and under itself to form intricate designs.

Bracelets may be made from both sheet and wire. Because no solder is used, these pieces will be of the open-end rather than the bangle type. A length of 6½ to 7 inches is the correct size, which allows for 1- to 1½-inch gap between the ends after bending so that it can be slipped over the wrist. If a bracelet mandrel is not available, any rounded wooden form can be used to form the bracelet. Use a rawhide mallet so as not to scar the metal.

A wire bracelet is best made by drawing the outline of the design on paper and then matching the bends one at a time over the drawing. Although the overall length of the bracelet is only 6½ to 7 inches long, the wire must be quite long due to all the curves and connecting lengths of wire between them. It is best to do all bending first, before cutting to length. In this way, you can make certain that enough wire remains to complete the design fully. Square wire of heavy, 8 or 10 gauge is more effective than round wire—flat surfaces are better light reflectors than round surfaces. Sections of the square wire may also be flattened; flattened areas are more in harmony with the flat surfaces of square wire than with round. A simple, easily made bracelet is shown in *Figure 172A*. Irregular-sized curves, wire length between curves, varied sloping of the wire lengths, flattened areas, and texturing—all may be used to change the appearance. Open-end bracelets are required to spring a small amount each time they are put on or taken off, which in time can make them brittle and cause them to break. This type of wire bracelet has the advantage of being a spring in itself by its design, so it is little affected by usage. It is easier to finish and polish the work before bending it into shape, especially the inner surfaces. Any small scratches on outside surfaces left by the mallet while bending can be easily sanded out before polishing.

One-piece bracelets from sheet metal should be made from heavy, 12- or 14-gauge metal. The heavier gauges withstand the constant springing action without crystallizing and breaking much better than the thinner gauges do. The length is the

Jewelry Without Solder   137

same as for wire; bending and finishing can also be carried out in the same manner. Different widths and shapes, cutouts, etching, and textures can be used to create a wide range of effects. *Figure 172B* shows a sheet metal bracelet which has been etched and oxidized for decoration before bending.

Sheet metal units can be made and connected together with jump rings to form a bracelet. To avoid spreading, the jump rings should be heavier than those which normally would be used if they were to be soldered. Ordinary bracelet findings can be used for connecting the two ends by using unsoldered jump rings or by making the hook and eye an integral part of the end pieces. Since this type of bracelet is not required to spring over the wrist or slip over the hand, it can be made smaller and to the desired size by measuring the wrist with a strip of paper. For decoration, the separate units can be treated in the same way as the single-piece bracelet. *Figure 172C* illustrates units which have cutouts for design interest.

Unsoldered coiled wire rings must have been among the first jewelry items made; they have been found in ancient tombs all over the world. There are two reasons for this: wire is easily worked, and coiled wire invariably brings to mind a coiled snake. The snake has always occupied a high place in ancient religions and embodied much that was mysterious or supernatural. Occult powers were credited to the snake, and these powers were believed to be imparted to the wearer of a snake replica. People today are still fascinated by this ancient design.

Unsoldered rings, however, are generally not as satisfactory as some of the other items. Both design and construction are limited; the rings must be made from heavier wire or sheet than would be used if the ends were soldered together to furnish support. A ring receives the hardest use of any piece of jewelry. Unless a ring is made from heavy material, it will bend out of shape and pinch.

There are fundamentally three ways of making the ring: it can be wrapped three or four times in a coil around a mandrel to form a snake ring, as in *Figure 173A*; it can be bent and the ends overlapped, as in *Figure 173B*; or it can be bent and left with a gap between the two ends, as in *Figure 173C*. The illustrations show the three methods simply, but many adaptations can be made in design. Different textures and oxidizing widen the variety still more. Wire of no less than 10 gauge should be used, and sheet metal should be 14 gauge in order to hold its shape when formed into a ring. Riveting can be done to hold the two ends solidly when the overlapping method is used, and so a lighter-gauge metal can be substituted in this case because of the added support.

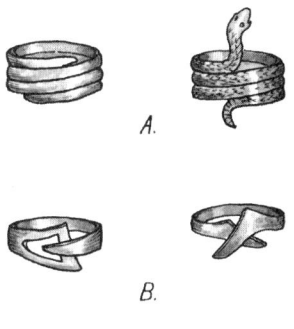

173

138 Jewelry: Queen of Crafts

Earrings and pendants can be made simply, and in one piece, from metal sheet and connected to earring findings or chains in several ways. These items do not require the strength necessary for rings and can be made from a lighter-gauge metal; 18- to 22-gauge sterling silver and 22- or 24-gauge karat gold have enough body and strength to make both earrings and pendants which will hold up well. If jump rings are used for connection, they should be heavier than would be normally used if soldered.

Any shape desired for an earring or pendant is first designed, transferred to the metal, and sawed out to furnish the blank. A hole is drilled in one end using a #50 or slightly smaller drill for a jump ring to connect the piece to the finding or chain, as shown in *Figure 174A*. A round projection similar to that in *Figure 174B* can be left at the top for the hole. No jump ring is necessary to connect these blanks to earrings, but a ring is necessary for use as a pendant in order for it to hang correctly on a chain. A long narrow projection may be left, as in *Figure 174C*, which is bent back to form a ring. A jump ring is required in this design for attachment as an earring but not as a pendant. *Figure 174D* shows a completed earring after some sawing has been done, and the piece has been slightly dapped to create a little form.

The partial sawing of a cutout can be used to form part of the design and also furnish the extended strip which is bent and used for an attachment ring. This idea is used on the triangular-shaped piece, with the strip bent backward to form the supporting ring, in *Figure 175*. A shows the metal shape drilled at the bottom for saw blade insertion and the two saw cuts; B shows the sawed flap bent upward and backward from a side view; and C shows the finished earring from the front. Flaps from cutouts or extended strips do not always have to be bent backward to form a ring with the ends hidden. *Figure 175D* has the top strip bent forward, with matching strips added onto the other three points and bent forward in the same manner to create an interesting design.

For earrings, early jewelry craftsmen made use of wire which required no solder. These usually took one of two forms for design: the spiral and its many modifications, or short lengths of wire dangles attached to a common jump ring. Coils can be varied in size, shape, length, and placement, as suggested in *Figure 176A*. If wire lengths are used as dangles they should be flattened at the jump ring end to allow them to fit in the ring without crowding and pinching. A hole for the ring is drilled through this flattened area for ring insertion; a #50 or slightly smaller drill will allow free movement

Jewelry Without Solder   139

of the dangles. *Figure 176B* illustrates three of almost any number of possible designs for wire dangles.

Necklaces can be made of unsoldered sheet metal units which are connected together with strong jump rings or with projections bent to form the ring for suspension on a chain or cord. Connection by jump rings is the same as illustrated earlier in the chapter for bracelets, and the narrow projections are the same as those used for attaching earrings to findings or pendants to chains or cords. Wire works easily and is attractive when formed into units to make up a necklace.

Next to chain, necklaces are the most flexible jewelry pieces; this must be taken into consideration in design and construction if the piece is to look attractive and feel comfortable when worn. A linked necklace, when connected and spread round and flat on a table, has two circumferences: the smaller, inner one, which is the one followed by the chain or cord, and the outer one, which is determined by the length of the units. The inner circle does not change when worn, but the outer circle spreads or contracts to some extent between the ends of the units as it rises from the front and goes over the shoulders and across the back of the neck. If flexibility is not provided, a stiff and clumsy appearance always results. Flat units with only one jump ring near the top for connection will automatically allow this spreading, as illustrated in *Figure 177A*. Units which have one or two projections bent to form a holding ring will accomplish the same thing. These pieces, however, according to their design, may have to be fixed in position on the chain or cord. Units which slip over a chain can sometimes bunch together in some areas and leave other areas blank except for chain. This happens when the top of a unit is narrower than the bottom. The formed rings can be attached through links to hold them in position, beads or tubing can be inserted between units, or each unit can be designed so that bunching does not occur. *Figure 177B* shows a shape which requires separators to maintain proper position.

Units which are wide enough on the top to touch each other along the full length of the necklace require no separators to keep them evenly spaced. This kind of designing was cleverly done by the Mycenaeans as early as 1400 B.C. Their work was done on thin sheet gold and stamped in relief for decoration. *Figure 178* is a copy of a sketch I made that shows two necklaces in the National Museum of Athens. These can be of help by providing a starting point for design; in the first there is repetition of a single unit, while in the other units of different shapes are alternated for a pleasing effect.

An alternative method of joining metal units for both

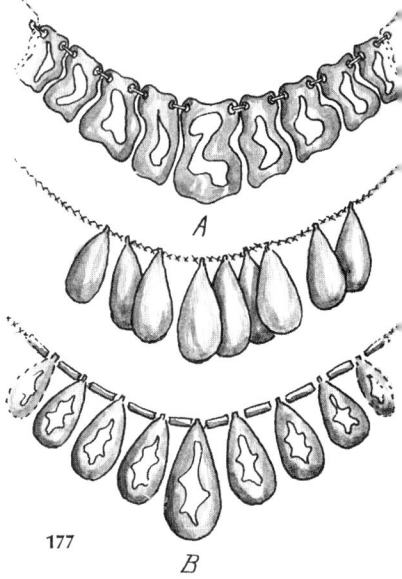

177

178

140　Jewelry: Queen of Crafts

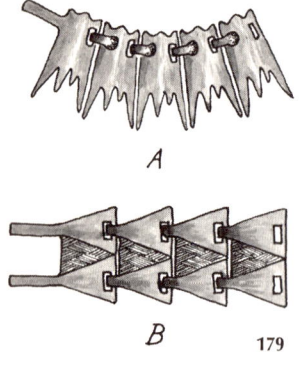

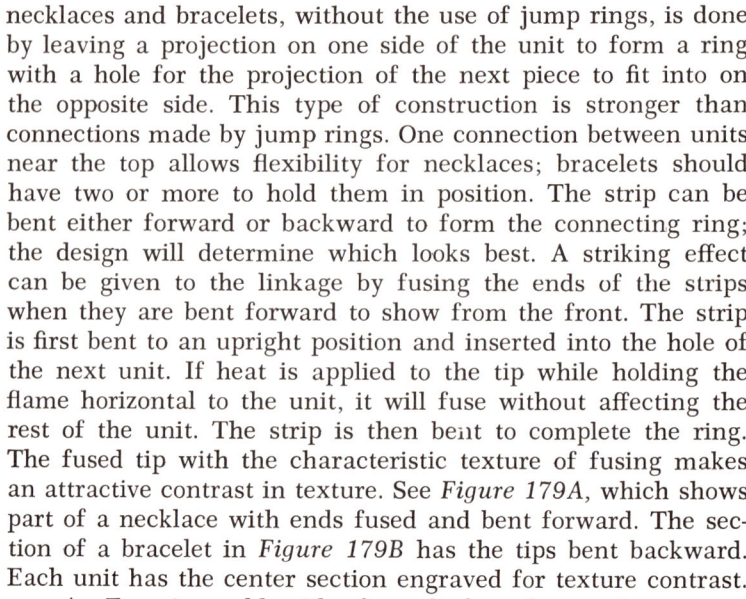

necklaces and bracelets, without the use of jump rings, is done by leaving a projection on one side of the unit to form a ring with a hole for the projection of the next piece to fit into on the opposite side. This type of construction is stronger than connections made by jump rings. One connection between units near the top allows flexibility for necklaces; bracelets should have two or more to hold them in position. The strip can be bent either forward or backward to form the connecting ring; the design will determine which looks best. A striking effect can be given to the linkage by fusing the ends of the strips when they are bent forward to show from the front. The strip is first bent to an upright position and inserted into the hole of the next unit. If heat is applied to the tip while holding the flame horizontal to the unit, it will fuse without affecting the rest of the unit. The strip is then bent to complete the ring. The fused tip with the characteristic texture of fusing makes an attractive contrast in texture. See *Figure 179A*, which shows part of a necklace with ends fused and bent forward. The section of a bracelet in *Figure 179B* has the tips bent backward. Each unit has the center section engraved for texture contrast.

An Egyptian goldsmith of nearly four thousand years ago is credited with the accomplishment of something which is the dream of all designers. He created an unsoldered wire necklace which was simple in design, easily made, had adequate strength, appealed to the people of his time, and still looks chic when compared with modern designs. This is a classic example of good design, seldom if ever matched. Several jewelry books describe this design; it can also be viewed in many museums and can be purchased today in some good jewelry shops. However, because this design is unique and fulfills its purpose so well, it will be illustrated and described here.

Wire of 18 or 20 gauge is all the material needed for a necklace using this design. Bracelets also can be made using the same units hooked together. The folded loop which joins the units is a double wire, which has much more strength than a jump ring. The wire should be annealed first and then cut into 6½-inch lengths; 40 to 44 of these lengths are enough for a necklace, half this amount will form a bracelet. (Units may be added or subtracted to match the size wanted by the craftsman.) Both ends of the wire are then filed to a point and bent into circles by using small round-nosed pliers (*Figure 180A*). These small circles are held flat in smooth-faced parallel pliers and the wire is pushed up against the small circles to form the coils. Both ends should be coiled evenly and equally, a little at a time, until the overall length is 1½ inches, as shown in *B*.

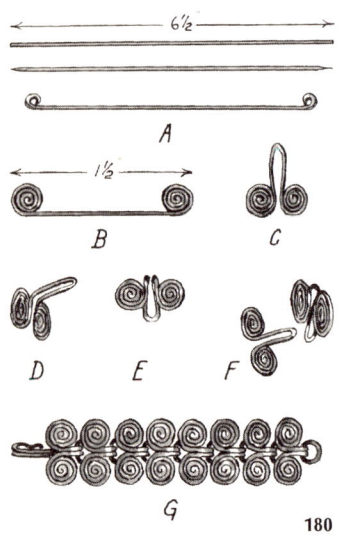

Jewelry Without Solder 141

The center is marked, and the coils are bent back toward each other. Round-nosed pliers can be used to hold it at the center, but a nail about ⅛ inch in diameter in a vise works better and does not scar the metal. The units should look like C when properly bent. The next bend is made by holding both coils with the parallel pliers; one side of the jaws should be even with the tops of the coils. Now the wire loop above the jaws can be pushed over with the thumb to look like D. A jump ring made of two turns of wire instead of one is slipped over this end loop, and the loop can then be pushed down against the coils, as in E. Other units are added, shown at F, by slipping the partially bent loop of one into the fully bent loop of another and bending it down against the coils. All wire units are the same except for the last one, which acts as a hook to join both ends at the jump ring. An additional 1¼ inches of wire is necessary for this unit to form the hook. A wire is cut 7¾ inches long and coiled from both ends until the overall length is 2¾ inches. It is then bent and inserted in the next coil the same as all the other units (C, D, E, and F). The end of the coil can be bent back on itself by hand to form the hook and complete the necklace or bracelet, as in G. *Figure 180* is, of course, not drawn to scale and shows only measurements, coiling, bending, and means of assembly.

Modifications can be made to this basic design—larger or smaller wire can be used for different effects, or longer lengths of wire can be cut for larger coils. Coils can be made on the units which are smaller on the end closer to the neck. This has a tendency to spread the necklace more evenly because of the difference of inside and outside diameters. The earrings shown in *Figure 176A* can be matched with a design for a necklace or bracelet.

Jewelry made from connected units of light-gauge wire can be designed in numerous ways which are effective and well worth the effort. There are books on the market devoted entirely to this form of jewelry for anyone especially interested. These books also include chain making, which is not covered here.

Heavy-gauge wire can be used without soldering for bracelets and necklaces which are composed of few units; the parts usually are shaped differently from each other, rather than in repeated units. This type of design is perhaps more modern, but care must be taken to ensure proper fit and correct drape, especially of necklaces, which turn out best when designed to fit the individual. Units are connected by hooks, jump rings, or by the extended strip-and-hole method. The piece shown in *Figure 181* has eight sections held together by hooks and shows

181

one possibility for this method of construction and design. The two pieces which form the lower section are riveted to hold them rigidly in position. This lower section can be designed in many ways for varied appearance; also, if the two end hooks are made so that the section can be unhooked rather easily, several of these different units can be made and substituted for use with the rest of the same necklace. *Figure 182* shows several different sections which could replace the one shown in *Figure 181*. Heavy wire is also used for necklaces made in one piece; these are spread to put them on, and the ends are then hooked together. This type must be very carefully bent and fitted across the back, front, and over the shoulders of the wearer, as there are no links to relieve the rigidity of the piece.

Necklace and bracelet units made from sheet material which have a fairly large flat surface can be set with stones, using the solderless method described in Chapter 5 under STONE SETTING. Wood, bone, ivory, plastic, or other pieces of metal can be attached to units by riveting. Etching, repoussé, dapping, stamping, piercing, texturing, and enameling can be used to vary design. Enamel work and stone setting should be done only if the article is not required to flex or bend.

Making unsoldered jewelry is a good way to start learning the craft; nearly all the working techniques can be employed at one time or another according to the designs and methods of construction. *Figure 183* shows earrings which were drilled, sawed, and partially fused, without soldering. The idea for the design came from a Ubangi warrior's shield; the rough texture and unevenness of the fused metal gives a primitive effect which would be lost if more sophisticated finishing were used. But as mentioned earlier, the solderless method has limitations; the joining of pieces by soldering gives such strength and so broadens the scope of work which can be done that the serious worker should learn how to solder correctly.

182

183

CHAPTER 7
JEWELRY USING SOLDER

A jade and gold dinner ring. This ring, because of its elongated shape, seems to lengthen short fingers and make the hand appear thinner.

Many times, as in the pin in *Figure 184*, soldering is absolutely necessary in order to execute the work, while in other cases it allows a less cumbersome means of attaching and holding pieces together with a large gain in strength.

There are five working techniques out of the forty listed in Chapter 5 that usually require the soldering process for successful work. They are appliqué, cloisonné enameling, laminating, finding application, and stone setting.

APPLIQUE

Appliqué, or the fixing of one piece of metal upon another, is usually done by using silver or gold solder to sweat-solder the joints between pieces. It is true that some larger pieces can

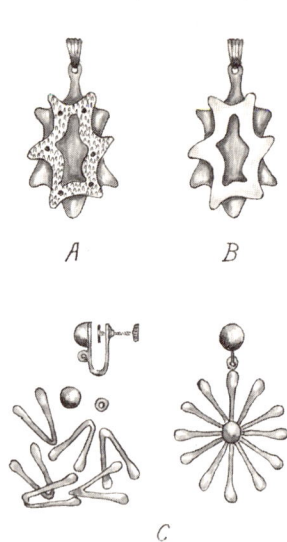

184

185

186

be attached by riveting, as mentioned before, but the rivet heads will necessarily show and the results are inferior to soldering. The rivets can be made less conspicuous by texturing, but if a smooth surface is desired soldering must be done. *Figure 185A* shows a piece attached by riveting and textured to make the rivets less obvious, while the piece attached in *Figure 185B* has been soldered. Good hard-soldering is also permanent, while it is possible for rivets to loosen. Very small metal sections, such as the one shown earlier in the etched bracelet in *Figure 172B*, can be easily soldered in place but would be a tedious problem if riveted. Wire, metal balls, beads, and other small pieces can be thought of as appliqué because they must be attached. Soldering is the best means of doing the work. Filigree work has to be done this way or an assembly must be made up of many small parts, as shown in *Figure 185C*.

CLOISONNE ENAMELING

Cloisonné enameling requires soldering because of the flat wire set edgewise onto the piece to be enameled. These wire enclosures hold the enamel in place and separate colors. Enameling covering plain surfaces or using the basse-taille, champlevé, Limoges, or plique-à-jour methods can be done on unsoldered as well as soldered jewelry because the enamel is either spread on the surface or applied to sunken or cutout areas. *Figure 186* shows the two soldering operations required to make and attach the wire. (See ENAMELING in Chapter 5.)

LAMINATING

Laminating was compared in Chapter 5 to plywood construction and described as a metal sandwich, in which advantage is taken of the varied colors of metals to create unusual effects.

Jewelry Using Solder   145

These layers of metals could be riveted together to expose the different metals at the edges, but soldering is really the only way to preserve the beauty of this work. After soldering, the laminated metal is often rolled or hammered to form a thinner, more workable sheet. It is then punched, dapped, or hammered into different levels which are later filed or ground off to expose the different metals. Riveting could not withstand much of this working. Even if a simple piece should be done in this way, the joints would be exposed in an unpleasing manner. Soldering leaves these joints almost invisible, the contrast of the colors of the metals giving the only indication of where they are joined.

FINDINGS

Findings for jewelry depend upon soldering for holding them strongly and inconspicuously together or in a fixed position. Perhaps soldering proves its worth to the craftsman for this type of work more than for any other. There are no substitutes in many cases; for example, hinges and catches cannot be riveted on, nor can the pad-type earring finding. Many different methods of linkage and suspension can be used if soldering is done. Soldering also makes it possible to reduce the size, increase the strength, and refine the design of unsoldered pieces which depend upon hooks, extended strips and holes, or heavy unsoldered jump rings to hold them together. Finger rings, as well as jump rings, are strengthened when the ends of the shanks are soldered together. Besides the gain in rigidity, possibilities for design are greatly multiplied by soldering. Chain can be made with each link soldered so that it will not separate under strain, as might happen if the links were merely bent together. Smaller gauges of wire can be used for the links, which will still be strong and long lasting. *Figure 187A* gives dependable methods of linkage which are possible only when soldered; many can be used for bracelets and necklaces as well as for pendants. *Figure 187B* shows wire wrapped around mandrels to form links for a chain. Separate links are made

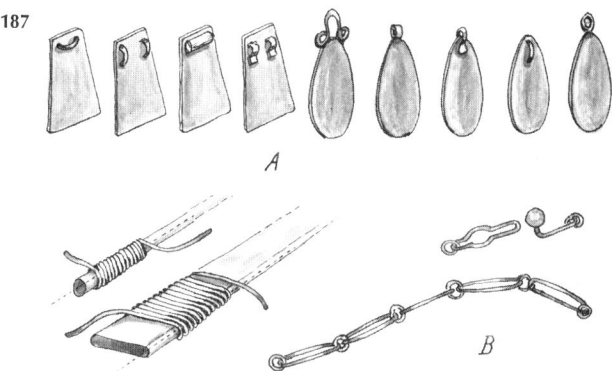

from these coils by sawing lengthwise of the mandrel along the dotted line in the figure. A connecting device is also shown which can be made when a ball is soldered to one end of a wire.

STONE SETTING

Stone-setting methods are also greatly expanded by soldering. Bezel settings, by far the best way to set cabochon-cut stones, can only be made by soldering. Gypsy settings do not require solder, but stones set from the bottom and held up by prongs must have these prongs soldered on. Cabochon settings that use extended prongs which are part of the backing metal expose the bottom of the stone. Cutouts with extended prongs for setting faceted stones lack the positive shoulder for the girdle of the stone to rest upon for strong support. This makes them usable only for pins, pendants, or other articles which do not receive hard treatment. Ordinary pronged settings, either purchased or handwrought, must be soldered in place, as well as the short pieces of wire used for pegging pearls. See STONE AND PEARL SETTING, Chapter 5, for all types of stone setting, both soldered and unsoldered.

GRANULATION

Granulation has been described in Chapter 5, but the process on jewelry pieces is not covered here under soldered jewelry because it is accomplished by colloid soldering, a process differing greatly from silver and gold hard-soldering.

CHAPTER 8
CAST JEWELRY

Melted casting wax was applied over a water-soluble wax core to make the model for this gold-cast pendant. The inner background was Florentined to contrast with the fused texture of the surrounding metal.

Cast jewelry differs from the handwrought in two ways: The first is that handwrought jewelry is built of separate parts of sheet and wire. Metal is added to a basic background or outline until the article is complete for structural or design purposes (*Figure 188*). It is compounded; it is synthesized. Cast jewelry, made from molten metal, is all one unit. All parts of a cast piece are homogeneous, much as a limb is an integral part of a tree (*Figure 189*).

The second difference between handwrought and cast jewelry is in the form of the materials used. Handwrought pieces, because they are usually made from a flat sheet, seldom lose this two-dimensional effect, regardless of the amount of forming that is done. Cast jewelry, because it depends upon a wax original which has been carved and built up into a three-dimensional form before casting, seldom loses this ap-

188

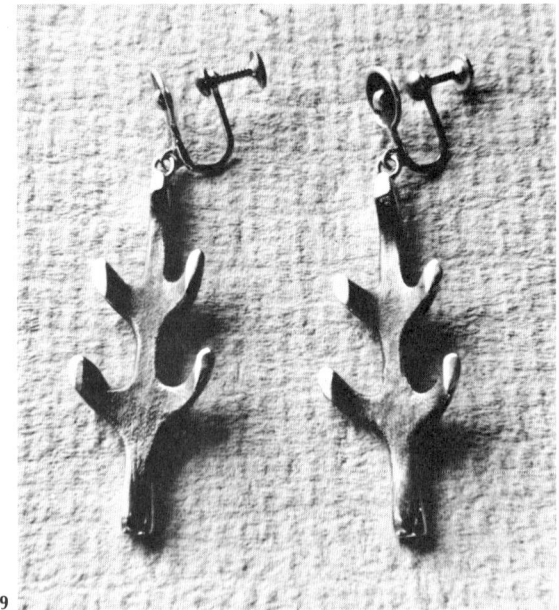

189

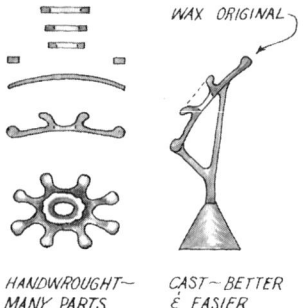

DO NOT CAST

190

HANDWROUGHT—
MANY PARTS

CAST—BETTER
& EASIER

WAX ORIGINAL

191

pearance of rounded form and seldom gives the effect of a shallow, two-dimensional shape. Thus, sculptural form is more easily attained by the casting method, but the word is seldom used here for a definite reason, as shown later.

Some craftsmen prefer to make all pieces out of sheet and wire. Handwrought jewelry to them is the only "real" jewelry. Casting to them is looked on as an inferior method. Other craftsmen cast everything and look askance at the "old fashioned" plodder who laboriously saws, forms, fits, and solders sheet and wire together. The results of each type of work is distinctive when the method is used to its best advantage. Identical pieces can be made using either method, but usually one or the other method is the best way to accomplish the job. *Figure 190* illustrates an article that is more easily handwrought than cast. *Figures 191* and *192* show an article which depends upon sculptural qualities for its main interest and is far better achieved by casting in one piece than by soldering separate pieces together for the same effect.

Casting is not the best method in all cases, and the same can be said about handwrought working. The two methods can sometimes be used together to advantage: for example, a cast piece with a handwrought, dapped, prong stone setting soldered in place; or a cast section soldered to a wire article where more bulk or complex curvatures would improve the monotonous flow of wire of one thickness and cross section. Both methods are here to stay, and the craftsman should understand the working methods, techniques, and inherent advantages and limitations of both. This knowledge will soon show that design is the key factor that determines which method of working is best suited to accomplish a desired result. If one or the other method is to be used, modification

Cast Jewelry   149

of design should be made where necessary to suit the method best. Either method may well be used for designs like *Figures 193* and *194*.

Lamination ("Marriage of Metals") is outside the range of casting. Different metals cannot be melted in the same crucible and cast to form the various stratas of separate metals required for this technique. Mixed and melted they only alloy themselves. Only soldered sheets of various metals can accomplish this. Casting can resemble fusion to a great extent. The plastic quality of the wax model and cast piece closely resemble the fusion of separate metal parts (*Figure 195*). Some kinds of textures that are possible for cast articles cannot be duplicated by stamping or carving or by any other technique of working sheet metal. One example is the depositing of hot wax droplets closely spaced upon a carved wax model; thus a series of small rounded mounds is created. This texture is just the reverse of a peened surface, which relies upon depres-

193

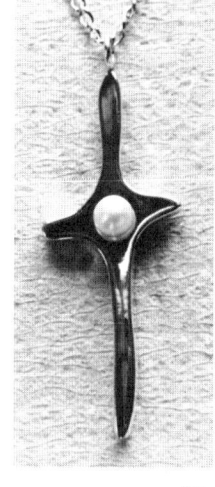

194

192

195

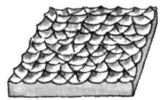
PEENED METAL

DRIBBLED WAX

196

sions for its characteristic texture. (See *Figure 196* for a comparison of the two textures.) Lost wax casting faithfully duplicates the model, even to fingerprints left in the soft wax. Textures can therefore be made in the wax which are next to impossible to duplicate in any other manner, and full advantage should be taken of this unique feature of casting. The wax can be manipulated while it is still in a liquid or semiliquid state; hot spatulas or other small tools can be pressed into or worked across solid wax; sharp tools can be used to chip or scratch; careful application of heat will smooth and blend—all these means and many others produced by experiment can be used for cast-metal texturing.

Texturing can of course be done on a cast article in the same ways as for any handwrought article. In fact, most of the working techniques are applicable to both. Cast objects can be sawed, filed, dressed up, and polished in the same manner; they may also be enameled, engraved, peened, etched, plated, and colored by the oxidation process. Soldering is the same, except in cases where a faulty or porous casting is worked on. The impurities are then brought to the surface by the heat, which makes it difficult to get a good joint; repeated heating and hot pickling or boiling in soda before soldering will usually correct this. Lamination, as explained earlier, cannot be done by casting. The techniques of chasing and repoussé are also not applicable to castings, because the forming created by these methods has been previously built into the wax model and appear in the resultant casting.

In most cases, the application of findings and the setting of stones are the same in cast articles as they are in handwrought articles. Prongs, however, may be cast as a part of the work, so a fabricated pronged setting is unnecessary. Bezels may be soldered on for cabochon stones or held by a method only possible by casting. In this holding method the stone is used as a pattern when making the wax model. For ease in handling, the stone is first attached to a short piece of dowel with sealing wax. The stone is then lightly oiled for later separation from the wax, and placed, as shown in *Figure 197,* in the desired position on the jewelry piece. Hot wax is transferred by spatula around the base and up the sides of the stone similar to a sheet metal bezel. Removal of the stone is done by warming the model in warm water and pulling the stone straight out from the wax. Refinements to the cooled, dribbled wax may be made before casting by trimming and scraping. Since slight shrinkage can occur during the casting process, it is well to enlarge the hole a small bit by scraping. If the wax surrounding the stone has been built up heavily, stone setting is made

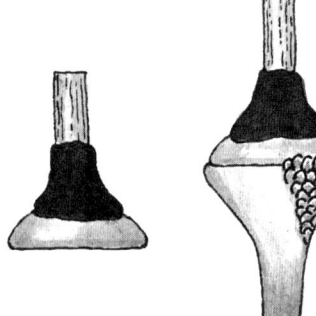
197

Cast Jewelry   151

easier by removing wax from the inside by undercutting the built-up bezel around the base where the stone will set.

Reproduction of an exact replica of a wax model in metal is the general use of wax in the casting process. Water-soluble wax is an exception, because it disappears by dissolving before casting. This wax is white, granular in structure, and can be sawed, filed, drilled, and sanded. It is used as a base, or core, over which regular casting wax is fixed. Sheet wax can be heated and molded over a formed piece of water-soluble wax, or full or partial coverage with casting wax can be done by dipping or by dribbling wax over its surface with a spatula. After any or all methods of casting-wax application have been made over the water-soluble wax, the thickness and outline of the applied wax is trimmed and trued to the dimensions required by the cast article. The piece is then placed in water, which dissolves the water-soluble wax and leaves only the wax which was molded and formed over it. This remaining casting wax is the finished wax model and is cast in the usual manner (see *Figures 198* and *199*). In this method, arched sections can be made; holes drilled through this type of wax and filled with casting wax produce internal structures within a piece which appear as tendons or steel trusses connecting and holding together parts of the surface. Water-soluble wax performs the function of supporting casting wax in a manner obtained in no other way. (Cristobalite investment cores are made in the same manner, but water-soluble wax allows the investment of the casting to be done all in one piece, which reduces the chance of separation between the core and the rest of the mold.) If casting is being done by the craftsman, this wax should be tried and experimented with because it offers many possibilities of design difficult or tedious to produce with any other method.

For more information on cast jewelry, refer to the following techniques in Chapter 5: DRAWING TRANSFER, CARVING, and CASTING.

198

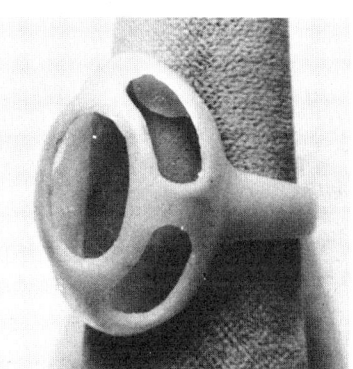

199

CHAPTER 9
GEMS

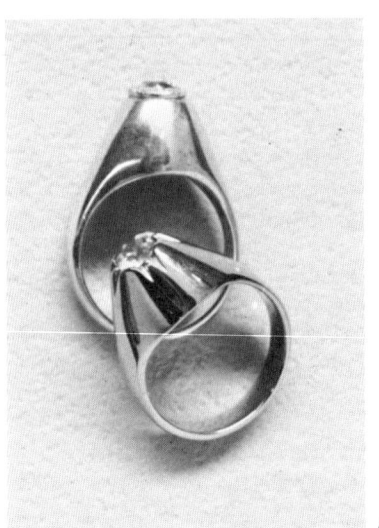

High pointed profile is distinguished feature of these two rings. The stones were set in a bezel and in a modified diamond setting so that no prongs might catch or snag clothing.

Although much fine jewelry is made solely of metal, most jewelry is composed of metal and gems which produce beautiful pieces of jewelry (*Figure 200*).

Perhaps the terms "stones" and "gems" should be clarified. The gems used in jewelry come from the three categories of substance: animal, vegetable, and mineral. Coral, ivory, and pearls are animal substances or animal by-products. Amber and jet are of vegetable origin, and so is the framework of petrified wood, in which slow mineral replacement changed the structure to stone but retained the wood pattern. Stones used for jewelry are minerals—inorganic, homogeneous substances having a definite chemical formula, such as diamond, C; sapphire, Al_2O_3; quartz, SiO_2. Minerals which possess beauty, along with other characteristics necessary for their use in jewelry, are therefore gem stones.

Gems

Gems can be discussed here in only a most limited manner. A full study of gems would cut a broad swath through mankind's scientific accomplishments, would fill libraries, and would most certainly be beyond the scope of this book.

Chemistry, physics, biology, gemmology, paleontology, geology, mineralogy, oceanography, and crystallography, along with other branches of science, furnish knowledge about gems. Complicated mining operations for minerals, pearl diving for pearls, dragging the ocean bottom for coral, big-game hunting and the finding of animal burial grounds for ivory are some of the means of acquiring gems. A study of all these subjects can be interesting but is unnecessary for the jewelry craftsman. Still, a little knowledge about gems can be of great help to the worker in choosing suitable material and in correctly identifying and evaluating what he is buying. Because of a little knowledge, I have saved fellow tourists hundreds of dollars. The money was saved by recognizing "bargains" being sold as jade that were actually of cheaper aventurine, and by recognizing high-priced but inferior pearls that were less expensive at reliable supply firms at home.

Dealers have extensive worldwide business connections, and thousands of dollars backing them, and they spend full time searching for all types of gems. There are very few valuable gems left unnoticed by the dealers. To get a real bargain the craftsman would have to be extremely lucky, would have to be expert in evaluating what he bought, and would have to be at the right place at the right time to take advantage of a sale. In this field the best assurance of getting value is buying from reputable dealers. Prices between dealers vary to some degree, so it is well to shop carefully before buying. This is most noticeable with less valuable gems: the semiprecious stones, synthetics, and cultured pearls. Precious stones—diamonds, emeralds, rubies—are more stable, and a lower price between dealers often indicates lower quality rather than a savings.

There are three main reasons why some materials are chosen for use with jewelry and are more or less universally classed as gems. Beauty heads the list. A gem which lacks beauty has no interest in itself and can only detract from the appearance of jewelry articles and defeat the purpose for which jewelry is worn. Since beauty is an intangible quality, and its concept is individual, this requirement for gems is wide and varied and includes such factors as color and texture.

Rarity is another requirement for a gem. This quality is fixed by nature. Although nature limits the amount, the demand for scarce and rather scarce gems is responsible for the classifi-

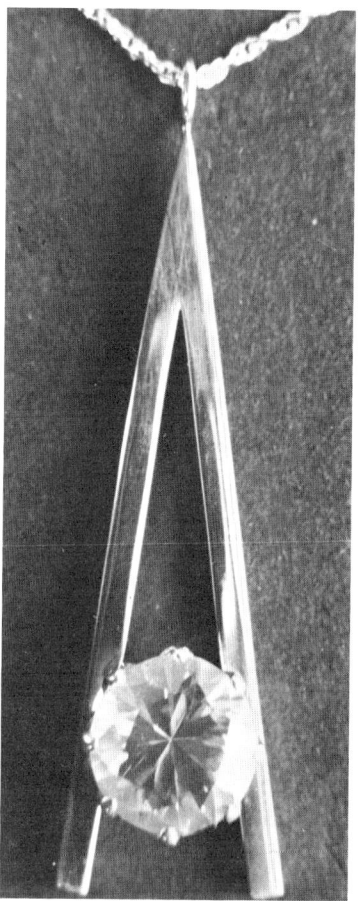

200

154   Jewelry: Queen of Crafts

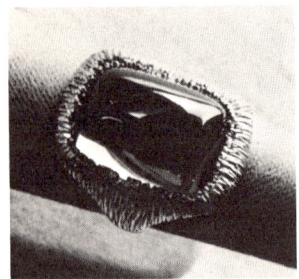

201

202

203

cation of stones as precious or semiprecious—a value division. Beauty is not enough. If roads were graveled with diamonds, who would stoop to pick one up? Diamonds, rubies, sapphires, emeralds, and pearls are classed as precious gems, all others as semiprecious.

The third requirement for a gem is hardness. This is a purely practical factor. A stone can be both beautiful and rare and yet be utterly useless to the jeweler because it is too soft to retain its beauty for any length of time. Hardness will be discussed at greater length.

All gems must possess three requirements of beauty, rarity, and hardness even though these may vary in degree and proportion. Gems also differ widely in another respect: their ability to transmit light. This ability makes them transparent, translucent, or opaque, qualities that apply to precious as well as semiprecious gems.

Transparent gems (*Figure 201*) are cut from crystals and allow light to pass through them—you can look through them. They are usually facet cut to take full advantage of the light entering the stone and being reflected back to bring out their greatest sparkle and brilliancy of color. The value of a good transparent stone is dependent upon what has been called the five Cs of faceted stones: cost, color, cut (workmanship), carat (weight, size), and clarity (degree of transparency, lack of flaws). Some may also be cabochon cut; this is frequently done when the color quality surpasses that of clarity. Among the transparent stones are diamond, ruby, sapphire, emerald, topaz, amethyst, and zircon.

Translucent gems allow light to penetrate them only partially (*Figure* 202). They cannot be looked through but only into; color is brought out in a soft subdued manner. Some of the transparent stones fall into this category as their clarity decreases. Amethyst, for instance, is translucent if clouded. Agate, moonstone, and opal are other examples of translucent stones. Faceting is seldom done on them; they are cut cabochon and depend more upon color and texture for interest, as they lack the sparkle and glitter of faceted gems.

Opaque stones are those which allow no light to pass through them (*Figure 203*). Colors, textures, and markings are the attributes of the opaque stones, as reflected flashes of light or transmitted muted colors are not possible where light does not penetrate. Jasper, turquoise, jade, aventurine, lapis lazuli, and malachite are but a few of the many opaque materials used for gems.

A craftsman should also be familiar with the terms "natural," "synthetic," and "imitation" when applied to gems. This is necessary not only to satisfy the worker's curiosity but will be of use to him in his purchases. If jewelry pieces are made for sale, it is mandatory that the seller have some knowledge of the difference because the buyer will want to know what he is getting. Complicated tests and delicate instruments are needed to identify correctly some stones and to establish whether they are natural or synthetic. Specific gravity, various optical properties, and crystal growth lines revealed by the microscope are some of the ways used to identify gems. It can be seen that identification is best left to the gemmologist and reputable dealer unless the worker wants to devote years of his time to the subject. For his purpose, faith in a jewelry supply firm and his own judgment of quality and price will be enough.

Natural stones are those which are formed by nature and are mined or found on the earth's crust. These are the minerals which ages ago took form due to seepage of chemicals, great pressures, tremendous heat, crystallization, and other natural processes. Some are plentiful, others are rare. The cost of these gems depends upon how rare they are, how much in demand they are because of beauty, perfection, hardness, and the cost of finding and processing them. Natural stones of good quality always demand a higher price than synthetics. The wide use and acceptance of synthetic stones has had little effect on the value of natural stones.

Synthetic stones are synthesized: compounded or manufactured by man. Their composition is the same as that of natural stones; they are composed of the same mineral and have many of the same physical properties. In fact, when synthetics were first introduced they were made from powdered natural stones of good quality but of very small size. Specific gravity, optical properties, and hardness are the same as the natural stones. They can be distinguished from the natural stones by microscopic bubble inclusions and curved growth lines. Natural stones have straight growth lines and irregular-shaped inclusions. The minerals which are now used generally for synthetics are those which compose the natural corundum stones (ruby and sapphire) and spinel. These stones have a hardness of 9 and 8, respectively. Minute quantities of added metallic oxides are responsible for color, the same as in natural stones. Since this can be controlled in the synthetic stone, many variations of colors are possible. This even makes it possible to synthesize stones which look like other natural stones but which in their natural state are composed of an entirely different mineral. This has two advantages: synthetics can be made which not only have a good appearance but also possess a hardness not found in the natural stone. Also, some

156 Jewelry: Queen of Crafts

types of natural stones have more flaws than others, especially when they are of any appreciable size. Synthetics with only microscopic inclusions can be made as substitutes for these.

Synthetic stones are good stones, and the craftsman can put them to good use in much of his work. They are quality stones, cheaply priced. Only the connoisseur of gems objects to them, and then, only because they are made instead of found. Jewelry pieces with mounted colored stones which are displayed in ordinary shops and sell for a moderate price are often made with synthetic stones. The large rubies, sapphires, and other stones mounted in fraternal rings and dinner rings can be used as examples. These synthetic stones can be bought for less than the price of a good pair of shoes. If they were natural stones of good quality the price would be astronomical. I have handled and examined such a natural stone in Switzerland, a ruby which had a price tag of $250,000. A $5,000 platinum and diamond ring mounting for this stone was designed and furnished gratis to the buyer of the stone.

The process of synthesis is used to duplicate semiprecious stones as well as precious stones. This is done not only because desirable hardness in the natural stone is lacking, as mentioned before, but also because of the rareness of natural semiprecious stones of larger size. Semiprecious natural stones of good quality and size can be quite expensive, contrary to what their classification tends to indicate. There is one big difference between natural and synthetic stones, precious or semiprecious: this is the factor of size and related cost. Synthetic stones vary but little in price as size increases; 2 carats cost about twice what 1 carat would cost. Natural stones become more rare as size increases, so a more geometrical price increase applies to them. A 2-carat stone can cost four to six times more than a 1-carat stone, and so on, as stone size becomes bigger. Most of the synthetics are transparent stones, but the asterism found in translucent gems is now duplicated. These are the star rubies and star sapphires of various colors. The price is much greater for these than for the clear ones, but it is still far less than that demanded for natural stones of equal quality. A star sapphire is shown mounted in a man's small-finger ring in *Figure 204*.

Imitation stones are the "junk" of the trade. They are made from paste (glass) or even plastic and are used on the cheapest costume jewelry for added glitter. They are not gems but are mentioned here because of a common misunderstanding about them. Many people do not know the difference in meaning between synthetic and imitation; the fact that stones can be synthesized makes some people assume that they, too, are

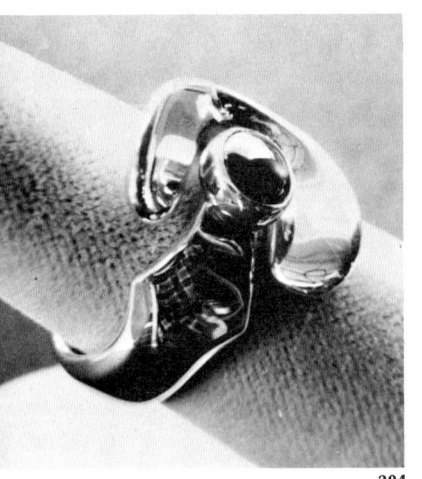
204

imitation. Imitation stones have none of the physical and optical qualities or hardness of either natural or synthetic gems. Needless to say, these cheap imitations are of no use to the craftsman and are not worth any time and effort to mount.

A unique stone which is neither natural nor synthetic is the grown, or cultured, emerald crystal. Arguments still go on over whether it is one or the other. It is synthetic to the extent that man assembles the ingredients and through a complicated and secret process gets emeralds as a result, but it is also natural because natural crystallization processes occur that make its formation possible. Gem experts and even the law courts are undecided just where this odd gem should fit. Even gem experts can be, and have been, mistaken when trying to differentiate between these stones and the mined natural ones. Chatham emeralds, as they are called, are not inexpensive like other synthetic stones. The cost is at least two thirds of the price asked for mined natural emeralds, and emeralds are precious stones.

Altered gems are offered by most gem suppliers. These gems—either natural, synthetic, or both together—have been treated or assembled. Color dyeing is often applied to such gems as amber, pearls, coral, turquoise, and agate. When used for pearls, coral, and turquoise, dyeing gives a good color to inferior material but proves unsatisfactory because of wear and fading. Agate, because of its small, close crystalline structure, is porous and receives dye readily and holds the color without fading. It is dyed more to obtain bright colors and band markings, which never occur in the natural state, rather than to camouflage a poor stone. These are good stones and well worth considering. The use of heat is another method of changing stone appearance. This is performed on natural stones which would otherwise be useless as gems because of poor color. Quartz, zircon, tourmaline, and topaz are some stones subjected to this treatment; after treating, these are good stones because the color changes are permanent.

Lamination of stones is another means of altering gems. Laminated stones may be made in two parts to form doublets or in three parts for triplets. Synthetic and natural stone and sometimes glass are used in various ways to make up the gem. The purpose is to provide a hard-wearing upper surface with good color showing through the table of the stone. Soft stones may be capped with clear, synthetic sapphire or spinel, or expensive material can be sliced into thin sheets and sandwiched between transparent, less costly stone. In some cases the bonding material furnishes the color. Synthetic stones which have a good natural-looking emerald color are hard to

158   Jewelry: Queen of Crafts

find; some doublets made from synthetic spinel which have a green-colored bonding material are superior in appearance to these synthetic stones. Color and structure are permanent, and only very close inspection will reveal the joint, usually only when inspected while still unmounted, as the joint is just below the girdle line. If workmanship and materials are good (no paste or glass used), these stones are very satisfactory and can be used with confidence so long as there is no deception. Their cost is about double that of synthetic stones, which still makes them a very good, reasonable buy.

205

Cultured pearls (*Figure 205*) are grown naturally enough, but here again some altering and tampering with nature separates them from the purely natural product. Most persons are familiar to some degree with the manner in which natural pearls are made by oysters. A foreign object, such as a grain of sand, enters an oyster, and as a defense against this irritation, the oyster secretes the same substance which makes up its outside shell over the irritant. This is an attempt by the oyster to protect itself by making the foreign body less irritating or to make it smooth so that it may possibly be expelled. This protective secretion builds up and hardens in layers. Many layers and several years later a pearl results. If it is perfectly round with a rose tint and is of good size, it is a gem of considerable value; it can even be valued at hundreds or thousands of dollars. Man has taken advantage of the oyster's behavior by learning to perform a delicate operation on the oyster to insert graded sizes of mother-of-pearl beads which act as irritants. Nature takes over and covers the bead in the same way as it does any other foreign matter. The value of this pearl is dependent upon how thick the protective covering is compared with the planted bead size. A heavy, many-layered covering gives body, sheen, and color, all of which raise the price for this superior item. Natural colors have a wide range: white, yellow, brown, gray, black, blue, green, and delicate rose, which is the most valuable. The location of production accounts for natural color. Pearls are also dyed but this process will be revealed by wear in time. It is best to purchase cultured pearls of natural color if mounted where they will be subjected to wear. Dyed pearls should be mounted so that they are protected as much as possible.

Half and three-quarter pearls show the thickness of the natural covering and the relative size of the bead core because of the ground flat area which cuts through both. X ray clearly shows this in full pearls which are not drilled, while a special instrument is used to see this in the hole of a pierced pearl. If the hole is large enough, a magnifying glass, or even the naked eye, can sometimes pick up the line where the bead core and the covering meet.

Quality and prices for cultured pearls vary greatly. Shopping is often necessary to get the quality, color, and sheen desired for a low price. As with synthetic stones, the public is sometimes confused by the terms "imitation" and "cultured" describing pearls. Imitation pearls are glass paste, either hollow and stuffed with coloring material or solid with a pearly covering. The first type looks and feels different; the second usually shows the covering near the hole and can be tested. If it is imitation, it can be peeled like an onion. Craftsmen should have no use for the cheap imitations. Cultured pearls are quality items at a reasonable price. They vary in cost from less than a dollar each for good small ones to several dollars each as size increases. There is nothing cheap about cultured pearls when they are of exceptionally fine quality, large, with sheen, and good color, and are perfectly matched to form a single piece of jewelry. Tiffany and Company of New York have offered a plain cultured pearl necklace with a diamond clasp for $110,000 and earrings for $15,000. These pearls were exceptional to be sure, but I mention them here to show that the jewelry craftsman can use good quality cultured pearls with pride and confidence.

A worker should have at least rudimentary knowledge of the terms used for the measurement and weight of gems. Since these differ from his familiar use of inches or fractions of inches for linear measurement and ounces and pounds for weight, confusion results until comparison is made between the English and the metric systems. The millimeter (mm) from the metric system is used for linear measurement of gems, especially for semiprecious cabochon-cut stones. The size of an oval stone listed in a catalogue as being 10 by 12 millimeters (10 x 12mm) can easily be visualized if it is remembered that 1 millimeter is very close to $\frac{1}{25}$ inch. Synthetic stones are also frequently listed in the same manner; a round brilliant-cut gem of 6 millimeters would be slightly less than $\frac{1}{4}$ inch in diameter. Linear measurement is thus quite simple.

Weight measurement becomes more complicated because of the introduction of more than one unfamiliar weight system. Rough semiprecious gem material of low value used by the lapidary for cutting is sold by the pound avoirdupois, the same unit used when purchasing groceries. More valuable rough material, boules of synthetic gem stones and faceted gems, are more often sold by the carat. Carat is perhaps the most familiar term used. It is $\frac{1}{5}$ gram, or 200 milligrams (metric system); the familiar ounce is equal to 28.35 grams in the metric system.

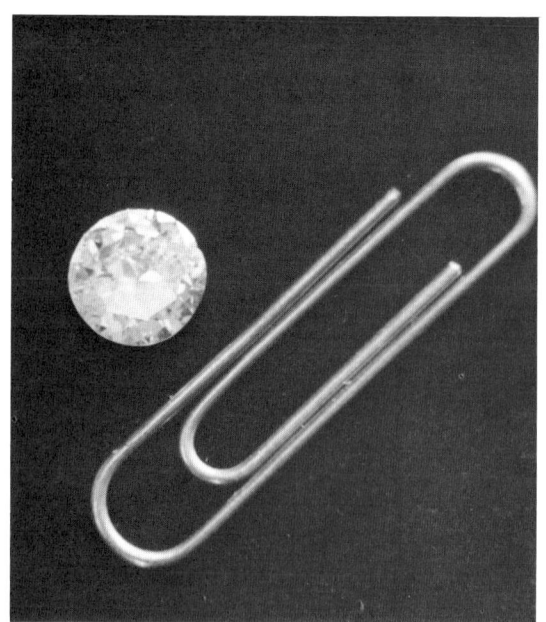

206 207

Familiarity comes with use so that a stone can be roughly estimated for weight. Although stones vary in weight, it may be of help as a beginning reference point to know that a ½-carat brilliant-cut diamond is about 5 millimeters in diameter; other stones are close in size and weight. The term "point" used for diamonds does not refer to the points created by the juncture of facets but to weight, each point being $\frac{1}{100}$ carat in weight. A 50-point diamond is a ½-carat stone. A magnified picture of a 46-point diamond is shown in *Figure* 206 in comparison with an ordinary paper clip. The same diamond appears in *Figure* 207 and will be mounted in the unfinished ring casting.

Natural pearls are sold by weight using the grain as a unit. Four pearl grains equal 1 carat in weight or $\frac{1}{5}$ gram metric. Cultured pearls, those which will be most often used by the craftsman, are sold by diameter size rather than grain weight; the millimeter is the basic unit, the same as mentioned before for stones. See the Appendix for weight systems and conversion table.

Hardness in gems was briefly mentioned before, but because of its importance it should be discussed more fully. Everyone is impressed early in life by the hardness of rock, but full appreciation of this quality of hardness comes later, usually when a person starts grinding and polishing stones. The author has never had a beginning student who was not amazed at the hardness of common stones, such as agate, especially if the student was already familiar with grinding hard steel. The common expression in our language "hard as a rock" points to the ultimate in this quality, but stones vary in hardness to a great extent and only those which are hard enough to withstand the wear and shocks given them while mounted in jewelry should be considered.

Hardness in stones is defined as, and determined by, the ability of one stone to scratch another, the one scratched or abraded being the softer of the two. An unscientific but good workable scale has been devised which is used for classifying stone hardness; this is Mohs' Scale of Hardness, which places all stones within a 10-point framework. These are shown below and progress from 1, the softest, to 10 in relative hardness:

1. Talc
2. Gypsum
3. Calcite
4. Fluorite
5. Apatite
6. Feldspar
7. Quartz
8. Topaz
9. Corundum
10. Diamond

There are many hundreds of known minerals, fifty or sixty of which are commonly used for jewelry. These do not exactly match the hardness of the ten listed minerals but often fit in between, and so one which will scratch quartz but will itself be scratched by topaz can be classed as 7½ in hardness, close enough for a craftsman's use. Just before the turn of the century a more scientific method of measuring hardness was found: a diamond point under known pressure left a scratch on a specimen which could be microscopically measured in width to exactly reveal its hardness. There is no need to elaborate on this method; it is mentioned here because of what it revealed about Mohs' scale. It showed that the difference in hardness was roughly doubled between each two numbers; i.e., a hardness of 5 was about twice as hard as 4, a hardness of 6 was about twice as hard as 5, and so on. This progression in relative hardness held true up to and including 9 (corundum—ruby, sapphire), but showed that the diamond, 10 on Mohs' scale, instead of being about twice as hard as corundum should have been given the number of 50 to place it in its real relative position to all other stones. This great amount of difference between the two hardest minerals is shown when using a grinding wheel; the sapphire can be easily ground and shaped in a few minutes, while a diamond-pointed wheel dresser will give years of service while grinding down and dressing up the same type wheel.

On Mohs' scale the human fingernail has a hardness of 2½, glass 4½ to 5, a good steel knife 6, and a file 6½. The ever-present dust which settles in all homes and must continually be removed from furnishings contains quartz to some degree. These tiny particles have a hardness of 7. It can be seen that a gem stone with a hardness of less than 6½ or 7 can become scratched when exposed to very common items. Knowing the hardness of a particular gem allows the worker to design his

208

209

jewelry in a way which will help protect the softer stones or to avoid them and substitute harder ones where hard usage is bound to occur. Men's rings receive the most wear of all jewelry; stones of a hardness less than 7 soon show this wear unless they are mounted so as to present a low profile or are recessed so that the metal rather than the stone takes the brunt of the constant abrasion. Women's rings are next for jewelry which receives the hardest use. However, softer material can be used for these rings mainly because women usually take better care of their jewelry. Soft materials, such as coral, pearls, and turquoise, will retain their luster when proper precautions are taken. Other jewelry items receive little hard use, so a much wider choice of stones can safely be made.

Toughness is another quality of some stones which makes them suitable for jewelry work. The ability to withstand shocks and blows without cracking or shattering is different from hardness. Diamonds can easily be cracked, so care must be taken even when mounting them. Jade is one of the toughest stones, although it is only 6½ to 7 in hardness. It resists breakage even when made into axe heads and knives, which was done by ancient peoples. It is fibrous in structure with no cleavage planes. *Figure 208* shows a piece of carved Oriental jade, or jadeite, mounted in a ring made from silver and brass. The stones in the parure in *Figure 209* are dark green nephrite jade mounted in yellow gold for a pleasing color contrast. Agate and rhodonite are other stones which possess great toughness. Because of their toughness and also because stones are cabochon cut, they resist abrasion out of proportion to their hardness and retain their beauty much longer than other stones of the same hardness.

Some of the more commonly used gems are listed in the Appendix showing their hardness on Mohs' scale.

CHAPTER 10
SIMPLE LAPIDARY

Metal work should accent or compliment the stones set in it. The black spotted and nearly clear agate set in this ring is enhanced by the white of the silver and the black oxidizing.

The natural grinding and polishing of stones which takes place in river beds gives them a rounded form, a surface which appeals to the touch and emphasizes colors and markings. It was only natural that first attempts to grind and polish stones were refinements of this haphazard forming. Stones were given true and pleasing shapes (round, oval, and so forth) and were domed on one side and flattened on the opposite side to make mounting possible. Few changes have taken place in these cabochon-cut stones. Better materials and equipment are now available to grind and polish them, but the results are today much as they were thousands of years ago. Cabochon cutting is ideally suited to opaque and translucent stones. It is also the simplest method of cutting and can be mastered by almost anyone in a very short time. The stones in *Figure 210* were made by a beginner in an hour.

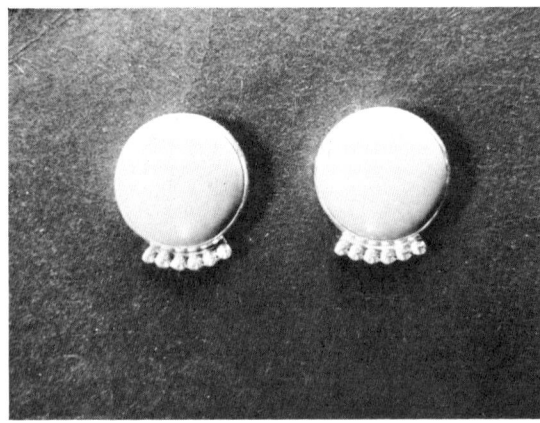
210

Facet-cut stones were next in origin, when it was found that facets on transparent gems added sparkle. The first attempts were merely flattening and polishing surfaces of the stone with no system or design, holding the stone in the hand while working. More control came later with the introduction of a peg with holes drilled in its sides which was mounted vertically alongside a horizontal lap. The gem was mounted on a dop stick, the other end of which was fitted into a hole in the peg; this would allow the stone to lie on the lap at the desired angle. Different angles for facets could be obtained by inserting the dop stick end into a high or lower hole in the peg. Working in this way the lapidary still had to space out his facets around the stone by sight alone. Today faceting heads are used which allow the worker to cut a perfectly round girdle on a stone, raise the head to get any desired facet angle relative to the girdle, and then turned to accurately number and space these facets around the stone. Degree indicators and height adjustments to one thousandth of an inch now take the place of sight and feel for faceting.

Different minerals have different optical properties. Now that these are known, angles of top and lower facets vary with the minerals to bring out maximum beauty in each case. This may all seem terribly complicated, but really it is not. Excellent books on lapidary work, listed in the Bibliography, give information on the optical properties of minerals and the facet angles for best results. Faceting heads come complete with instructions for their operation. The great variety of faceted forms makes this type of gem cutting a craft in itself, so space cannot be devoted to it here.

Lapidary equipment is expensive for the hobbyist whose main interest is making jewelry. He should purchase the inexpensive faceted synthetic stones and cabochon-cut semiprecious stones rather than invest money, up to $1,000, in costly diamond slabbing saws, grinding and polishing units, and faceting heads and laps. However, there is much satisfaction to be derived from cutting stones and mounting them in jewelry pieces of one's own design and making, and some craftsmen do prefer to cut their own. Cabochon cutting is quite simple and machinery can be held to a minimum for this work.

It was suggested before that a worker interested in lapidary should join a lapidary group or school class whenever possible in order to use and become familiar with equipment before purchasing his own. If this cannot be done the following equipment will be adequate for his work: a small trim saw, a unit of two grinding wheels, and a unit for sanding and buffing. These can be purchased as single units or all combined. A large slabbing saw is not really necessary because craft shops and suppliers' catalogues furnish slabbed stock of all materials.

With this equipment at hand the first step in cutting a cabochon is to mark the desired shape on the stone slab. Heavy plastic sheets with cutouts in a variety of shapes and sizes are used for this. The marking is done with an aluminum pencil after placing the chosen cutout over the stone in the best location. Conservation of material, avoidance of fractures or unsightly inclusions, and direction of bands or markings in the stone should all be considered for exact location of marking. The next step is to saw this cabochon blank out of the slab. The trim saw cuts in a straight line, so the blank is cut into a rough 6- or 8-sided figure for round or oval stones; square and rectangular stones are of course cut along their four sides. In the cutting at least 1/16 inch of material should be left outside the marked line. Only slight pressure is needed to make these cuts; because of the extreme hardness of stones and the subsequent slowness of cutting, there is a tendency by beginners to apply too much pressure on the stone against the saw blade. Allow the saw to do the cutting; as long as the stone is firmly held against the blade it will do its work. Excessive pressure only shortens the life of the saw by dislodging the embedded diamond particles. After trimming, the rough blank is ready for the next step, grinding.

Silicon carbide wheels are used for the grinding operation, and all grinding must be done while wet, as the heat generated by dry grinding would fracture the stone. Wheels composed of two grit sizes, #100 and #220, are enough for simple cabochon lapidary work; these will accomplish the grinding of all stones that the craftsman will normally use and leave them in a smooth enough condition for polishing. The rough grinding is first done on the #100-grit wheel, which is the coarser of the two, to give form to the stone. This is followed by grinding on the #220-grit wheel, which is more a smoothing operation than a forming one.

The outline of the stone should first be ground to perfect shape, or contour. Stones of 5 to 6 millimeters or less will have to be attached to a dop stock for holding, but stones over this size can be held by hand for outline grinding. By holding the stone in a horizontal position the marked outline can be seen. The stone is then brought up to the revolving wheel so that the edge is almost perpendicular, or parallel with the wheel surface, in order to get a nearly straight or slightly beveled outline edge. There is no danger of grabbing and tearing the work out of the hands as in buffing, so the work can be held at angles of 3, 4, or 5 o'clock on the wheel according to how close or far away from the wheel the worker stands or sits, how tall or short he may be, or how he chooses to tilt the stone from a horizontal position. The worker takes a comfortable position for grinding and a line of sight down and past the touching point of the wheel and stone will determine the amount of tilt to the stone that he must maintain to grind a good outline (see *Figure 211*).

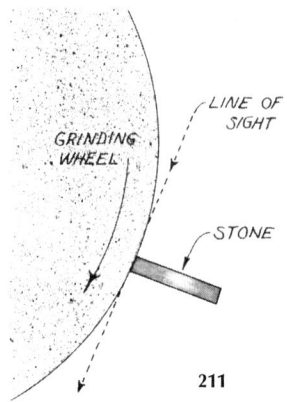

211

All grinding should be done in a deliberate, smooth manner, and very little pressure should be applied. If stone and wheel are in contact, grinding is taking place. Here again, allow the wheel to do the work. Short, jerky jabs at the wheel will soon put it out of balance. Working on one small area of wheel surface rather than moving over the whole face while grinding soon puts grooves in the wheel. Bonding material used in grinding wheels is purposely made to allow gradual sloughing off of particles; this allows fresh, sharp particles to come to the surface and also avoids the buildup of waste material which would clog the wheel. Wheels do get out of balance and become grooved even with the best of care. When this happens it is better to dress the wheel up as soon as this is first noticed rather than to keep working. Further grinding only aggravates the wheel condition and can check or chip the stone.

Lapidary work is a safe craft, but there is one precaution which should be taken. Grinding wheels are used wet, usually with a small stream of water flowing over them. While grinding, this water is thrown evenly outward to the surface of the grinding edge and balance is maintained. But water seeps to the bottom of the wheel when it is not in motion, so that after a few minutes the bottom is heavy and the top is light, making the wheel unbalanced. Present-day wheels are strong and well made, but they can explode if suddenly turned up to full speed while they are greatly unbalanced by water. This can be

Simple Lapidary 167

avoided by turning off the water after grinding and allowing the wheel to turn long enough to throw out excess water. If the equipment stands for some minutes before using again, it is well to give an experimental on and off switch to the motor to make certain that water buildup has not created a dangerous unbalance. This testing is especially important when more than one worker is using the same equipment; the previous worker could have failed to turn off the water or run the wheel long enough after grinding to dry it.

Grinding to the marked line should be done gradually all around the stone rather than cutting down to the line in one small area and moving further along the stone in separate stages. After most of the excess stone has been removed, the plastic pattern used for marking can be used to inspect the stone. By placing the stone in a hole one size larger than marked, high and low spots in the outline can be spotted and corrected so that the stone will exactly fit the marked pattern.

After the outline has been ground, work on the stone is done with the stone attached to a dop stick as shown in *Figure 212*. Wooden doweling of ⅛-, ³⁄₁₆-, and ¼-inch, diameters cut into 4- or 5-inch lengths make excellent dops for small, medium, and large stones, respectively. Regular stationery sealing wax works well for attaching the stone to the dop stick. The stick of wax is first heated slowly to melting point with a torch, and the end of the dop is rubbed over it to pick up wax. This can then be formed into a cone with a wet finger and thumb (sealing wax clings to dry skin and cannot be shaken off, so make certain the fingers are wet and work the wax with care until it is almost solid again). It is easier to charge several dop sticks at a time by melting wax in a tin can and dipping them two or three times for wax buildup; this also provides reserve dops for further work. Hot wax and cold stone do not make a good joint. To mount the stone it should first be warmed slowly with a torch to a temperature which is almost uncomfortable to the touch; the wax at the end of the dop stick is then melted and pressed against the back of the stone. Wet fingers are used again to mold the wax cone up from the stone and to center the stone on the stick. The stone should be as level as possible in all directions across the stick when held upright.

Since cabochon forming is done entirely by sight and feel without the use of mechanical aids other than the motor-driven wheels, it is only natural that many different approaches and steps taken to complete the work are advocated by different craftsmen. Some would have the beginner start by grinding a bevel on the stone edge sloping inward to the top of the stone at a 25°, 26°, or 27° angle while leaving a small portion at the

168   Jewelry: Queen of Crafts

bottom of the stone perpendicular to the base. The most common error in beginning grinding is to make the stone too flat and to leave too thin an edge around the stone. This not only gives a poor appearance to the stone but is hard to mount and the stone is easily cracked. Grinding the steep angle first, as just noted, leads the inexperienced stone cutter into this common error. There is a simpler and easier way to begin forming which reduces chances of ending up with an unsightly, flattened cabochon.

Holding the end of the dop stick in one hand for turning with the fingers of the other hand in back of the stone for control and guidance, the surface of the edge of the stone is first slightly ground to further true up the shaping which was done while the stone was roughed out. All workers are familiar with a 45° angle, so this angle is judged by sight (no exact measurement of degrees is needed) to grind a bevel around the top of the stone. The lower edge of this bevel should be approximately at the center of the stone edge, as shown in *Figure 212A*. Further forming is done by grinding off the ridges left by the first 45° bevel and progressing by smaller circular bevels to form the contour into a rounded line from the bottom of the stone to the top. Rough grinding on the #100-grit wheel is completed when the stone is formed like that shown in *Figure 212B*.

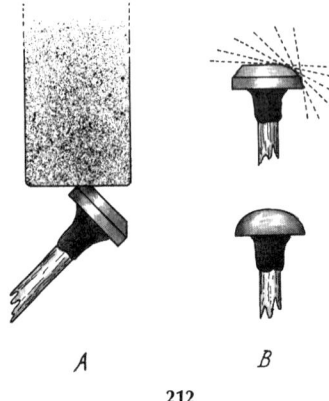

212   A   B

If proper forming has been done, the #220-grit wheel is needed only to remove the coarser scratches left by the #100-grit wheel. Very little pressure is needed for the second grinding. The stone is turned so that the bottom of the stone edge is smoothed first, and then by gradually changing the angle of the dop stick while grinding, all of the surface of the stone is smoothed from bottom to top. The small remaining beveled surfaces should be almost imperceptible. If the stone is of very hard material, these slight ridges can be removed by rocking the stone lightly against the wheel to grind across the ridges. Softer stone can be sufficiently smoothed by the next step, sanding.

Sanding can be done on wet or dry sanding cloth. Dry sanding is more commonly used in nonprofessional shops and only one grit size is necessary for amateur work if proper grinding has been done. Cloth of #220 grit smooths a stone sufficiently for polishing, especially after it has been used a short time. Special work may require cloth of #400 or even #600 grit but are not necessary for 90 percent or more of the lapidary work a jewelry craftsman will encounter. Sanding is not a forming process but a means of smoothing and removing scratches left by grinding. The stone is sanded in the same manner as when grinding on the #220-grit wheel: the stone is turned and the angle gradually increased until all the surface has been smoothed. Rocking the stone gently across the sanded circles further smooths the stone and removes even the smallest flat areas which might be left from grinding. Sanding creates a great deal of heat in the stone especially when done on dry cloth. The stone should be sanded with very little pressure and checked frequently to avoid checking or "burning." The stone and dop stick should be carefully washed and scrubbed after sanding to remove all traces of grit before polishing is started. Even one grain of grit embedded in a polishing buff can cause havoc with the polishing process.

There are many buffs for polishing: different types of cloth, felt, leather, and wooden discs. Polishing agents such as cerium oxide, tin oxide, chromium oxide, and commercial preparations with trade names, such as Linde A polishing powder, are used. These all have their places for specific jobs, but most work can be done with a felt buff and inexpensive tin oxide or cerium oxide. Oxides are mixed with water and only polish when wet and kept wet during use. The buff is charged with a watery to creamy mixture, using a brush, and the stone is buffed all over the surface to remove the fine marks of the sanding cloth. Best polishing occurs when the buff is not too wet or too dry, a point which will be recognized by experience as a pulling of the stone is felt. In buffing a good solid pressure is used for best results. The stone should be examined with a small 10- to 15-power glass at intervals to determine when all scratches have been removed. The stone can be removed from the dop stick when polishing is completed by placing the dop stick and stone into ice water to chill and then prying off the stone, or by directing flame carefully at the base of the stone to slowly soften the wax, which can then be cut off by sliding a knife across the back of the stone.

If the polished stone is translucent or is to be mounted where the back can be seen, it should be turned over and remounted on the dop stick and the back lightly ground, sanded, and polished for a finished appearance. Opaque stones set in solid-backed bezel settings do not require the back of the stone to be polished. In either case, however, there is one last important step to take before the stone is finished. A small 45° bevel should be made around the stone base to allow for any solder which might have formed a small fillet between the metal backing and the bezel ring into which the stone will be mounted. This will help prevent chipping or cracking the stone during setting (see *Figure 166* under STONING in Chapter 5).

Six phases of the work between rough stone and finished

213

214

jewelry pieces are shown and explained in the following figures. *Figure 213* shows a small block of jade embedded in plaster of paris for secure holding and accurate and economical cutting. The whole block has been clamped in the slabbing saw vise and aligned with the saw blade in order to obtain the maximum number of slices. In *Figure 214*, the block has been cut into uniform slabs having the correct thickness needed for cabochon cutting. An aluminum pencil and stencil were used to mark the outlines for trimming in *Figure 215*. *Figure 216* (right) shows the rough octagon shape after trimming on the trim

Simple Lapidary 171

saw, and next to it are two stones which have been given the first outline grinding. Also included is a cabochon mounted on a dop stick, and one which has been completed. Bezels have been made to fit the stones in *Figure 217*, and wax models have been carved which have their upper portions the correct size to hold the bezels and stones. These models were cast in gold, dressed up, and polished, and the bezels were soldered in place. *Figure 218* shows the matched set completed, the woman's ring on the left, the man's on the right.

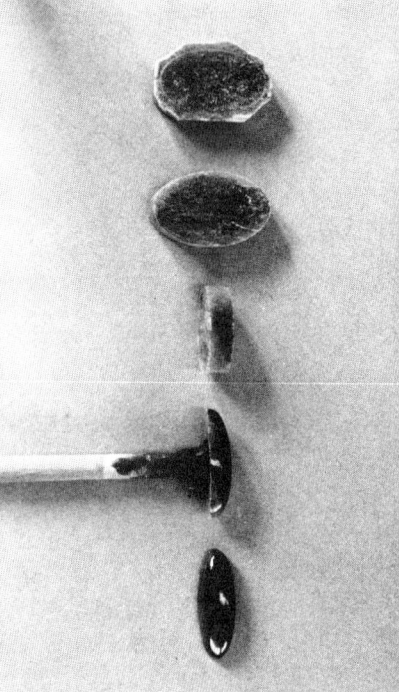

216

215

217

218

219

220

Three bola ties of quite different design are shown in *Figure 219*. The stone on the left tie was cut from red jaspar which has a white quartz inclusion running down the center. A simple mounting was made to draw attention to the stone itself. The center tie was made from Persian and Arizona turquoise with red coral for the eyes. Twisted wire and bead wire outline the mask, and oxidizing removed the brightness of metal to harmonize with the primitive design. The triangular cabochon in the right-hand tie was cut to follow the triangular marking in the agate as closely as possible. The stone had interest enough; therefore, a simple setting was made.

The cabochons mounted in the pendant and earrings in *Figure* 220 were cut from rhodochrosite. This stone is much too soft for mounting in rings but is suitable in this case. The original rock slab was carefully picked and marked to take advantage of the pink and white stripes in the stone. When possible, it is best to get the material for stones used in a set out of the same piece or slab of rock. The color and stripes will be the same, which makes the job of matching much easier.

Obviously this short discussion of lapidary work is only an introduction to a fascinating art. The worker who purchases his own equipment will want much more information than is offered here, so he is referred to the texts given in the Bibliography. The chapter should be of some aid in evaluating lapidary work done by others and help a craftsman in making his purchases. It is hoped that these few pages might awaken interest in lapidary work and get the beginner started on his own.

APPENDIX

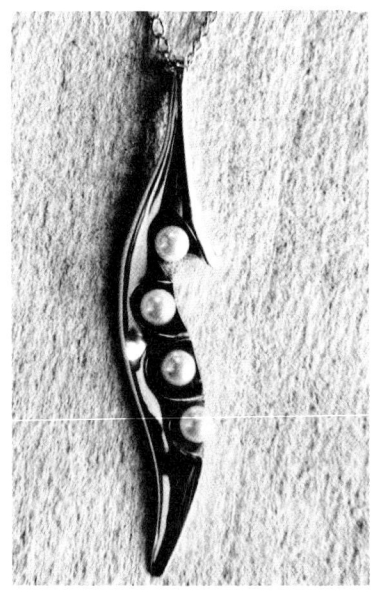

Repetition, like peas in a pod, is present in the design of this silver pendant.

ABBREVIATIONS FOR WEIGHT TERMS

Avoirdupois—Av or Avoir
Carat—ct
Grain—gr
Gram—g
Kilogram—kg
Milligram—mg

Metric—M
Ounce—oz
Pennyweight—dwt
Pound—lb
Troy—Tr

WEIGHT SYSTEMS AND COMPARATIVE CONVERSION TABLE

Systems Used for Precious Metal and Stone Weight

Avoirdupois (U.S. standard): 1 pound = 16 ounces
Metric: 1 gram = 0.0353 ounce avoirdupois
Troy: 1 pound (12 ounces) = 373.2 grams metric
    1 ounce = 20 pennyweights
    1 pennyweight = 24 grains

Appendix

Conversion

1 ounce avoirdupois = 0.912 ounce troy (28.35 grams metric)
16 ounces avoirdupois = 14.6 ounces troy
1 ounce troy = 480 grains troy (31.1 grams metric)
1 ounce troy = 20 pennyweights troy (1.1 ounces avoirdupois)
1 pennyweight troy = 24 grains troy (1.555 grams metric)
1 pound avoirdupois = 453.6 grams metric (7,000 grains troy)
1 pound troy = 373.2 grams metric (5,760 grains troy)
1 gram metric = 15.43 grains troy (0.032 ounce troy)
1,000 grams (1 kilogram metric) = 2.2 pounds avoirdupois (35.26 ounces)
1 grain troy = 0.065 gram metric
1 carat metric = 200 mg. metric, 3.086 grains troy, 0.007 ounce avoirdupois, 4 pearl grains,* or 100 points**

   *Pearl grains do not belong to the three basic weight systems and should not be confused with the troy grain.
   **Point weight is used for diamonds, 100 to the carat.

1 pearl grain = ¼ carat metric (0.772 grain troy)

COMPARATIVE LINEAR MEASUREMENTS

1 millimeter = 0.03937 inch (about 1/25 inch)
10 millimeters = 1 centimeter (0.394 inch)
1 meter = 39.37 inches

CENTIGRADE AND FAHRENHEIT TEMPERATURES

	Freezing	Boiling
Centigrade	0°	100°
Fahrenheit	32°	212°

Conversion

If degrees are given in Centigrade, multiply degrees by 9/5 and add 32 for Fahrenheit temperature.

If degrees are given in Fahrenheit, subtract 32, then multiply remainder by 5/9 for Centigrade temperature.

SILVER SOLDER MELTING AND FLOWING TEMPERATURES

	Melting Point	Flow Point
Easy	1240° F	1325° F
Medium	1275° F	1360° F
Hard	1365° F	1450° F

PRECIOUS METAL ALLOYS

Fine silver: pure, or 1000/1000 silver
Sterling silver: 925/1000 fine silver and 75/1000 copper
Coin silver: 900/1000 silver
Continental silver: charms or jewelry purchased in Europe and stamped 800 or 830 are 800/1000 or 830/1000 silver
Fine gold: pure, or 24 karats
Karat gold: 18-karat gold is 18/24 or ¾ gold. Alloying metals used singly or in combination and mixed with gold include copper, zinc, silver, or iron depending upon color desired.

METAL MELTING TEMPERATURES AND SPECIFIC GRAVITY

	Fahrenheit	Centigrade	Specific Gravity
Copper	1981	1083	8.93
Gold*	1945	1063	19.36
Lead	621	327	11.37
Nickel	2645	1452	8.85
Platinum	3224	1773	21.45
Silver	1761	962	10.56
Sterling Silver	1640	893	10.40
Tin	450	232	7.29
Zinc	787	419	7.14

*Fine gold.

NOTE: *Karat golds of different colors vary widely in melting temperature: 14K green, 1765°; 14K red, 1715°; 14K white, 1825°; 14K yellow, 1615°.*

TABLE OF COMPARATIVE RING SIZES

British	European	American	British	European	American
A				54	
	38				7
		1		55	
	39		O		
B				56	
	40		P		
C				57	8
	41		Q		
		2		58	
D			R		
	42			59	
E					9
	43			60	
		3	S		
	44			61	
F			T		
	45			62	
G					10
	46		U		
		4		63	
H			V		
	47			64	
I					11
	48			65	
	49	5	W		
J				66	
	50		X		
K				67	
	51				12
L			Y		
	52	6		68	
M			Z		
	53			69	
N					13

NOTE: *Inside diameters in inches for the three systems start and end as follows: British (0.4750") to Z (0.8625"); European 38*

(0.4762") to 69 (0.8647"); and American 1 (0.486") to 13 (0.875"). The British sizes advance by 0.0155"; the European by 0.0125"; and the American by about 0.032". The craftsman is usually concerned with ring sizes rather than diameters by linear measurement. The above table shows close comparisons in systems—all can be converted to another within a few thousandths of an inch by their relative placement on the table. EXAMPLE: British size R is equal to 58½ European or 8½ American.

NUMBERED DRILLS AND DECIMAL EQUIVALENTS IN INCHES

No.	Inch	No.	Inch	No.	Inch
1	.228	21	.159	41	.096
2	.221	22	.157	42	.093
3	.213	23	.154	43	.089
4	.209	24	.152	44	.086
5	.205	25	.149	45	.082
6	.204	26	.147	46	.081
7	.201	27	.144	47	.078
8	.199	28	.140	48	.076
9	.196	29	.136	49	.073
10	.193	30	.128	50	.070
11	.191	31	.120	51	.067
12	.189	32	.116	52	.063
13	.185	33	.113	53	.059
14	.182	34	.111	54	.055
15	.180	35	.110	55	.052
16	.177	36	.106	56	.046
17	.173	37	.104	57	.043
18	.169	38	.101	58	.042
19	.166	39	.099	59	.041
20	.161	40	.098	60	.040

STERLING SILVER WEIGHT

Round Wire		Half-Round Wire	
B&S gauge	Weight, oz per ft	B&S gauge	Weight, oz per ft
¼"	3.23	5/16"	2.52
4 (ga)	2.15	¼"	1.62
6	1.36	4 (ga)	1.08
8	.852	6	.680
9	.676	8	.426
10	.536	9	.338
12	.337	10	.268
14	.212	12	.169
16	.133	14	.106
18	.084	15	.084
20	.052		
22	.033		
24	.021		
26	.013		

(Courtesy of Allcraft Tool and Supply Company, Inc., Hicksville, N.Y.)

STERLING SILVER WEIGHT

Sheet B&S gauge	Weight, oz per sq in	Square Wire B&S gauge	Weight, oz per ft
8	.701	¼″	4.00
10	.558	4 (ga)	2.74
12	.443	6	1.73
14	.351	8	1.085
16	.278	9	.861
18	.221	10	.682
20	.175	12	.429
22	.139	14	.269
24	.110	16	.169
26	.087	18	.107
28	.070		

(*Courtesy of Allcraft Tool and Supply Company, Inc., Hicksville, N.Y.*)

STONE HARDNESS SCALES

	Mohs	Brinell	Pfaff
Diamond*	10		
Corundum	9	667	1000
Topaz	8	304	459
Quartz	7	178	254
Feldspar	6	147	191
Apatite	5	137	53.5
Fluorite	4	64	37.3
Calcite	3	53	15.3
Gypsum	2	12	12.03
Talc	1	3	

The relative hardness of 10 assigned to diamond on Mohs' scale is misleading—a jump to about number 50 would be more correct for showing the relative hardness between 9 and 10.

SHEET METAL AND WIRE B&S GAUGES AND DECIMAL EQUIVALENTS IN INCHES

Gauge	Inch	Gauge	Inch	Gauge	Inch	Gauge	Inch
1	.289	10	.102	19	.036	28	.013
2	.258	11	.091	20	.032	29	.011
3	.229	12	.081	21	.028	30	.010
4	.204	13	.072	22	.025	31	.009
5	.182	14	.064	23	.023	32	.008
6	.162	15	.057	24	.020	33	.007
7	.144	16	.051	25	.018	34	.006
8	.128	17	.045	26	.016	35	.0056
9	.114	18	.040	27	.014	36	.005

GEM STONES AND HARDNESS (MOHS' SCALE)*

- 10 Diamond
- 9 Ruby, transparent and star
    Sapphire, transparent and star
- 8 Alexandrite
    Cat's-eye, Oriental
    Crysoberyl
    Spinel
    Topaz
- 7 Agate
    Amethyst
    Aquamarine
    Aventurine
    Bloodstone
    Carnelian
    Citrine
    Emerald
    Garnet (almandine)
    Garnet (pyrope)
    Garnet (rhodolite)
    Iron pyrite
    Jasper
    Kunzite
    Morganite
    Onyx
    Quartz, smoky
    Sardonyx
- 7 Tiger's-eye
    Tourmaline
    Zircon
- 6 Garnet (demantoid)
    Jade (jadeite)
    Jade (nephrite)
    Labradorite
    Moonstone
    Obsidian
    Peridot
- 5 Hematite
    Lapis lazuli
    Opal
    Rhodonite
    Turquoise
    Variscite
- 3 Azurite
    Azurmalachite
    Coral
    Ivory
    Jet
    Malachite
    Pearl
    Rhodochrosite
    Serpentine
- 2 Amber

Listed alphabetically by number. Some stones within each number group are harder than others and may almost reach the next number in hardness.

SOME SUPPLY SOURCES

Allcraft Tool and Supply Co., Inc. 215 Park Avenue Hicksville, N.Y. 11801	Tools, findings, books, metals
Anchor Tool and Supply Co., Inc. 12 John Street New York, N.Y. 10038	Tools, findings, metals, kilns
Dick Ells Company 908 Venice Boulevard Los Angeles, Calif. 90015	Casting equipment and accessories
Foredom Electric Company, Inc. Bethel, Conn. 06801	Flex-shaft equipment and accessories
Grieger's Incorporated 1633 East Walnut Street Pasadena, Calif. 91106	Tools, findings, books, metals, stones

180   Jewelry: Queen of Crafts

T. B. Hagstoz and Son 709 Sansom Street Philadelphia, Penn. 19106	Tools, findings, metals, books
C. R. Hill 35 West Grand River Detroit, Mich. 48226	Tools, findings, metals, enamel supplies, kilns
Francis Hoover 12449 Chandler Boulevard N. Hollywood, Calif. 91607	Unusual stones, cut and rough material
Jewelgems P.O. Box 1000 Thousand Palms, Calif. 92276	Findings, cultured pearls
Karlan and Bleicher, Inc. 136 West 52nd Street New York, N.Y. 10019	Findings
Sam Kramer 29 West 8th Street Greenwich Village New York, N.Y. 10011	Exotic woods, stones, ivory
Plummer's Minerals 4720 Point Loma Avenue San Diego, Calif. 92107	Stones, cut and rough material
R & B Artcraft Co. 11019 S. Vermont Avenue Los Angeles, Calif. 90044	Tools, findings, books, metals
Silvercraft Suppliers P.O. Box 282 Rosemead, Calif. 91770	Sterling and fine silver, sheet, wire
C. W. Somers and Company 387 Washington Street Boston, Mass.	Tools, findings
Western Ceramics 1601 Howard Street San Francisco, Calif. 94103	Enameling equipment, kilns, books
Western Manufacturing Co., Inc. 149 Ninth Street San Francisco, Calif. 94103	Enameling equipment, books
Wildent Corporation 2330 Beverly Boulevard Los Angeles, Calif. 90057	Karat golds, refining

Most suppliers furnish catalogues free upon request.

GLOSSARY

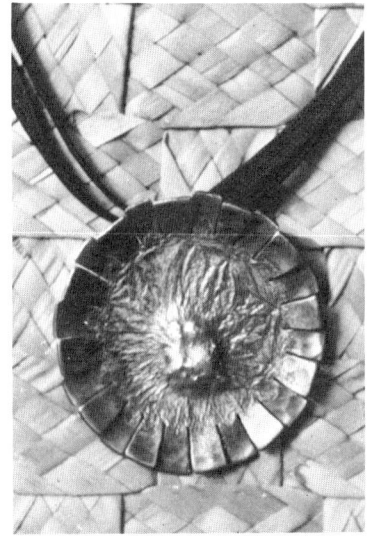

Both texture and color differences are present in this copper and silver pendant. Silver scraps were placed in the center and fused and melted to form the flowing lines radiating outward.

Abrasive: A substance used for cutting, wearing away, or smoothing a surface.

Adamas or *adamant:* Hard, unyielding. Ancient name of diamond.

Aigrette: A hair or hat ornament made from precious metals in the form of a plume or spray.

Alcohol lamp: A lamp used for heat rather than light having a wick and fueled with alcohol.

Alloy: A mixture of metals. Base metals added to precious metals to effect a physical change, such as to increase hardness.

Amorphous: Not having a definite crystal structure.

Annealing: A metal-softening process accomplished by heat and slow cooling.

Appliqué: The placing and attaching of one piece of metal upon another.

Arkansas oilstone: A natural stone used for the final polish on cutting tools, such as gravers.

Asteriated or *asterism:* Showing a star effect, such as in a star ruby or star sapphire when cut *en cabochon.*

Avoirdupois: U.S. weight standard—16 ounces to a pound. Not used for precious metals. See TROY.

Axis: Direction in a crystal.

Bangle: An inflexible bracelet that must be slipped over the hand.

Baroque: A pearl of irregular shape. See BLISTER PEARL.

Basse-taille: An enameling process for which the metal surface has been carved to hold the enamel.

Bench pin: A small block of hardwood attached or clamped to the bench for supporting work to be filed or sawed.

Bezel: The metal stripping forming the "box" into which a cabochon stone is fitted and held in place.

Blister pearl: A blister from the shell having a flat back. Regular pearls are formed in the flesh of the oyster and are round or baroque in shape.

Bloom: A soft, nonshiny finish on metal. Acid can give a bloom to gold or silver by eating away alloy metal, thus leaving microscopic indentations.

Bobbing compound: A buffing compound which is faster and coarser than tripoli.

Bort or *boart:* Impure diamond crushed for cutting and polishing purposes.

Brass: A copper and zinc alloy.

Brilliant cut: The most popular cut for round facet-cut stones, in which there are 58 facets, regardless of size.

Briolette: A pendant-shaped stone entirely faceted, usually pierced for use as a pendant or in a necklace.

Brittle: The quality of being easily chipped or broken by a shock or blow.

Bronze: A copper and tin alloy.

Brooch: An ornamental pin worn at the breast.

Burnish: To polish by friction or rubbing.

Burnisher: A hand tool with a hard, polished surface, usually curved, which is used to remove scratches, to give a finish to metal, or to set a bezel, or prongs, over a stone.

Burn-out: A heat process which removes the wax model from an invested flask for casting.

Burr: A rough edge left on metal after filing or drilling.

Cabochon: A stone cut with a rounded top without facets. The bottom may be flat, concave, or convex.

Cameo: Any gemstone or other substance carved in relief.

Carat: A weight standard for gems—$1/5$ gram or 200 milligrams.

Carborundum: A trade name for synthetic corundum.

Casting: The process of pouring or forcing molten metal into a mold. Also the cast piece.

Champlevé: Enamel work done by removing metal from the piece so as to leave sunken areas for the enamel with separators between colors.

Chasing: A work method of lining with tools on the front of a piece, as opposed to repoussé, which raises a design from the back. Both methods are usually used in conjunction with each other.

Glossary

Chatoyancy: The shifting band of light reflection best illustrated by such stones as cat's-eye and tiger's-eye.
Chinese white: A white compound in small-block form used on metal for design transfer. It is applied with a wet brush, and after drying, carbon paper may be used to transfer the design.
Cire-perdue: Lost wax casting method.
Cleavage: The property of splitting along planes of a crystal.
Cloisonné: Enamel work using small metal strips to form cells into which the enamel is placed and fired.
Corundum: A mineral known as ruby or sapphire when of gem quality and as emery when impure and used as an abrasive.
Cratex wheels: A trade name for rubber-bonded abrasive wheels produced in various sizes, shapes, and grit sizes.
Cristobalite: A heat-resistant plaster containing silica used for investment in metal casting.
Crown: That part of a faceted stone above the girdle.
Cryptocrystalline: Formation in stone composed of microcrystals. Agate is a quartz form of this type of formation.
Crystal: The solid form of certain minerals having a definite atomic structure.
Culet: The small facet at the bottom of a brilliant-cut stone.

Dapping: Doming of metal by using a dapping die and punches.
Dop stick: A small rod of wood or metal similar to a pen holder used to hold a stone for grinding and polishing.
Doublet: A stone consisting of two parts cemented together.
Douzième: A linear measurement equal to $74/1000$ inch.
Drawplate: A steel plate having graduated holes used for reducing wire diameter.
Ductile: A property of metal which allows it to be drawn without breaking, as into wire.

Electrostripping: A method of cleaning used just before plating metal.

Facet: A small, flat, polished surface on a stone.
Fetter chain: A chain having long, narrow links.
Fibula: An ancient decorated pin.
Filigree: Jewelry having a lacelike or threadlike quality made from wire.
Findings: The term used to designate catches, hinges, studs, earscrews, and other small accessory pieces used on jewelry.
Fine: Pure metal without alloy.
Fire scale: The discoloration found on the surface of metal after prolonged high heat. In silver, the copper alloy has been driven to the surface.
Fisheye: An improperly proportioned faceted stone. Cut too shallow, the stone has a dead, lifeless center area.
Flask: The metal cylinder which holds the wax pattern and investment in the lost wax (centrifugal) method of casting.
Florentine: A texture on metal made by using lined gravers.
Flux: A substance that prevents oxides from forming when metal is heated and that picks up impurities when metal is melted. Borax is the base of most hard-soldering flux.
Form: Three-dimensional as opposed to two-dimensional shape.

Forming: Giving a third dimension to flat sheet by various working methods.

Gauge: A measure of thickness used for wire and sheet metal.
Gilt: An extremely thin film of gold.
Girdle: The outer perimeter of a stone which defines its shape. The edge of a stone which is held by the setting.
Gold filled: Gold on the outside, base metal on the inside—a metal "sandwich."
Gold plate: Gold covering added by the electroplating process.
Grain: A unit of weight used for pearls. One grain is ¼ carat.
Granulation: Small granules fixed upon a piece by colloid soldering.
Gravers: Hand tools for engraving or carving metal.
Grit: Loose abrasive material.

Handwrought: Made from sheet and wire rather than being cast.
High-speed steel: A superior alloy steel. When used for twist drills it holds an edge longer than ordinary carbon steels.
Hue: Another name for color. A tint is lighter and a shade is darker than the color, or hue.

Inlay: Decorative material fitted or inserted into another material and finished with all parts forming a smooth, common surface.
Intaglio: Carving into stone rather than in relief as in a cameo.
Intarsia: Inlay of mosaic.
Investment: A high-heat-resistant plaster material which is used in lost wax (centrifugal) casting. See CRISTOBALITE.
Investment flask: See FLASK.

Jadeite: A crystalline type of jade. Oriental, or precious, jade.
Jig: A fixture used to make duplicate parts.
Jump ring: Small ring or link used to connect parts of jewelry pieces.

K or Kt: Abbreviation for karat.
Karat: specifies purity of gold. Pure gold is 24K. Gold of 14K is 14/24 gold and 10/24 alloy metals.

Lamination: The soldering together of several layers of sheet metal.
Lavallière: Small jeweled pendant worn with low-cut dresses.
Limoges: Enamel work resembling painting.
Liver of sulphur: Potassium sulphide, a chemical used to tarnish, or "antique," metals.
Luster: Appearance of reflected light from a mineral or metal, e.g., greasy luster, satin luster.

Malleable: A property of metals which allows them to be formed easily without breaking or splitting.
Mandrel: A tapered steel spindle used to shape and size metal pieces such as rings, links, and bracelets.
Marriage of Metals: Lamination. A Mexican term for this type of work.
Matte finish: A nonshiny, velvety texture on metal or stone.
Matting: A pebbled or grained surface texture applied to metal.

Glossary   185

Millegrain: A small-beaded texture applied around set stones.
Mirror finish: A mirrorlike polish of extremely high gloss.
Mohs' scale: A scale of hardness much used to classify stones based on the ability of one stone to scratch another, ranging from 10 (diamond) to 1 (talc).
Motif: Main feature or theme of a design.
Muffle: Giving indirect heat, as in a muffle furnace.

Nephrite: A fibrous type of jade.
Niello: Inlay work on metals using an alloy composed of silver, copper, lead, and sulphur placed in depressions and fired.

Opal: A noncrystalline form of silica. When it possesses the characteristic flashes of color, it is known as precious opal.
Opalescence: A play of colors or sheen found in some stones.
Opalized: Converted into opal, as in opalized wood.
Opaque: Opposite of transparent, or impervious to light.
Orientation: Cutting a stone in reference to the crystal axis for star stones and in reference to stone formation as in tiger's-eye.
Oxidize: To color or "antique" metal. A chemical union between metal and oxygen.

Parures: A set of jewels to be worn together.
Paste: Glass imitation stones.
Patina: The darkening or coloring on a metal surface. See OXIDIZE.
Pavilion: That part of a facet-cut stone below the girdle.
Peened: A texture made with a peen hammer, usually characterized by small rounded indentations over the surface of a metal.
Pendant: A jewelry piece suspended by a chain around the neck.
Pennyweight: A unit of troy weight—20 pennyweights to an ounce troy.
Pickle: A water-acid solution used to clean metal and remove flux and oxides after soldering or high-heat application.
Piercing: Cutting through a solid metal background to form a design.
Pitch: A semihard substance upon which metal is embossed and chased.
Pitch bowl: A heavy cast-iron bowl for holding pitch.
Plique-à-jour: Enamel work on filigree or pierced work having no backing, the effect of which is similar to a stained-glass window.
Point: Unit of weight used for diamonds—100 points to 1 carat.
Potassium sulphide: See LIVER OF SULPHUR.
Prongs: The small metal fingers which are used to hold a stone in a setting.
Pusher: A tool with a blunt end used to set bezels and prongs over stones in settings.
Pyrex: The trade name of a commercial glass having a high heat tolerance, used in kitchen utensils.

Quench: Fast cooling of metal in water or pickle solution.

Reconstructed stones: Stones made by fusing fragments of natural stones.
Reducing flame: A flame which will allow little, if any, oxygen to combine with metal.

Repoussé: A design which is hammered or pressed from the back of a metal piece.

Ring clamp: A clamp closed by a wooden wedge to hold small work for filing, drilling, buffing, sawing, and other working methods.

Ring gauge: A set of rings attached to one large ring, used to measure finger sizes of rings.

Ring mandrel: See MANDREL. Markings on a ring mandrel show standard ring sizes.

Rolled-gold plate: The same as gold filled except gold is thinner.

Rouge: An oxide of iron used as a polishing compound for high gloss in buffing metal.

Satin finish: A satinlike polish less brilliant than a mirror finish.

Scale: The oxides that form on metal, usually from high heat.

Scale-off: The commercial trade name of a scale and oxide preventive cream used in enameling to prevent formation of fire scale.

Scratch awl: A pointed tool used for layout work and used to mark lines by scratching the metal surface.

Seat: The section or area that a stone rests upon in a setting. See SHOULDER.

Shank: That part of a ring that fits the finger. The part of a twist drill that fits into a drill chuck.

Shape: Two-dimensional design, flat.

Shoulder: The seat in a prong setting.

Silicon carbide: An abrasive manufactured in the form of grit, wheels, and cloth for grinding and sanding stones.

Sparex No. 2: The commercial trade name of a pickling compound, superior to acid and less dangerous.

Spindle, tapered: A threaded fitting attached to a motor shaft to hold buffing wheels.

Sprue: That part of a wax model which connects the carved wax jewelry piece to the outside of the flask or the resultant metal attached to the cast object.

Stake: Heavy metal tools fitted into a bench for forming larger sheet metal objects, used by the silversmith more than by the jewelry maker.

Star setting: A setting which has the table of the stone nearly flush with the metal. Engraved rays striking out from the stone give a star effect.

Sterling: A standard of silver purity—sterling is 925/1000 parts fine silver and 75/1000 parts copper.

Stripping: Removal of fire scale by using a pickling solution.

Synthetic stones: Stones made by fusion using the same chemicals found in the natural stones.

Table: Top flat facet of a gem.

Tang: The end of a graver or file that fits into a handle.

Tempering: The term generally used for the two processes of hardening and later the controlled softening of steel to a limited degree.

Template: A pattern.

Transfer wax: A beeswax and tallow mixture used to coat metal so that a design may be transferred.

Translucent: Allowing partial transmission of light.

Transparent: Allowing nearly perfect transmission of light. Transparent stones are usually cut with facets.

Triplet: The same as doublet, except for being composed of three parts glued together instead of two.

Tripoli: A fast-cutting buffing compound. Usually followed by buffing with rouge for a high gloss.

Troy: Weight system for precious metals—12 ounces to a pound, 20 pennyweights to an ounce.

Trumming: Polishing by rubbing over an abrasive-charged string.

Work hardened: A physical change (crystallization) in metal brought about by hammering, bending, and other forming methods.

BIBLIOGRAPHY

Matched pair of silver pins. Contrast between shiny silver tips and the central portion was made by oxidizing over the textured metal.

JEWELRY

BAERWALD, MARCUS, and MAHONEY, TOM, *The Story of Jewelry.* London–New York, Abelard–Schuman, Ltd.

BAXTER, WILLIAM T., *Jewelry, Gem Cutting and Metalcraft.* New York, McGraw-Hill Book Company, 1950.

BOVIN, MURRAY, *Jewelry Making, for Schools, Tradesmen, Craftsmen.* Forest Hills, L. I., N.Y., Bovin, 1956.

BOWMAN, JOHN J., *The Jewelry Engravers Manual.* Princeton, N.J., D. Van Nostrand Company, Inc., 1954.

CLEGG, HELEN, and LAROM, MARY, *Jewelry Making for Fun and Profit.* New York, David McKay Company, Inc., 1951.

CURRAN, MONA, *A Treasury of Jewels and Gems.* New York, Emerson Books, Inc., 1962.

DAVIS, MARY L., and "PACK, GTETA," *Mexican Jewelry.* Austin, University of Texas Press, 1963.

FLOWER, MARGARET, *Victorian Jewellery.* New York, Duell, Sloan and Pearce, 1951.

Bibliography

FRANKE, LOIS E., *Handwrought Jewelry*. Bloomington, Ill., McKnight and McKnight Publishing Co., 1962.

HARDY, R. ALLEN, and BOWMAN, JOHN J., *The Jewelry Repair Manual*. Princeton, N.J., D. Van Nostrand Company, Inc., 1956.

HIGGINS, R. A., *Greek and Roman Jewellery*. London, Methuen and Company, Ltd., 1961.

HOLMES, MARTIN, F.S.A., *The Crown Jewels*. London, Her Majesty's Stationery Office, 1960.

HUGHES, GRAHAM, *Modern Jewelry*, New York. Crown Publishers, Inc., 1963.

HUNT, W. BEN, *Indian Silversmithing*. New York, The Bruce Publishing Company, 1960.

KUZEL, VLADISLAV, *A Book of Jewelry*. London, Allan Wingate, Ltd., 1962.

MARTIN, CHARLES J., *How To Make Modern Jewelry*. New York, The Museum of Modern Art, 1949.

MERA, HARRY P., *Indian Silverwork of the Southwest*, Vol. I. Globe, Ariz., Killian Printing Service, 1959.

NEUMANN, ROBERT VON, *The Design and Creation of Jewelry*. Philadelphia, Chilton Company, Book Division, 1961.

OSTIER, MARIANNE, *Jewels and the Woman*. New York, Royal Books, Pyramid Publications, Inc., 1962.

PACK, GRETA, *Jewelry and Enameling*. Princeton, N.J., D. Van Nostrand Company, Inc., 1953.

ROGERS, FRANCES, and BEARD, ALICE, *5000 Years of Gems and Jewelry*. New York, J. B. Lippincott Company, 1947.

ROSE, AUGUSTUS F., and CIRINOS, ANTONIO, *Jewelry Making and Design*. Worcester, Mass., The Davis Press, Inc., 1946.

SHOENFELT, JOSEPH F., *Designing and Making Handwrought Jewelry*. New York, McGraw-Hill Book Company, Inc., 1960.

SNOWMAN, A. KENNETH, *The Art of Carl Faberge*. London, Faber and Faber Limited, 1962.

SUTHERLAND, C. H. V., *Gold*. London, Thames and Hudson, 1959.

WIENER, LOUIS, *Hand Made Jewelry*. Princeton, N.J., D. Van Nostrand Company, Inc., 1960.

WILSON, H., *Silverwork and Jewellery*. London, Sir Isaac Pitman and Sons, Ltd., 1962.

WINEBRENNER, D. KENNETH, *Jewelry Making*. Scranton, Pa., International Textbook Company, 1955.

ZARCHY, HARRY, *Jewelry Making and Enameling*. New York, Alfred A. Knopf, Inc., 1959.

LAPIDARY

DAKE, DR. H. C., *The Art of Gem Cutting*. Portland, Mineralogist Publishing Company, 1956.

FOSHAG, W. F., "Exploring the World of Gems." The National Geographic Magazine, (Dec., 1950).

Gem Cutting, Lapidary and Jewelry Arts. Grieger's Encyclopedia and Guide for Rockhounding, Pasadena, Grieger's Inc., 1960.

GUMP, RICHARD, *Jade: Stone of Heaven*. New York, Doubleday and Company, Inc., 1962.

The Lapidary Journal, San Diego, Calif.

LEECHMAN, FRANK, *The Opal Book*. Sydney, Australia, Ure Smith Pty. Limited, 1961.

MCDONALD, LUCILE SAUNDERS, *Jewels and Gems*. New York,

Thomas Y. Crowell Company, 1940. Out-of-print, but available at bookstores specializing in old books.

PEARL, RICHARD M., *How to Know the Minerals and Rocks.* New York, McGraw-Hill Book Company, Inc., 1955.

QUICK, LELANDE, and LEIPER, HUGH, *Gemcraft,* Philadelphia, Chilton Company, Book Division, 1960.

SHERIDAN, MICHAEL, *How To Polish Rocks and Gems.* Los Angeles, Spotlite Books.

SPERISEN, FRANCIS J., *The Art of the Lapidary.* New York, The Bruce Publishing Company, 1961.

SWITZER, GEORGE S. and CULVER, WILLARD R., "Rockhounds Uncover Mineral Beauty." The National Geographic Magazine, (Nov., 1951).

WEINSTEIN, MICHAEL, *The World of Jewel Stones.* New York, Sheridan House, Inc., 1958.

WHITLOCK, HERBERT P., *The Story of the Gems.* New York, Garden City Publishing Co., Inc., 1940.

WOOLF, BELLA SIDNEY, "Fishing for Pearls in the Indian Ocean." The National Geographic Magazine, (Feb., 1926).

ZIM, HERBERT S., and SHAFFER, PAUL R., *Rocks and Minerals.* New York, Simon and Schuster, Inc., 1957.

DESIGN

DOWNER, MARION, *Discovering Design.* New York, Lothrop, Lee and Shepard Company, 1947.

ENCISO, JORGE, *Design Motifs of Ancient Mexico,* New York, Dover Publications, 1953.

MEYER, FRANK SALES, *Handbook of Ornament.* New York, Dover Publications, Inc., 1957.

PEPPER, STEPHEN C., *Principles of Art Appreciation.* New York, Harcourt, Brace and Company, 1949.

SPELTZ, ALEXANDER, *The Styles of Ornament.* New York, Dover Publications, Inc., 1959.

INDEX

Silver square wire and sheet were used for this classic design. The oxidized background gives depth to this flat pin and also contrasts sharply with the three white pearls.

Acheson, George, 102
Acetylene heat units, 34–36, *Figs. 39, 40*
Acetylene-oxygen torch, 108
Annealing, 40–41, *Fig. 42*
    chasing and, 58
    dapping and, 62
    forming and, 88
    repoussé and, 58
    stamping and, 114
    wire, 65
Antidotes, for acid, 78
Appliqué, 41–42, 143–144, *Figs. 43, 44*
Art, aboriginal, 11, *Fig. 14*
Asbestos, 22
Auctions, 2–3

Bails, 85
Balls, 85, *Fig. 95D*
Basse-taille, 70, *Fig. 81A*
Beads, 85, *Fig. 95D*
Beeswax, 63
    as lubrication, 65–67, 106
Belt buckles, *Fig. 20*
    solderless, 135, *Fig. 13*
Bending, 42–43, *Figs. 45, 46*
Bezel, 116–119, 146, *Figs. 134–137*
Bone, 11, *Fig. 14*
Bracelets, solderless, 136–137, 140–141, *Figs. 172A–C, 179B, 180*
Brass, 20–21
    coloring of, 59–60
Brooches, 82–84, *Fig. 93*
Buffing, 43–45, 131, *Figs. 47, 48*

Buffing motor, 36
Bunsen burner, 32
    for soft soldering, 108
Burin. See Gravers.
Burnout, 50–51
Burnout ovens, 32–33, 50
Burnisher, 30
Burnishing, 45, 131, *Figs. 49A–C*
Burnishing tool, 131
Button eyes, 84, *Fig. 95C*

Cabochons, 21, 116–120, *Figs. 133–136*
    forming and polishing of, 165–173, *Figs. 210–220*
Calipers, sliding, 28–29
Carborundum stone, 25, 31, 34, 102
Carving, 45–47, *Figs. 50–53*
    as different from modeling, 47
Casting, 47–57, *Figs. 54–66*
    centrifugal wax, 48
    equipment, 32–33, *Fig. 37*
    machine, 32, 48–51, *Fig. 60*
    materials, 21–22
    reasons for failure, 53–54
    temperatures, 51
    use of wax, 47–57, 150–151, *Fig. 198*
Cast jewelry, 147–151
    appliqué and, 42
    compared to handwrought, 147–150, *Figs. 189, 191, 192, 199*
    finding application to, 150–151
    as resembles fusion, 149, *Fig. 195*
    texture, 149–150, *Fig. 196*
Catches,
    box, 85
    foldover, 85
    safety, 83, *Fig. 94*
Cementing, 22
Center punch, 28
Champlevé, 70, *Fig. 81B*
Chasing, 57–58, *Figs. 67A–D*
    annealing and, 58
    materials, 22
    repoussé and, 57–58
    tools, 131
Cire-perdue, lost wax casting, 47–57, 150–151
    equipment, 33
Cloisonné enameling, 70, 144, *Fig. 81C*
Coin mounts, 85
Colloid soldering, 91–92, *Fig. 102B*
Coloring, 12, 58–61, *Figs. 68–71*
    of pearls and stones, 157

Copper, 20–21
    coloring of, 59
    enameling and, 71–72
Counterenameling, 73
Crystalon. See Sanding.
Cuff links, *Fig. 19*
    findings, 82–84

Dapping, 61–62, *Figs. 72, 73*
    annealing and, 62
Dapping punches, 31
Debubblizer, 21–22, 49
Design, 4–18
    abstract, 18, *Fig. 32*
    balance, 10–11, *Fig. 12*
    basic, 6
    decoration, 12–13, *Figs. 17–18*
    form, 8, *Figs. 6, 7*
    function, 13–17, *Figs. 19–30*
    line, 6–7, *Figs. 2, 3*
    nonobjective, 18, *Fig. 33*
    proportion, 10, *Figs. 10, 11*
    realistic, 17, *Fig. 31*
    shape, 7–8, *Figs. 4–6*
    structure, 9–10, *Figs. 8, 9*
    unity, 11–12, *Figs. 13–16*
    volume, 8–9, *Fig. 7*
Design transfer, materials, 22–23
Die, dapping, 61
Dowels, 23
Drawing transfer, 62–64, *Figs. 74, 75*
Drawing wire and tubing, 64–66, *Figs. 76A, B*
Drawplates, 64–65
Drawtongs, 64–65
Drilling, 66–67, 132, *Figs. 77A, B, 78*
Drill press, 36
Drills, 66–67
    gauges, 29
Ductility, loss of, 40
Dust collector, 36

Earrings, 11, 55–56, *Figs. 14, 30, 47*
    solderless, 138–139, 142, *Figs. 174–176, 183*
Earwires, 81–82, *Fig. 92*
Electrolyte, 68
Electroplating, 68–69, *Fig. 79*
    equipment, 33
Electrostripping, 69
    equipment, 33
Emery cloth, 102–103
Enameling, 69–74, *Figs. 79, 80A–E*
    basse-taille, 70, *Fig. 81A*
    champlevé, 70, *Fig. 81B*

cloisonné, 70, *Fig. 81C*
counterenameling, 73
en plein, 69
equipment, 33–34, *Fig. 38*
history, 69
limoges, 70, *Fig. 81D*
materials, 23
plique-à-jour, 70–71, *Fig. 81E*
special effects, 73, *Fig. 82*
Engraving, 74–76, 132, *Fig. 86*
Equipment,
    casting, 32–33, *Fig. 37*
    electroplating, 33
    electrostripping, 33
    enameling, 33–34, *Fig. 38*
    lapidary, 37–38, 164–166
    power, 36–37, *Fig. 41*
    soldering, 34–36, *Figs. 39, 40*
Etching, 76–78, 132, *Figs. 87–89*
    materials, 23

Fabergé, Carl, 69
Faceting, 121, 164, *Fig. 143*
Ferrous metals. See Tempering.
Filigree, 144
    piercing and, 97
    soldering of, 111–112, *Fig. 127*
Findings, 9, 21, 72, *Figs. 8, 9, 91–97*
    application of, 81–87, 94, 150
    discoloration of, 96
    jump rings, 85–87, *Figs. 97, 98*
    pin stems, 82, 84, *Fig. 93*
    riveting of, 101
    safety catches, 83, *Fig. 94*
    soldering, 145–146
    types of, 81–87
Files, 79–80, *Fig. 90*
    riffle, 29
Filing, 79–80, *Figs. 90, 91*
Fire-scale, 41, 44, 71–72
Flex-shaft tool, 36–37, *Fig. 41*
Flux, hard solder, 110–112
    soft solder, 108–109
Forming, 87–88, *Fig. 99*
    annealing and, 88
Fusing, 88–90, 132, *Figs. 100, 101*

Gas heat units, 36
Gauges,
    drill, 29
    ring, 29
    spring, 28
    wire and sheet, 29
Gems, 152–162, *Fig. 200*
    altered, 157–158
    beauty of, 153–154
    characteristics of, 153–154
    definition of, 152
    hardness of, 154, 160–162
    imitation, 156–157
    laminated, 157–158
    measurement and weight of, 159–160, *Figs. 206, 207*
    Moh's scale, 161–162
    natural, 154
    opaque, 154
    precious, 154
    rarity of, 153–154
    synthetic, 154–155
    toughness of, 162, *Figs. 208, 209*
    translucent, 154, *Figs. 202, 204*
    transparent, 154, *Fig. 201*
Goggles, safety, 45
Gold, 10, 128
    casting of, 51
    coloring, 59–60, *Fig. 69*
    enameling and, 71
    gauges used, 20
    granulation and, 91–92
    as hard solder, 109–111
    oxidizing of, 24
    plating, 68–69
Granulation, 90–92, 132, 146, *Fig. 102*
Gravers, 30, 45, 74–75, *Fig. 84*
Gypsy setting, 120–121, 146, *Fig. 140*

Hammers, 87–88
    ball peen, 95
    chasing, 30, 58
    peen, 94–95
    planishing, 30
    straight peen, 29
Handwrought jewelry, *Figs. 188, 190*
    appliqué and, 42
    compared to cast jewelry, 147–148, 150
    lost wax casting and, 54–55
Hard solder. See Soldering.

Investment, 49–51
    dental, 47
    measuring, 49
    mixing, 49–50
Jade, 12, *Fig. 15*
Jadeite, 12, 162

194 Jewelry: Queen of Crafts

Jewelry, personality and, 17
    Indian, 113, 115
    religious, 14, *Figs. 23–25*
    symbolic, 14, *Fig. 22*
Jump rings, 85–87, *Figs. 97, 98*

Key rings, 85
Kilns, 71–72
    enameling, 34

Laminating, 92–94, 144–145, 149, *Figs. 103, 104*
    casting and, 149
    finding application and, 94
    "marriage of metals," 92–93
    oxidation and, 94
Lapidary, 163–173, *Figs. 210–218*
    equipment, 37–38, 164–166
    materials, 23–24
Limoges, 70, *Fig. 81D*
Liner. See Graver.
Lost-wax casting. See Cire-Perdue.

Malleability, loss of, 40
Mandrel, ring, 42
"Marriage of Metals." See Laminating.
Materials, casing, 21–22
    cementing, 22
    chasing, 22
    design transfer, 22–23
    enameling, 23
    etching, 23
    lapidary, 23–24
    metal, 20–21
    oxidizing, 24
    repoussé, 22
    sanding, 24–25
    soldering, 25
    stones, 20–21
Mercury, 68
Metal, 20–21
Mica, 71
Modeling, as different from carving, 47
Moh's Scale of Hardness, 161–162
Monogram letters, 85, *Fig. 95D*
Mordants, corrosive compounds, 78

Natrolon. See Sanding.
Necklaces, solderless, 139–142, *Figs. 181, 182, 177–180*
Niello, 12, 75

Oxidation, coloring and, 59, *Figs. 68, 104*
    lamination and, 94
    reduction of, 25
Oxidizing, 12, 94, 132, *Fig. 105*
    materials, 24
    See also Coloring.

Pad eyes, 84, *Fig. 95C*
Pearls, cementing, 22
    coloring, 157
    cultured, 158–159, *Fig. 205*
    price of, 21
Pearl setting, 125, 127, *Figs. 155–163*
Peening, 94–95, 133, *Figs. 106–109*
Pendants, 10, 11, 15, 16, 46, *Figs. 10, 11, 12*
    solderless, 138–139, *Fig. 174*
Pendant loops, 85
Pickling, 96–97
    compound, 111
    discoloration of findings and, 96
Piercing, 97–98, *Figs. 110, 111*
    filigree, 97
Pins, 9, 46, 82–84, *Fig. 93*
    solderless, 135–136, *Fig. 171*
Pitch, 22, 58
Plating. See Electroplating.
Platinum, 128
Pliers, 28
Plique-à-jour, 70–71, *Fig. 81E*
Polish, as texture, 100, *Fig. 112*
Polishing, 98–100, 133, *Fig. 112*
    stones and metal, 100
    tumbling, 100
    See Buffing
Prong settings, 85, 146
    for pearls, 125, *Figs. 155, 156*
    for stones, 120–123, *Figs. 138, 139, 144–154*
Punches, 113–114
    dapping, 61–62, *Fig. 73*
    in forming, 88

Repoussé, 100–101, *Figs. 113, 114*
    annealing and, 58
    chasing and, 57–58, *Fig. 67*
    materials, 22
    See Chasing
Rhodium, 68
Rings, 8–9, 46–47, *Figs. 18, 29, 50–52*
    castings of, 48–50
    gauges, 29

shanks, 85, *Fig. 96A*
solderless, 137, *Fig. 173*
Riveting, 41, 101–102, 144, *Figs. 116, 118, 185A*
    of findings, 101
Rouge, 43, 99, 131

Sanding, 102–103, *Fig. 117*
    carborundum, 102
    crystalon, 102
    emery cloth, 102–103
    materials, 24–25
    natrolon, 102
Saw blades, 105–106
Saw frames, 105–106
Sawing, 103–107, *Figs. 118–120*
Scale-off, 23
Setting. See Stone setting
Silver, 10, 41, 128
    casting, 51
    coloring, 59–60
    enameling and, 71–72
    gauges used, 20
    as hard solder, 109–111
    plating, 68–69
Solder, 41
    gold, 20
    hard, 109–111
    silver, 20, 109–111
    soft, 108–109
Soldered jewelry, 143–146, *Fig. 185B*
    appliqué, 41–42, 143–144
    cloisonné enameling, 144
    enameling, 69–74
    findings, 145–146
    granulation in, 90–92, 146
    laminating in, 92, 94, 144–145
    pins, *Fig. 184*
    stone setting, 146
Soldering, 107–113, *Figs. 121–126*
    colloid, 91–92, *Fig. 102B*
    equipment, 34–36, *Figs. 39, 40*
    of findings, 81–87, 145–146
    hard solder, 109–111
    laminating and, 93
    materials, 25
    soft, 108–109
    temperatures, 113
Solderless jewelry, 135–142
Spring rings, 85
Stamping, 113–115, 133, *Figs. 128–130*
    annealing and, 114
Stamps, 114–115
Stones, 20–21
    coloring, 157

imitation, 156–157
natural, 154–155
opaque, 154, *Fig. 203*
synthetic, 154–156
Stone setting, 10, 115–124, 133, *Figs. 131–154*
    bezel, 116–119, 146, *Figs. 134–137*
    on cast jewelry, 150
    gypsy setting, 120–121, 146, *Fig. 140*
    pegged, 85, *Fig. 96B*
    prong, 85, 120–123, 146, *Figs. 96B, 138–139, 144–154*
    wax, 149, *Fig. 197*
    wire, 116, *Fig. 131, 132*
Stoning, 127–128, 133, *Figs. 164–166*
Sulphides, 59
Sulphuric acid, 23
    antidotes, 78

Tempering, 128–130, 167
    ferrous metals and, 129
    temperatures, 130
Texture, 12–13, *Fig. 17*
    on bezels, 119
    on cast jewelry, 149–150, *Fig. 196*
    color and, 60, *Figs. 70, 71*
    Florentine, 75, 132, *Figs. 83, 85*
    Millegrain, 133
    peening and, 95, *Figs. 108, 109*
    polish and, 100, *Fig. 112*
    stamping, 115
Texturing, 130–134, *Figs. 168–170*
    buffing, 131
    burnishing tools, 131
    chasing tools, 131
    drilling, 132
    engraving, 132
    etching, 132
    fusing, 132
    granulation, 132
    oxidizing, 132
    peening, 133
    polishing, 133
    stamping, 133
    stone setting, 133
    stoning, 133
Tie clips, findings, 84, *Fig. 95B*
Tie tacks, 84, *Figs. 21, 95A*
Tools, 26–38, *Figs. 25, 35, 36*. See also under particular tool
Tracing, as design transfer method, 63

Tragacanth, 23
Tripoli, 43, 99, 131
Trumming, 133–134, *Figs. 169, 170*
Tumbling, See Polishing.

Wax, 21, 45–57
    in casting, 151, *Fig. 198*
    in design transfer, 63–64, *Figs. 74, 75*
    elimination, 50, 51
    water-soluble, 151, *Fig. 198*
Wire, 64
    annealing of, 65
    drawing, 64–66, *Figs. 76A, B*
    gauges, 29
Wheels, silicon carbide, 24

739. SANFORD 55758
27   Jewelry: queen of crafts
SAN

6/96 (5)   4/94
1/98 (6)   1/98